CULTURAL HERITAGE OF LADAKH HIMALAYA

CULTURAL HERITAGE OF LADAKH HIMALAYA

Prem Singh Jina

KALPAZ

Cultural Heritage of Ladakh Himalaya

Rs. 790

ISBN: 978-81-7835-745-4

Published in 2009 in India by
Kalpaz Publications
C-30, Satyawati Nagar,
Delhi-110052
E-mail: kalpaz@hotmail.com
Phone : 9212729499

Laser Type Setting by: Quick Media, Delhi
Printed at : Young Art Press, Delhi - 92

Dedicated to
Mrs. Manju Jina
and
Manvendar

Contents

PART-II

Preface

Cultural Heritage of Ladakh narrates the old Dard and Buddhist Cultures of Ladakh. Once it was long and almost inaccessible to the outside world, being relatively isolated among its high mountains and often politically closed off. Therefore, it had closed relationship with Tibet after 10th century. In 1959 Chinese invaded, and occupied the same. Ladakh, however, fortunate to preserve the Buddhist Culture under Mahayani tradition till today. In the present monograph I have endeavoured to high-light some important cultural treasures of Dards and Buddhists. I hope my this effort will fulfil the basic requirements of Research scholars teachers and tourists of the world, who want to know about the same.

Prem Singh Jina

Acknowledgements

I would like to express deep appreciation to Dr. (Mrs.) Kapila Vatsayayan, Chairperson, India International Centre, Lodhi Road, New Delhi for rendering help-as-and when required.

I would fail in performing my moral duties if I forget to mention Mrs. Manju Jina, Principal, Hira Convent School, P.O. Bari Mukhani, Haldwani, District Nainital (Uttrakhand), who helped me in various ways in completing this book.

I am also greatful to the authors by whose thought and works, I have benefited immensely.

Prem Singh Jina

List of Tables

List of Figures

PART–I

1

Village Dictionary of Ladakh

In Ladakh maximum villages are pronounced in Tibetan language. They are nemed after an old tradition or on the importance of the concern places. Here follows the details :

Achinathang: It is a part of Skurbuchan and derived by two Bodhi words 'Achina' and 'Thang', which means 'At the foot of mountain' and 'Plain area' respectively. Therefore, it is a village situated at the foot of mountain.[1]

Lat. 33°31′

Long. 76°43′

Achinathang is a neat village on the right bank of the Indus river, situated on a plateau of river–alluvium, 200 feet above the water. Near the village we can see some shallow pits, which are said belong to Baltis who were gold washers, dug gold from the pits, later carried down to waterside to wash the same.[2]

At Achinathang the Indus valley begins to be rather less confined. The road along it is such that one can ride, bellow this valley narrows considerably, thus is damaged often by falling rocks and debris.[3]

Agham or Ugham: It may also pronounce as Agyam. Here follows the details :

Lat. 34°18′

Long. 77°54′

Lat. 10°500′

It is a village in the Nubra sub-division of Leh district, situated on the left bank of the Shyok river, at the junction of the Digar stream. In olden days it was considered the Third march from Leh about 31.5 miles from Leh on the winter route by the Karakoram pass to Yarkand.[4] Thus, after crossing Shyok river one may reach Agyam, which is about 03 hours on foot journey. It has 09 Buddhist houses and 110 big animals viz. horse, yak etc.

Alchi:

Lat. 34°14′

Long. 77°14′

Locals belive that the name of village derived from the Drigung Ka'gyud's main deity Apchi in the following way:

Apchi pa va	≥	Apchi pa
Apchi pa	≥	Abchi
Abchi	≥	Alchi

Thus, Alchi is the corrupted form of Apchi pava. Some scholars say it is corrupted from Aachik[5]. In olden days one famous artist lived in the above village, people called him 'Aba chik' which latter corrupted to the present name in the following way:

Aba chik pe yul	≥	Aba chik pe
Aba chik pe	≥	Aba chik
Aba chik	≥	Aa chik
Aa chik	≥	Al chik
Al chik	≥	Alchi

Alchi is situated at the left bank of Indus river, was under the Kardari of Saspol.[6] In olden day a common trek passes through this village to Zanskar via the Strakspir pass, which was opend for traffic from 15 th June every year.[7]

Amdi: It is two hour journey from Khema in Nubra sub-division of Leh district. During summer Tangyar villagers come here with their animals for grazing. They have four or five houses.

Aranu: It is situated in Nubra sub-division of Leh district, has 30-35 Buddhist houses and about two hour bus journey from Nyungstet.

Anley: In Tibetan language it is equivalent Vamle. 'Vam' is the symbole of tantra 'Ae-vam' or kalachakra tantra.[8]

In general speaking it spells as 'Hanle'

Lat, 32° 47′

Long 79° 04′

Elev, 14, 276′

This village is situated on the left bank of the Hanle river. There is a fine monastery, built on the summit of a steep hill which rises abruptly out of the plain. Once this monastery had a large animal population.[9]

Hanle has about 6 or 8 miles diameter pasture ground. Several streams are very tortuous and sluggish, wind over its surface. These are frequently 3 feet or more in depth, contain multitudes of small fish, a species of carp. The surface of plain is saline, where not swampy, covered with coarse grasses. It is very uneven, being covered with knolls. In some parts there are extensive patches of doma (Tib. furze).[10]

The streams all converage to a point at the north-east and of the plain and uniting into one, continue their course down an open velley a northerly direction towards the Indus. It can scarcely be doubted that it had at one time been a lake, which had gradually silted up.[11]

Basgo: In Tibetan language equivalent Bamgo. It is derived by two Tibetan words 'Bam' and 'go' (or mgo) meaning 'cow' and 'head' respectively. Today it is corrupted from 'Bamgo' in the following in the due course of time.

Bam-mgo ≥ Bamgo

Bamgo ≥ Bazgo

Bazgo ≥ Basgo

Lat, 30° 14′

Long 77° 20′

This village is situated at the right bank of the Indus and about 15 miles below Leh, at the foot of the Basgo thang or plateau Bellow says:

"This undulting plateau is the first bit of open ground we have seen since crossing the Photo-la. It is an arid waste, with hardly a blade of vegetation to vary the bare nakedness of the soil. From the plateau we descended to the Basgo hallow; it is a fertile and populous tract, and picturesque in the clusters of its Buddhists monuments and neatly built dwelling houses amidst a general spread of fields and fruit trees."[12]

Owing to its sheltered situation Basgo is reckoned the warmest winter residence in Ladakh. It had a large 'Shahram' or polo ground. The monastery is built on a towering rock.[13]

Bogdang: This village is derived from 'Bia' and 'Thang' which means 'Hen' and 'Field' respectively. Thus 'Bogdang' from the distance looks like hen, can be explained as :

Bia-Tang ≥ Biadang

Biadang ≥ Begdang

Begdang ≥ Bogdang

It is Shia muslim dominant, came under Indian Republic affter 1971 Indo-Pak war.

Brangsa Saser:

Lat, 35° 2′ 43″

Long 77° 50′

Elev 15, 240′

Once it was a camping ground on the summer Karakoram route, at the north foot of the Saser pass. It had a small collection of stone-wall enclosures to protect the traveller and his cattle from the icy blasts that blew down from the Saser pass. The Shyok river is forded opposite the camp.[14]

Burtsi:

Lat. 35° 10′

Long. 75° 05′

Elev. 16, 000′

It was a halting place on the Karakoram route to Yarkand, between Bulak-i-murghai and Kizil Angiu, on the Dipsang plain.[15]

Burtsi:

Lat. 36° 05′

Long. 99° 12′

It was a halting place of Hayward's route by the Changchenmo valley, about 30 miles from Nischu and 24 miles from Kizil Jilga, north-west of Tso-Thang.[16]

Chati (Tib.Tse-ti) It is four hour bus journey from Leh in Nubra, has 25 Bauddhist houses, 300 goats and sheep, and about 20 yaks.

Chiron: It is one hour joureny from Tegar in Nubra sub-division of Leh district.

Changga (Tib. byang dg'a): It is 3 km from Karu. One can reach here after crossing Karu bridge near Leh, has 40 Buddhist houses.

Chanagundor Piliskimbo:

Lat. 34° 36′

Long. 76° 08′

Elve. 8, 675′

This village has about 80 muslim houses on the right bank of the Dras river, on the road from Srinagar to Leh, situated between Tashgam and Kargil. It is about 127 miles from Leh. According to Bellow:

"Travellers going to Baltistan halt here or at Krikitchu, on the opposite bank. The village stands on a high bank of granite boulders. There is a little cultivation. It is Piliskimbo by the Tartars. The journey from Tashgam to Kargil is generally done in one march.[17]

Charak:

Lat. 34° 24′

Long. 76° 32′

It is a small village on Leh-Srinagar road, situated at the west end of the Namik La between Mulbec and Kharbu, 84 miles from Leh.[18]

Charasa (Tib, ca-ra-sa):

Lat. 34° 40′

Long. 77° 37′

It is situated in Nubra sub-division of Leh district, on the right bank of the Nubra river, and the most conspicuous place in Nubra. At one time it was the most important place, here lived the hereditary rulers of Nubra who ruled under the raja of Ladakh. The houses of Charasa are built on an isolated steep-faced rock, composed of hard porphyry which stands up away from the mountain-side; it is some 200 yards long and 150 feet high. All the upper part of it covered with white buildings: The loftiest of them is the monastery; they were formerly dependended by a wall of which parts still remain-running along the rock at varying intervals, and flanked by towers, with the exception of lamas. The people of the village live on the rock in winter only; for summer they have other dwellings scattered about by their fields, but for warmth in winter they crowd to their old fortress. Here the buildings are crowded so close togather. The space occupied is so completly, roofed over-pathways and all that when filled with human beings and with cattle, it must indeed be warm. It has 40 Buddhist families one can reach here after crossing a bridge over Nubra river, sometime this river is also called by locals as Siacan. It is well connected by road, has one hour bus journey from Panamik and has about 110 cattle in which horse population is comparatevely more than other animals.[19]

Some historians believe that the origional name of Charasa was lchakrasa, which means, 'A place where iron ore is found'. In fact there are two settlements e.g. Chamschen and Charasa, later under the last J&K Govt. settlement they were taken under one name as 'Charasa'. Thus the name of the village corrupted from lchakrasa in the following manner.

lchakrasa	≥	Chakrasa
Chkrasa	≥	Charasa

Chiktan

Lat. 34° 30′

Long. 76° 34′

The name of the village is derived after the collection of villages as 'Chiktan'. It is a part of Kargil has settlemente at the bottom of Kanji valley contains about 600 houses. The inhabitants are Muslims. Rajas Rasanpur and Hasan Khan lived here.[20]

Chilling: It is said that during 10th century many Kashmiri artists came Ladakh along with Lotsava Rinchen Zangpo. They latter employed for decorating Buddhist temples and 'Tsokhor'. In due course of time some of them settled down in Chilling. Kashmiri people are called 'Khatsepa', later pronounced as Khatseling, means 'Kashmiri place', the same gradually corrupted to the present name 'chilling' in the following way.

Khatsepa ling	≥	Trepaling
Trepaling	≥	Chipaling
Chipaling	≥	Chilling

Chamrey: It is pronounced as 'Chemray' or 'Chemre'. Once was under the Kardari or collectorate of Ladakh province. In these days Chamrey, Kharu, Igu Nagla, Shara, and Sakti were included in one group. Chamrey and Sakti then had about 150 houses. The cash revenue was collected Rs 4,000/—, besides taxes in kind.[21]

According to some Ladakhi scholar Chamrey can spelled as lchi-thi, means throne of an importan person. Sometime Ladakhi called it 'Che-bde' means neat toung.[22]

Choglamsar: The village is situated at 8 km from Leh town. It is Buddhist dominant, has one gonpa and monsque.

In Bodhi language it is spelled as lcog-lam-gsar. The name of choglamsar village is derived from two Budhi words 'lcog-yog' and 'lam' means 'winded' and 'pass'. Therefore via Choglamsar two circular passes go to Leh–One through Spituk to Leh other through Sabu to Leh. Some say it is derived from 'Kyoklamsar' words 'Kyok', 'lam' and 'Sar' which means 'Turn', 'path' and 'place'. In brief choglamsar means a place where path turns to various directions to Leh town.[23]

Besides, it is also derived from 'Chok' and 'Tsal' which means 'Tent' and 'Garden' respectively.[24]

Choglamsar was also famous for Chokse (i.e. Ladakhi table). Therefore, it is also known as choklsel; a place of 'Chokse'.

Chamshen: The name of this village is derived from Chambachenmo, which means a village where one big 'Chamba' or 'Matreya' (or Future Buddha) on a rock is engraved.[25]

Chang-ga: This village is 3 km from Karu near Hemis monastery in Leh district. It has 30 Buddhist houses. Moorroft called it 'Chunga'.

It has following geographical details :

Lat. 33° 57′

Long. 77° 46′

Thus, Changa village is situated at left bank of the Indus between Marselang and Leh.[26]

Chumathang

Lat. 33° 22′

Long. 78° 25′

Elev. 13, 600′

It is situated on the right bank of the Indus below the junction of the Puga rivulet, there is one hot spring. The temperature of this hot spiring water was recorded by H. Strachey about 170°F. Once it was under the Hemis Kardari.[27]

Some people believe that the name of this village is derived by two Bodhi words 'Chu" and "Thang' means 'Water' (or River) and 'Plain'. As the village is situated on the bank of Indus river along the big plain, called 'Chumathang'.[28]

Some say it is derived from 'chu' and 'khol', which means 'Water' and 'Boiling' or a place of hot spring.

Chushul:

Lat. 33° 35′

Long. 78° 43′

Elev. 14, 200′

A large village of about 100 houses with Government store house, Government High school, Committee Hall. It is situated about 10 miles south of the Pangong lake. Between Chushul and Pangong lake, we can see hot springs which possess medical properties. The temperature of spring water recorded about 96°F, and has neither taste nor smell. There are two routes here to Nima Mud on the Indus.[29]

1. The eastern one via eastern Chushul Valley and Tsaka La
2. The western route via the Chushul and Thato (or Nurpa) passes.

The eastern path is better rout for trek. A route also leads from here along the Pangong lake and via Tankse to Leh striking the Changchenmo route at Lukung. [30]

There is another route to Tankse and Leh via Kongta la and Lungchu valley.[31]

Close to Chushul is the narrowest part of the Pangong lake, which is easily crossed by masak rafts; this is the shortest road to the Changchenmo velley. A road also leads from here across Changthang to Polu and Khoten; this was the route traversed by Pandit A.K.[32] In olden days the frontier near Chushul was very carefully watched by men from Rudok, who were jealous of Europeans entering in their territory.[33]

Local scholars believe that once chushul was under water, as a result it is derived by two Bodhi words by 'Chu' and 'Shul' means 'water' and 'residue'. Therefore, it came into existence after drying up the lake.[34]

Chushot: It was under the Ladakh Kardari or collectorate, consists three parts the lower, middle and upper. Here follows the details :

(*i*) **Chushot Gongma:** This is the upper part. In Ladakhi language Gongma means upper portion or low land of the region.

(*ii*) **Chushot Shama:** The middle part is called Chushot Shama.

(*iii*) **Chushot Yogma:** The last or lower part of the village is called Chushot Yogma

Chushot is named after two Bodhi words 'Chu' and 'Shot' means 'water' and 'low land'. As this village is situated along the bank of Indus river at low land, called Chushot. It is Shia muslim dominant village in Leh district, about 10 km far away from Leh town.

Da (or Dah): In Tibetan language equivalent 'Arrow'. It is said in olden days when Dards started settling along the Indus banks in Ladakh, their hero 'Gil Singhe' shot arrow, which struck a rock in the above village and went into several metres inside. Therfore, on the direction of his hero, Dards settled down there and named after 'Arrow' or 'Da' as Dah. Besides, one more story is said that once the ancestors of Dards had organised annual festival at the upper portion of Indus gorge. During function Devis and Devatas were dancing with a Devi, unfortunately one Dard did nonsense activities with Devatas. Thereafter , Devatas decided that they would not stay with them and asked to go to the place where shooted arrow had fallen. Dards then settled down there.[35]

Here follows geographical details :

Lat. 34° 37′

Long. 76° 33′

Elev. 9, 690′

Dah village is a frontier part of Ladakh, situated on the right of the Indus below Hanu Yogma. There is a fort which was built to protect the inhabitants from the Balti raiders. Here Buddhist Dards have colony.[36]

Dras

Lat. 34° 26′

Long. 75° 49′

Elev. 10, 144′

It is situated on the left bank of the Dras river. Traders and English explosers from Sunamarg used to take halt at Dras, the second march after crossing the Zoji-la pass, on the route from Srinagar to Leh, 15 miles from Matayan and the same distance from Tashgam the next march. In short Dras has a collection of 50—60 hamlets dispersed over the inequalities.[37]

It is the second coldest place of the world and highest show fall place of Purig. This is owing: "To the great depression in the Himalaya, at the head of the Dras river, which allows the constantly humid vapours of Kashmir to pass to the north of the mountanins, where they become condensed by the cold, and are precipated in rain or snow, according to the season of the year."

Dras area extends from Zoji-la to Chanagund, near Kargil. It is a collection a half a dozen hamlets dispersed over the inequalities of a spacions basin in these close set hills. There was a small square fort in Dras with bastions at each corner and over the entrance wall was 20' high; garrion had one Jemadar and ten sepoys; the fort was commanded within one km. It was in a fair state of repair. It had a garrision of fifty men, and adjoining was a Tehsil or Collectorate of the Thandar of Dras region. There was a telegraph line from Dras to Skardu, a single wire carried on poles without insulators. The Skardu wire followed the Dras, Suru and Indus rivers, there used to be telegrapic communication between Dras and Srinagar, but the snow on upper part of the Sind valley, and from there to Dras, destroyed the line frequently. As a result telegrams were sent by hand between Dras and Sonamarg.[38]

Demcok: It is also spelled as Demjok, in Tibetan language equivalent 'Demchok' or 'bdeychok'. It is named after Buddhist deity 'Dechok', in Sanskrit equivalent to 'Cakrasamvara'. There is a famous white hill called Lhari Karpo, which is believed to be the abode of 'Cakrasamvara'. The village 'Demcok', is situated at the border of China in Leh district.[39]

Deskyit:

Lat. 34° 33′

Long. 77° 36′

Elev. 9, 950′

A village on the left bank of the Shyok, opposite its junction with the Nubra river. It is one of the largest villages in Nubra, and is the Sub-Division headquarter of Nubra. In olden days more than fifty houses paid taxes. Thomson remarks : "It is one of the largest villages of Nubra and contains fifty-eight houses, forty three of which pay taxes. Two smiths and two carpenters live here. The resorces of the village as said to be twenty horses, fifity three horned cattle and over a thousand sheep and goats. The cultivated lands of the village lie on a sloping bank rising rather steeply out of the plain. Many apricot trees grow among the houses, large enough to afford a shade under which a tent could be pitched here much of the plain in encrusted with soda."[40]

In 1998 I visited there, saw good cultivation, had many big apricot trees near houses, one Govt. High school one State Govt. Dairy farm, Lamdon Junior Model School and State Govt. Hospital. Today it has good market with Tourist Banglow, Assistant Commissioner's office, good number of Double hamp camels which are used for tourists. People seems me happy. 'Deskit' means happiness and confort.[41]

Diggar: It is a village where people keep 'Demo' in large number. Demo is a female Yak. The village has good Demo population as such the name derived after 'Diggar'.[42]

Domkhar: In olden days one 'Khar' or fort was built here, later it pronounced as 'Domkhar'. This village is spread along the mountain towards high region, and popularly known as 'Domkhar Gongma' and 'Domkhar Yogma'. 'Domkhar Gongma is surrounded by high mountains, while entering in the village, there is a high chancess of stone falling on the road, 'Domkhar Yogma' is along the main road, has fertile land and water for irrigation. Here walnut, apricot trees can be seen in good number.

Durbuk: It is deriyed from 'Do' and Khook, means 'last part of the valley and 'Hidden portion' . This village is located near Pela pass, can only be visible after descending from the pass, therfore known hidden village of the valley or 'Dorkhook', which later corrupted to the present name in the following way:

Dorkhook	≥	Dokhook
Dokhook	≥	Dubhook
Dubhook	≥	Durbook
Durbook	≥	Durbuk

Futtoksir:

Lat. 34° 04′

Long. 76° 54′

Elev. 13, 900′

The village is situated on the route Kishtwar to Leh via Zanskar, between Yelchung and Hafata, or lies north–west of the Singa La and South-east of the Sirsir La. The valley here is partially cultivated, the fields forming a narrow belt, parallel to the stream, once under Lamayuru Kardari.[44]

The name of the village is derived from 'phi' and 'thosa' means 'high pasturelands along the mountain slopes' and 'Location'. Hence at the location on high altitude the village is corrupted to 'Fotoksar' as :

Futtoksir	≥	Futoksar
Futoksar	≥	Fhutoksar
Fhutoksar	≥	Fotoksar

Garkon:

Lat. 34° 37′

Long. 76° 30′

This is the border village lies on the right of the Indus river. It is most curious in its situation, consists of very narrow strips or ledges of flat watered ground, between separate stages of a great river-cliff, so that on one side is a precipitous fall of ground, while the other vertical cliff overhang the narrow fields, which receiving their radiated heat quickly, ripen their crops; even at night the place does not lose its heat. Water is led over the fields from a ravine which comes from the high mountains. Apples, apricots and mulberry are cultivated in company with cereals on the narrow space and flourish well with the combination of warmth and moist atmosphere. Nowadays tomato and grapes are also cultivated in large quantity.[45]

Gera: This village is situated in Leh district and named from Skyitra which means 'Good garden' or 'A place where no water shortage' one can finds fruit, popular and willow trees in good number. The name of the village is corrupted in the following way:

Skyitra	≥	Gyitra
Gyitra	≥	Gitra
Gitra	≥	Gera

Gya (Tib. gya): It is 25 km from Leh, has following details

Lat. 33° 40′

Long. 77° 45′

Elev. 13, 500′

The village is situated at the left bank of the stream along the Leh-Manali highway, has 40-50 houses with a wide area of cultivation. Villagers grow wheat, barley and peas. It is one of the most elevated villages is Leh district. There are some poplar trees with a considerable size. The Runse monastery crowns a rocky hill on the oppisite bank of the stream. It was a helting place on the route from Kulu to Leh, lies north of the Tagalang pass had one rest house, traders then got ration in small quantity.[46]

Gyik:

Lat. 33° 33¢′

Long. 78° 12¢′

A small village on the right bank of Indus river, half way between Upshi and junction of Puga rivulet.[47]

Hemi: The village is named after 'Ha' which is formed on a rock in the rivine of Hemi.[48]

Hemi Shukpachan: The name of the village is derived by two Bodhi words 'Hay' and 'Shukpa' means 'Boulders' and 'Shukpa tree' (of pencil oedor). The village, therefore, has boulders and 'Shukpa trees' in large number.[49]

Himya: It is situated in the middle of big boulders, and derived its name from 'Hem' and 'Nya' means 'Boulders' and 'Base'. The village is located on the base of heap of boulders, has 35 Buddhist houses.[50]

Hunder: This village is in Nubra valley near Deskyit, has two monasteries, one near the stream along the road, other just above on the mountain. It is derived from the Tibetan word 'Snontar', which means first settled village, hence tribes first settled down here during their early migration to Nubra.[51]

Hunder Dok: This village is upper side of Hunder in Nubra valley, earlier it was used for animal grazing by the Hunder villager. Later some of the families from Hunder settled down and the village named after 'Hunder Dok'.

Igu (Tib. dbyib-dgu): This village is in Leh district on the left side of Leh-Manali high way. It is mamed after its nine corners, 'Iff-gu', has 60 Buddhist houses and 5 km from Karu.

Ieeg: It is in Leh district near Shara village, 10 km from Shara on the left of the main road, has 5-6 Buddhist houses.

Inca: It is derived from 'Ian' and 'tsa' means 'Located in a distance' and 'land'. This Inca means a village which is located at a far off distance. It is about 3 km from Nubra (of Siacan) river in Kincu valley in Nubra sub-division of Leh district.

Kanji: A river in Baltistan rising in about latitude 34° 10' and longitude 76° 36", and flowing into the Indus some 5 miles above Dah village. It is also called the Sangluna river. The portion of the valley in which Kharbu situated is wide, skirted by gently sloping hills, which at some distance on the left bank rise into high mountains, but on the right only attain a moderate elevation, Alluvium occurs, indurated into a hard conglomerate. Kanji valley forms a part of Kargil district.[52]

The Leh-Srinagar road passes for some distance down this valley, entering by the Fotu-la pass and leaving by the Namika la, From it a branch road leads to Kanji and then into Suru by Kanji la. The another road leads down the valley to the Indus. It has the following geographical location.[53]

Lat. 34° 14′

Long' 76° 40′

The village has 30-40 Shia muslim houses, and derived its name from 'rkan' and 'Ji' which means 'Base' and 'four'

Hence, village is situated at the base where four mountains meet.[54]

Karsha:

Lat. 33° 32′

Long. 76° 58′

A village in Zanskar of Kargil district, nearly opposite 'Thonde' a few miles below the junction of the Zanskar river, with a tributary from the north. It is the largest village in Zanskar region, lies in a ravine at a considerable distance from the river, and from the steepness of the slope on which it is built, presents rather an imposing appearance the level tract between the Karsha and river is covered. with cultivation.[55]

Khalsar: It is in Nubra sub-division of Leh district, has four hour journey from Leh, 25 Buddhist houses of about 150 soules, 30 horses, 14 zos, 13 ass and 120 goats & sheep.

Kung to: It is in Nubra, has about 2-3 Buddhist houses, and half an hour journey fron Agyam village.

Kyung-ru: It is in Nubra, has 5-6 Buddhist houses and about one hour journey from Lhabab village.

Khemra: It is in Nubra, has 25 Buddhist houses, 1000 sheep and goats, 50 yaks, 30 horses and 50 ass, and about one hour journey from Kyung-ru.

Khardong: It is on way to Nubra valley, about 80 km from Leh town, has one Gelukpa gonpa under Shankar monastery. 95 Buddhist houses, two Primary schools, one Medical center and one Dak Banglow.

Lag zujg (Tib. lag-gzhu) It has 25 Buddhist houses and about 150 sheep goats.

Lhabab: It is in Nubra about half an hour journey from Skil-na village, has three houses. with 50 yaks.

Marselang (Tib. mar-tse-glang): It is about one km from Kulu in Leh district, has 40 Buddhist and 2-3 Muslim houses. In 1989 agitation Muslims left their houses, when peaceful atmosphere had taken place they returned back. Here follows further details:

Lat. 33°50′

Long. 77°45′

Elev. 12,200′

This is a village on the left bank of the Indus, 22 miles above Leh. It had rest house and supply depot, Near this travellers used to stay at the camping ground. There are routes from Leh to Kulu and Garo pass and has extensive cultivation on an alluvial platform on both sides of a deep ravine, through which a stream flows from the west into the Indus river. It has considerable plantation of poplar and willow on the roads up the left bank of the Indus to Upshi and up the Shang valley and over a pass to Gya.[56]

Matho:

Lat. 34°0′

Long. 77°42′

A village about 150 houses, lies near the top of a sloping allavial fan 3 miles to the left bank of Indus river. It was under the kardari of Hemis and had jagir of king of Ladakh.[57]

The name of village is derived from Mangtro, which means where wheat grow in good quantity.

Meru: It is along the Leh-Manali highway,10 km from Upshi and has 15 Buddhist houses.

Mangyu: The name of this village is derived from 'Soman-rgyu', which means herbal materials for medicines. Here many herbal and aromatic plants grow along the slopes on mountains. As a result the village is known 'Mangyu.[58]

Nang (Tib. nang) It is about 25 km from Leh and 10 km from Thiksey on the left side corner, has 50 houses of about 200 soules.

Nyungstet (Tib. nyung-tet): It is in Nubra valley, 2 hours journey from Sarsoma has 55 Buddhist houses.

Panamik: It is in Nubra valley in Leh district has 40-50 Buddhist houses and one hot spring. Tourist can visit this place. It has one Tourist Rest House.

Piyucan (Tib. pi-yu-can): It is in Nubra valley, 20 minute journey from Khalsar, has 3 Buddhist houses, 20 soules and 50-60 cattle.

Puk-pho-tse (Tib. phug-po-ce): It is in Nubra, 10 miles from Panamik, has 20 Buddhist houses.

Phuktse: It is near Shara **nala** in Leh district, has 150 Buddhist houses.

Phu: It is situated on the upper side of Shara **nala,** has 50 Buddhist houses.

Romche: It is situated just below the Taglang la pass on the Leh-Mnali road, 4 km from Gya, has 10-12 Buddhist houses.

Rong pe Rong: It has one or two houses, 80 yaks and 100 sheep & goats.

Ranibagh: It is 15 km from Tarshit, has two Buddhist houses.

Rong-do (Tib rong-mdo): It is two hour bus journey from 'Tsa-ti' in Nubra, has seven houses and 50 cattle.

Shamphuk: It is in Nubra, 2 km from Hundar, has one Druk-pa monastery.

Skuru: It is 10 km from Skamphuk, has 100 houses, one gonpa, Dak Banglow, and one Higher Secondary school.

Shyang (Tib. Shang): It is in Leh district, 15 km from Marselang at the right side of Indus river, has 45 Buddhist houses.

Sarsoma (Tib Sa- so-ma): It is in Nabra, half an hour bus journey from Tak-sha, has 4-5 Buddhist houses.

Stok (Tib, rtog): It is near Leh, derived its name from Bodhi word 'Tog', means 'The top of mani wheel', has one gonpa of Gelukpa tradition. Here dethroned family of Ladakh king dynasty live.

Sakti (Tib. gres-khri): It is near Leh, derived its name by 'Ser' and 'Thi', means 'Gold' and 'Throne', In olden days one Ladakh king had gold throne at this village, thereafter it is known as 'Ser-thi', which through the ages corrupted into the present name as:

Ser-thi	≥	Sar-thi
Sar-thi	≥	Sak-thi
Sak-thi	≥	Sak-ti

Sumda: When Kashmiri artists settled down at Chilling village, a man 'Sumdo' did not get proper place at Chilling, came to the present side and settled down. Subsequently, other tribes came and started cultivation, the village then known 'Sumda' after 'Sumdo'.[59]

Skurbuchan (Tib. skin-brus-chan pron. Skyurbuchan): In olden days skin (Ibex) in large number used to come here for grazing. They dug the ground during winter and eat the roots of grass. We can find many pits, dug by Ibex, called later Skurubuchan'.[60]

Some say the name of the village is derived after the pulm plantation. It is said that once a brave man killed village enemy in 'Skir-mish'. Thereafter, villagers started to plant pulm fruits in memory of the brave man. The pulm tree is called 'Kham Skyur'. 'Kham' means 'fruit' and 'Skyur' means 'sour taste'. Thus 'Skurubuchan' named after 'Skyur' fruit plantation.

Skil-na: It is in Nubra valley, after travelling via Kung, we come to the above village, which has only 1-2 Bnddhist houses.[61]

Summur (Tib. gsum-yur): It is about 10 minuts bus journey from 'Lag-zung', has 250 Buddhist houses and a few muslim houses (ioe. 2-3 in number); has 250 zos, 30 sheep & goats and 270 other big animals.

Stang: It is not settled area, and comes under Tangyar village, where villagers send their animals for grazing.

Shara: It is in Leh district and 8 km from Upshi, has 100 Buddhist houses.

Sharmos: It is situated in Indus Valley near Shara village, has 250 Buddhist houses.

Terche: It is in Nubra valley, 2 km from Udmaru, has 40 Buddhist houses, one Primary school, one Middle school and a gonpa on the mountain.

Tangyar: It is in Nubra, has 40 Buddhist houses, half an hour journey from Amdi, has good cultivated land on the Kava hillock.

Tuna: It is 5 km from Shara, situated opposite to the shara village, has about 10-12 Buddhist houses.

Tokula: It is 3 km from Liktse at the corner of the valley, has 20 Buddhist houses.

Tarshit: It is 2 km from Liktse, situated at the right of the Indus river, can be reached by bus after crossing the river, has 30 Buddhist houses.

Tirit: It is in Nubra, has about 43 Buddhist houses, consist 50,000 sheep & goats. Near the village, there are number of pasturelands viz. Tirit Phu, Ose khar, Skoce, Phonglas Rigu Dugsa, Ishe Bande, koptar ground, Tarcokcan Sagyang etc. Here Nubra Kalon has 20 goats, 80 cows, 06 horse, 25 camels etc. King Jigmet wangchok wife was from Tirit. At present Nubra Kalon who has large portion of land, started to arrange tourist camp in this remote area. It is about 6 km from Koyam Dompa and 20 minutes bus journey from Khalsar.

Tak-sha: It is 20 minutes bus journey from Puk-po-tse, has 30-35 Buddhist houses.

Udmaru: It is 2 km. from Skuru has 30 Buddhist houses, 01 Primary School, 01 Middle School and one Dak Banglow.

Upsi (Tib'aub-shi): It is 8 km from 'Igu' situated on the left of the Leh-Manali road, has 108 Buddhist houses.

Notes and References

1. Sonam Phuntsog; 'Ladakh', 2000: 195-200.
2. Gazetteer of Kashmir and Ladak; Vivek Pub. House, Delhi; 1974 (Reprinted): 162.
3. Gazetter of Kashmir and Ladak; *op. cit.,* 162. Quoted from the book of F. Drew on Ladakh.
4. *Ibid.,* p. 164.
5. Sonam Phuntsog; *op. cit.*
6. Gazetteer of Kashmir and Ladak; *op. cit.,* 166.
7. *Ibid.*
8. Sonam Phuntsog; *op. cit.*
9. Gazetteer of Kashmir and Ladak; *op. cit.,* 354.
10. *Ibid.*
11. *Ibid.*
12. *Ibid.,* 214
13. *Ibid.*
14. *Ibid.,* 235
15. *Ibid.,* 246
16. *Ibid.*
17. *Ibid.* Bellow in Gazetteer of Kashmir and Ladak.; *op. cit.,* 252.
18. Cuningham in Gazetteer of Kashmir and Ladak, *op. cit.,* 260.
19. F. Drew in Gazetteer of Kashmir and Ladak.; *op. cit.,* 260.
20. Aylmer in Gazetteer of Kashmir and Ladak; *op. cit.,* 269
21. *Ibid., op. cit.,* 270.
22. Sonam Phuntsog; *op. cit.*
23. *Ibid.*
24. *Ibid.*
25. *Ibid.*
26. Moorcroft in Gazetteer of Kashmir and Ladak; *op. cit.,* 278.
27. H, Strachey is Gazetteer of Kashmir and Ladak; *op. cit.*
28. Sonam Phuntsog; *op. cit.*
29. Gazetteer of Kasmir and Ladak; *op. cit.,* 747.

30. *Ibid.*
31. *Ibid.*
32. *Ibid.*
33. *Ibid.*
34. Sonam Phuntsog *op. cit.*
35. *Ibid.*
36. F. Drew is Gazetteer of Kashmir and Ladak; *op. cit.,* 281.
37. Gazetteer of Kashmir and Ladak; *op. cit.,* 303.
38. *Ibid.*
39. Sonam Phuntsog; *op. cit.*
40. Thormson in Gazetteer of Kashmir and Ladak; *op. cit.,* 289-'90
41. Sonam Phuntsog; *op. cit.*
42. *Ibid.*
43. *Ibid.*
44. Gazetteer of Kashmir and Ladak; *op. cit.,* 315.
45. *Ibid.*, 324.
46. *Ibid.*, 348.
47. *Ibid.*
48. Sonam Phuntsog; *op. cit.*
49. *Ibid.*
50. *Ibid.*
51. *Ibid.*
52. Gazetteer of Kashmir and Ladak; *op. cit.,* 364.
53. *Ibid.*
54. Sonam Phuntog; *op. cit.*
55. Thomson in Gazetteer of Kashmir and Ldakh: 364.
56. Gazetteer of Kashmir and Ladak; 590.
57. *Ibid.*: 594
58. Sonam Phuntog; *op. cit.*
59. *Ibid.*
60. *Ibid.*
61. *Ibid.*

2

Dards : An Indo-Aryan Race in Ladakh

The Himalayas is the original home of many ancient tribes, like other tribes Dards migrated Ladakh from various entrance points beginning from pre-historic to early christian era.

Ethnologically Dards are of the Indo-Aryan stock. They are the survivors from Alexander's troops, who after their general's departure scattered over Indus valley lying between 'Kylindrine'and 'Daradri'.

There is no definte time when Dards migrated towards Indus valley. However, migrated to Ladakh in many batches, later settled down along Dras, Skardu, Dah, Hanu, Garkon, Darchik, Skrubuchan, Khalatse etc.

Today Dards who are in Kargil district adopted Islam. The rest became Buddhists, after Muslim invasion in 14th centrry A.D. Dards, who were settled down in Dras, and at the boarder of Kargil district towards Leh embraced Islam. In the consequence they cut off from their original traditional customs and folklores.

Moreover, Dards of Dah, Hanu, Darchik, Achinathang, Gaskon etc. though accepted Buddhism, but able to preserve their ancient old Aryan culture and tradition.

At the beginning Dards were migrated Ladakh from Gilgit and scattered along the banks of Indus river in Lower Ladakh. Only a few groups went to upper Ladakh. But were driven away by the nomads. Therefore, they had to confine themselves to lands in Lower Ladakh.

Some Ladakhis believe that thousand years ago four Drok brothers arrived in the Indus valley via Gilgit. On their way one brother returned to Gilgit, the other three settled down in Dah, Hanu Garkon etc. as evident from the following song:

Song.1[1]

(Translation)

Then they went (and) arrived at Rong-Churgyud, Ouncle;

At Rong- Churgyud; love (to you) O gods:

Is that not, then, a pleasure ground, O gods! (There are) currents at Gusur

(And also) at Goartokumar; love (to you) O gods!

Is that not, then, a pleasure ground, O gods!

Skardo god is near the willows; love O gods!

Is that not, then a pleasure ground, O gods!

Shiggar near chambrozhing, O gods!

Is that not, then, a pleasure ground, O gods!

Kyeris (is) near chumghog, O gods!

Ghasing manthrokhar (is) near the gravel; love O gods!

Parkudda is underneath the midst of the sky; love O gods!

Gabis is near the forest of pecil cedars; love, O gods!

Ganogse (is) near the holy willow tree; love O gods!

Kyishur (is) near the Oasis of the gods; love, O gods!

Hanu is near Handragmir; love O gods:

With Samd is the beginning

The youths of the two Oases are happy,

O, we honour the Mande de mande mande-shin

Let us dance,

O, Mandede mandeshin!

O, This little field !

Mandede mamdeshin!

O, this little field!

In Dah village, there is a several metres long rock tunnel. Locals believe — Once Dards Magspon 'Gil-Singe' was on a hunting tour, He shot an arrow from Mal-Mal-Khatu at this rock.

Thereafter, the village got the name 'Dah' The following song also clears that the Dard ancestors were hunters.

Song-2

(Translation)

At Brashal and Gilgit;

One hundred youths appear.

In the fertile village of Satsil;

One hundred maids appear,

They from a great assembly at Gilgit;

The lion-king of Gilgit appear at the head of the dancers.

Then all you girls twirl your hands; to greet us!

All you boys, clap your hands to greet us;

Hurrah for love! well done, hello!

On the Ambir bass it makes' "tarag" !

Take the arrow then the bow,

The arrow- shafts and the heads

O boy that art clever at hiding!

O boy clever at climbing;

O boy, clever at imitating then antelope's cry;

O boy, clever at getting out of right,

An ibex can be seen,

Ibex can be seen in a herd!

Now take the arrow, O boy!

Then take the arrow - shafts and heads,

O boy that art clever at driving them together;

O boy that art clever at driving them heaps;
Thou that art clever at singling out the best;
Thou that art clever at shooting them!
Offerings of flour, butter, milk, and water,
Must now be brought! However to thee, O god!
Now cut the flesh with a sharp knief:
Roasted meat must be offered!
Cut it to pieces!
Give a mouthful to each of one hundered boys!
They will cary the meat in their pockets of leather;
They will give some to father and mother, O boy!
They will make presents of it to our hundred girls, O boy!
Now we have happiness and abundance, O boy!

The above folklore proves that the fore fathers of 'Dah' migrated from Gilgit latest by seventeenth century A.D. They consider Kesar as their formost hero, An old Drokpa tells this story:

> "To us he (Kesar) is the son of heavenly god, who sent him down to earth in a human form to help human beings. He even changed his appearance and turned himself the grab of a beggar. When he was looking for the land of princess Breugmo. Her parents rejected him, He then performed many feats of bravery, and was accepted as a son-in-law by them. When the king of China got ill, it was, Kasar who, healed him. The daughter of the Chinese king eloped with 'Kesar' who was chased by the dragonds. After overcome many hazards, he reached his place and lived with his two queens. The later of the epic deals with Kesar's battles with 'Jinni' of the north.

Besides, Dards have many heroes viz. 'Dani', 'Melo', etc. 'Dani' belonged to 'Sicili'. 'Melo' founded Hanu village. The folklore dealing with their ancestors are sung during annual Harvest festival in the following reasons:

1. Their ancestors cultivated land in Drok-yul and were first to attend to the computation of time,
2. Their ancestors sowed the precious seeds to the bosom of mother earth,
3. Their ancestors hoped for good production, which would increase their wealth and happiness for their families, and
4. Their king sowed a portion of land on an auspicious day. He is the first furrow sprayed some gold dust and hoped that in future his countrymen would have bumper crops of golden wheat and barley.

The festival is celebrated in every three years interval, called Chhaipo Sarupalha Bono-na, means 'festival of fertility'. It begins with 'Lha-bab' who leads the group of worshippers. Later they are welcomed at a festival ground by Dokpas at their traditional costumes, and dance with full gay, sing their folk songs. Here follows some of them.

Song.3[2]

(Translation)

(This is) the day of the good constellation of the stars.

The day when the rygastod rises.

In the peasure-garden.

The youths gather,

The maids gather,

They arrange the beer

They bring crudled milk,

They bring milk,

They bring milk offerings,
They bring flour-offerings,
They bring butter-offerings,
They bring dumplings (of) flour and butter;
They put on flowers :
Wild marguerities
They bring Rhubarb-flowers,
Meadow-flowers, the shepherds,
They bring alpine butter-cups,
Then to the prospering village,
They bring calendulas,
They put on large marigolds,
They put on fresh marigolds,
They put of straw-flowers,
They put on centrifolias,
They put on wild roses,
They put on ambar flowers,
They put on clusters of kanimal flowers
they put on coats of sheep-wool,
They put on girdles of sheep-wool,
Honour to thee, O God!
Keep us without illness!
Let us trust in Gods!
Assemble, O Gods!
Assemble, O men!

The above song reveals:

(*i*) rgya-stod (Tib. rgyal-stod) is one of the luna mansions.

(*ii*) The inhabitants of Drok-yul offer flowers to their gods, live in heaven, earth and under-world.

(*iii*) They offer flowers to their gods.

(*iv*) They offer flowers to their gods and goddesses before starting auspicious work.

Song.4[3]

(Translation)

How did the erath first grow?
At first the earth grow on a lake
What grew on the water?
Meadow grew
What grew on the meadow?
Three hills grew.
What are the names of three hills?
The name of one hill is 'White Jewel'.
What is the name of second hill ?
The name of second hill is 'Red Jewel".
What is the name of third hill?
The name of third hill is 'Blew Jewel'.
What grew on three hills?
Three trees
What are the name of three trees?
The name of one tree is 'White sandle'
The name of second tree is 'Red sandle'
The name of third tree is 'Blue sandle'.
what are on the three trees?
Three birds.
What are the name of three birds?
The name of first bird is 'Wild Eagle'
The name of second sbird is 'Barndoor Hen'.
The name of third bird is 'Black bird'.

Thus from the above song we understand that:

In the beginning there was ocean in the world. Later it shrinked into big lakes, gradually earth grew up. In this way at first vegetation grew, therafter birds and other animal beings started to take place.

Song.5[4]
(Translation)

Rise then quickly, O uncle !
Our bodies are well-shaped, O uncle !
Our hair is (like) a king's willow O uncle !
Our pig-tails are shinning and curly O uncle !
Our foreheads are (like) rising sun, O uncle !
Our eyes are radiant, O uncle !
Our eye - brows are raised O uncle !
Our ear - rings are of god, O uncle !
Our teeth are (like) pearls, O uncle !
Our lips are swelling, O uncle !
We are assembled, O uncle !
Change sheep wool dress, O uncle !
Change beautiful head covering, O uncle !
Change beautiful scarf, O uncle !
Change beautiful flows, O uncle !
Hurrah, hurrah, hurrah hurrah!

The above song informs that during the annual harvest festival all young boys and girls of Drokpa (Dard) families assemble at the assigned place. During festivity they choose their life partners and exchange their views with regard to fertility in their married lives. Girls attract boys by praising their beauty, before enterning into marriage. They are allowed to change their valuable costumes and express their great exclaming thrim, thrim .... On this occasion wide kissing scene make the atmosphere warm and empressive. The partners love each other without any heritation, and sing the following song.

Song.6[5]
(Translation)

Let us show love to each other.
Look at the village.

The hen eating green grass.
Hurrah ... Hurrah ... Hurrah !
Show then, ... O show love !
The hen is lying down in the village.
Love ..., let us express love !
In the village of foxes, let us
Show love to tach other!
Kyishur is the village of mice,
There are good places, belong to father land!
Let us show love to each other !
In the lower village barley is ripening,
In the middle village golden barley is ripening,
In the upper village barley is ripening,
In kyishur, peas and barly are ripening;
Happiness has come,
Honour to thee, O God !
O friends, clap,
Hurrah ... hurrah !

Dard women are strikingly beautiful and have hospitable nature. They are fond of flowers, decorate their caps with red 'Shoklo, which they plucked during summer, drived and stocked for the whole year.

In conclusion Buddhist Dards are able to preserve ancient old Aryan tradition, whereas who are converted Muslims, unable to preserve the same.

References

1. Francke, A.H. 'The Eighteen Songs of the Bono-na festival (Bono-Nayi lu athrungsh'; The Indian Antiquary Vol. XXXIV, 1905, Swati Pub., 1985:93.
2. *Ibid.*
3. *Ibid.*
4. *Ibid.*
5. *Ibid.*

3

Khalatse : A Village of Dards

In 1981, I had meeting with old people of Ladakh and Hoshiyarpur, they were involved in Central Asian trade activities. An old Hoshiyarpur trader informed me, in olden days they got gold dust from Tibet in exchange of Indian spices, wheat, sugarcandy etc. Then another old Ladakhi told me about the Dards who were engaged in gold trade, had their colonies in Khalatse area. After the gap of four-five years I visited Khalatse, and came to know from their folk tales, there were gold digging ants about dog size nearby to their villages. Their ancestors were gold diggers. Migrated from Gilgit, settled down along the belt in between Khalatse and Dah Hanu side along Indus river. Herodotus, a Greek writer very early mentioned about the gold digging ants. Here follows the account which he gives about them:

"Besides these there are Indians of another tribe, who live at the border on the city of *Kaspatyrus* and the country of *Paktyika*: these people dwell north-ward of all the rest of the Indians, and follow the same mode of life as the *Baktrians.* They are more warlike than any of the other tribes, from them the men are sent forth who go to procure the gold. For it is in this part of India that the sandy desert lies. Here in this desert there live amid the sand great ants, in size somewhat less than dogs, but bigger than foxes. The Persian king has a number of them, which have been caught by the hunters in the land whereof we are speaking. These ants make their dwellings underground, and, like the Greek ants, which they very much resemble in shape, throw up sand-heaps as they burrow. Now the sand which they throw up is full of gold. The Indians when they go into the desert to collect this sand take three camels and harness them together, a female in the middle, and a male on either side in a leading-rein. The rider sits on the female, and they are particular to choose for the purpose one that has just dropped her young: for their female camels can run as fast as horses, while they bear burdens very much better. The Indians reach the place where the gold is, they fill their bags with the sand and ride away at their best speed: the ants, however, scenting them, as the persians say, rush forth in pursuit. Now these animals are so swift, they declare, that there is nothing in the world like them: if it were not, therefore, that the Indians get a start while the ants are mustering, not a single gold-gatherer could escape. During the flight the male camels, which are not so fleet as the females, grow tired, and begin to drag first one and then the other: but the females recollect the young which they have left behind, and never give way or flag. Such, according to the Persians, in the manner in which the Indians get the greater part of their gold: some is dug out of the earth, but of this the supply is more scanty."[1]

According to ancient Greek legend. Once a fruitless expedition against the gold-digging ants undertaken by the Athenians with troops of all arms, and provisions for three days, as expressed below:

> "A mound of gold-dust heap been seen on Mount Hymettus guarded by the warlike ants: whereupon they armed themselves and set out against the foe, but returning to Athens after much expenditure of labour to no purpose, they said mockingly to each other".[2]

In 1788, Major James Rennel admitting the exaggeration of gold-digging ants story.[3] Later in 19th century historians had the opinions that gold-diggers were not really ants, it had simply been a confusion between the names of the ant and some animal of larger size. However, the idea of resemblance was especially grouunded on the larger animal's mode of digging its burrow, or excavating the earth with any other object. This animal can be identified with marmot found every where cold desert.[4] I saw them in larger number at Spang Chenmo and at larger plain near Taglang la.

According to the Greek historian, the Indians who went in search of the gold lived in the neighbourhood of the city of Kaspatyrus and of Paktyika. The inhabitants of Paktyika were Afghans, who in the west called as Pashtun. Kaspatyrur may be spelled as Kaspapyrus or Kasyapura and was the ancient name of the capital Kashmir.[5]

Dards were the tribes, settled down along the banks of Indus, knew Pushtu, the Afganisthan language, but their native tongue was Sanskritic Jdion. Mirizzet Ullah, the travelling companion of Moorcroft visited Ladakh during 1812 also confirmed that Dards knew Pashtu:

"The houses of this country from Matqagin to this place are all wrecked and deserted. Last year a great number of inhabitants were carried off by bands of Dards, an independent tribe who live in the mountains three or four days, march north of Diriras, and speak Pashtu and Darads."[6]

In 1865–66 Britist Government sent some Pandits from Srinagar to explor Eastern Tibet. The first expedition undertaken in the same year for Lhasa later a Pandit reported:

"He saw Thok-Jalung an important gold field in the province of Nari Khorsum with a large excampant of Tibetan miners, and took the opportunity to gain information relative to the working of mines".[7]

At the third expedition in 1868 another Pandit reached Rudok, on the frontier of Ladakh visited the gold fields of Thok-Nianmo, Thok-sariung and Thok-Jalung.[8]

The Pandit also gave information some more gold fields of Thok-Munuak, Thok-Ragyok, Thok-Ragung and Thok-Dalung.[9]

Thus the expeditions of goldmine discovery made by pandits reveal that the situation of all gold fields in Tibet were same as Khalatse gold fields. They did not find gold digging ants except Tibetan mineres. Pandit stayed at Thok. Jalung from 26th to the 31st of August 1867 says, "Never in any of hills travels did he experience such piercing cold as at that place, and the director of the miners informed him that in winter all the miners are dressed in furs, since one could not live at that season without them. At the height of about 16,330 from the sea-level when Tibetan miners were engaged with fur coats, from distance looked like animals. They cover their faces almost resemblance to apes. Their customary mode of saluting one another is to loll out the tongue, grin, nod, and scratch their ear... when they sleep, draw their knees close upto their heads and rest on their knees and elbows.[10]"

The Dards of khalatse might be slept in the way described above. The account received by Herodotus that: "They made themselves subterranean dwellings,"[11] Therefore literally applicable to the miners of Thok-Jalung. The gold digger ants were infact gold miners who exacavate the earth, heap up at the mouth of the pit like moles. Pliny, says: "The gold is dug up by them in winter and the Indians carry it off in summer."[12]

The Pandit tells about Thok-Jalung miners "...spite of the cold, the diggers prefer working in winter; and the number of their tents, which in summer amount to 300, rises to nearly 600 in winter, they prefer the winter, as the frozen soil then stands well, and is not likely to trouble them much by falling in."[13]

Megasthenes informs that the gold digging ants lived by hunting this statement seems to be wrong as Tibetan gold miners procure their food by hunting the wild Yak and animals. Hence, gold digging ants may be gold miners.

Herodotus said that gold-digging ants had high speed, attacked their enimies in a ferocious manner. In my opinion, Tibetans and Dards used to have dogs to safe gaurd grazing of their animals. The dogs were bigger than the normal size. They were very clever in hunting wild beasts. Mir. Izzet ullah pointed out Tibetan dogs had large heads, long hair, a formidable amount of strength, and great courage. Therfore, it would be possible when strangers endeavoured to take out gold, the gold miners alongwith their dogs attacked them. Therefore, Herodotus might be wrongly interpreted Tibetan dogs as 'gold' digging ants.

In conclusion the gold digging ants were Dards, settled down along the Khalatse area at the banks of Indus, were engaged in gold digging works during winter season and pitched their tents some seven or eight feet below the surface of the ground, so as to keep out the wind. They prefered winter, as the frozen soil then stands well, and was not likely to trouble them much by falling. Besides, during winter they had sufficient time to dig gold, as most of the time they lived with their families along the Indus banks near Khalatse.

Refferences

1. Frederic Schiern & Tranlated by Anna M.H. Childers:' The tradition of the gold-digging ants, In: 'The Indian Antiquary; Vol. IV, 1875: 225.
2. *Ibid.*
3. *Ibid:* 226
4. *Ibid.,* & Conf Link, Die Urwelt and das Alterthum (Berlin, 1821–22), I. 258.
5. Frederic Schiern; *op. cit:* 227.
6. *Ibid.* & voyage dane l'Asie centrale, in Klaproth's Magasin Asiatique, 11.3-5; Conf. Wilson's preface to Moorcroft and Trebeck's Travels, I. X Viii.
7. Frederic Schiern; *op. cit:* 228.
8. *Ibid.*
9. *Ibid.*
10. *Ibid.* 229.
11. *Ibid.* 230.
12. *Ibid.*
13. *Ibid.*
14. *Ibid.*
15. *Ibid.*

4

Stag Rimo Gonpa (Tib. stag rimo dgon pa)

Stag Rimo monastery is situated in Zanskar region of Kargil district in Ladakh region. It was founded by Zanskar king in 1617. In the beginning it was a small Buddhist temple, on a remote hillock in Zanskar. In the early 17th century king Dechok Namgyal requested villagers of Zanskar to donate their lands for the stablishment of the above monastery. After sometime Chosje Nawang Gyaltsen[1] visited Zanskar and met king at Padum.[2] Chosje preached Zanskar queen and villagers. He requested villagers to donate their children to strengthen the Buddhist monastic tradition. Later Lama Nalzor Cinba visited the site, instead of preachings he retreated there. His deceased body is preserved in Skudung (Tib. sku gdung) Chorten[4] at the monastery.

Nalzor Cinba founded the tradition of meditation in Stag-Rimo. It is a branch of Bardan monastery. The Bardan Gonpa society and the head of this monastery used to appoint Lopon or head lama for Stag-Rimo gonpa. This tradition continued up to Lopon Ti-zin (Tib,. slob-dpon khri 'adzin).[6]

Till sixties Lopon and lamas of Stag-Rimo were invited by the Bardan monastery in every auspicious ceremony. On the arrival at Bardan they used to welcome with music played by Tung[7] and Gyaling[8]. Today this tradition is almost stopped. Lopon of the monastery now-a days is selected in a democrative way from the Stag-Rimo itself. In order to preserve the old tradition every year some lamas are sent to Bardan monastery during annual festival, who participate in 'Cham'.[9]

Stag-Rimo is located in the centre of beautiful forest surrouned by lash green pasture grounds. During summer, the white monastery building with their lamas in the middle with green forest looks like flower in which bees are going and coming for their food. Winters are difficult. Sometimes lamas of the monastery have to go far away for drinking water, usually they store snow during autumn season in order to avoide water crises.[10]

In the monastery one old and beautiful statue of Vajra Warahi can be seen. Besides, there are many Buddha, Boddhisattva statues and thankas are placed.

ANNUAL PRAYERS

Nungnas (Tib. snyung nas): During summer season lamas of the monastery perform Nungnas prayer.[11]

In winter season lamas of the monastery perform Zitho Tamba Rigya (Tib zhio kro dampa rigs rgya), Chotchok (Tib. gcot tsodgs) etc. rituals. They do not go anywhere, reside at the monastery, and practice philosophical debates.[12]

The incarnation of lama Tashi Stemphel (Tib. blama bkris bstan 'aphel) is the head lama of the monastery. His full name is Skjabye Skathul Nawang Tonyot Jigdal Dorje (Tib. skyabs rje stag sbrul dag dbang don yod ajigs bral rdo rje). The lamas under his direction used to do daily prayer of chagya chenpo (Tib. phyag rgya chen po) and Lancik skesjor (Tib. lhan cik skyes sbyor). Besides, they make mandala and perform rituals of Igya (Tib. Yig bgya), lame nalzor (Tib. bla m'ai rnal 'abyor) and Naro chostuk (Tib. rna ro chos drug).[13]

The monastery does not have many lamas, that is in between 20 – 30. However, at a time one may see 10 lamas at least in the monastery, who look after the monastic activities very well.

Notes and References

1. Chosje Nawang Gylatsen: In Tibetan language it is equivalant chos–rje ngag dbang rgyal mchen
2. **Padum:** Once the capital of the ancient kingdom of Zanskar. It is the present day administrative headquarter of the region. Its old part copmrising inter connected abode houses and several chortens.
3. **Nalzor Cinba:** In Tibetan language equivalant rnal 'abyor, he was one of the famous siddha, in Zanskar and belonged to Druk-pa K'agyud tradition.
4. **Skudung (Tib. sku gdung) chorten:** It contains the dead body or sometimes the deposition of the dead otherwise customarily being by burial for a prominent lama or rimpoche of the concern monastery.
5. **Bardan monastery:** 12 km south of Padum, Bardan is an isoiated monastery with about 40 Dukpa monks in residence. Founded during the 17th century as the first ever centre of the old, unreformed Drukpa monastic order in Zanskar. It controls several small Dukpa establishments in the region, including the famous Sani monastery.
6. **Jamyang Gyaltsen (ed,):** The history of Ladakh monasteries', All India Gonpa society, Leh-Ladakh; 1995: 389-90.
7. **Tung:** It is a musical instrument which is used during prayers and annual monastery festival "cham".
8. **Gyaling:** This gonpa musical instrument is used during prayers and annual festival of the monastery.
9. **Cham:** This is the Tantric dance, perform by lamas of the monastery during annual festival.
10. Jamyang Gyaltsen; *op. cit.*
11. *Ibid.*
12. *Ibid.*
13. *Ibid.*

5

Buddhist Engraved Images in Ladakh

In Ladakh early traces of Buddhism are found in the form of the Buddhist Images, engraved on rocks and stones. Here follows the details:

Maitreya image at Hunder: I visited Nubra first time in 1991, thereafter in 1998. On both the occasion I visited Hunder[1] and saw some Buddhist images on stones at the bank of stream and just below the Hunder bridge. These images were not clearly visible. However, after intensive study I understood that one image would be of Maitreya.[2] I measured its height and width as :

Hegiht: 6 feet

Width: 1½ feet

Just near to the above I saw another image of Buddha[3] on the other side of the stream. It also has 6 feet in height and 2 feet wide.

Rohit Vohra saw two more images of Maitreys. But I did not see. These images are made according to Gandhara art.

Maitreya image at Tirche: This engraved image lies on a huge rock just outside the village along the left bank of Shyok river. Here follows the details: Art: Gandhara

Height - 10½ feet

Width - 4 feet along the chest

Maitreya image on Sod in Purig: This image is engraved on a rock about late 10 century A.D.

20 cm deep carved five Buddhas at Padum: On the slope of the ridge towards the river, a little below the Padum town there is a huge boulder of about 12 feet in height. From here on the north side looking towards the town, there are five engraved images of Buddhas, popularly known Gyal va rig nga in Sanskrit equivalent Five Dhyani Buddhas. These figures are all much above life-size, and cover six square yard land.

All the above images are seated on lotus throne. The figure in the middle represents Maitreya, the future Buddha of the next Kalpa, the rest Buddhas are said to be representations of present and three proceeding Kalpas. Maitreya is the only figure which is furnished with a crown with three points. Like the others, he is seated on a lotus throne, underneath there are two lions. His hands almost touch each other in front, the left hand covering the right, but right hand is a little above the left. The Buddha to the left of Maitreya has a pair of peacocks under the throne, and his finger tips touch each other in front. The second to the left of Maitreya has two **garudas** underneath his throne. He holds up his right hand as if in the act of teaching. Two rest Buddhas on the right of Maitreya touch the ground with their right hands. Underneath the pictures of these five Dhyani Buddhas[4] there is a long row of pyramidical chaityas, and below them a row of men wear hats with three points, like Maitreya. Above the five Buddhas, at both ends of the row, there are two square recesses bored into the rock, which evidently served for the reception of beams. Thus it appears that there used to be a hall erected in front of the boulder, and that the sculptures formed the back wall of the hall.

Five Standing Buddhas: Near the above five Dhyani Buddhas there are five image of standing Buddhas of six yards high, and Chaityas of all sizes, carved on the same rock in other places and in a less deep style of relief.

Five Standing Buddhas: At little higher up the river, on the slope, there are five standing Buddhas on a big boulder, underneath of these images lions, peacocks and garudas are carved. These emblems were seemed much later date, as the artist did not know where to carve the emblems.

Maitreya Sculpture at Sani Village in Zanskar: This sculpture was first time documented by Franke in 1909, later David L. Senellgrove described this during his visit 1974-75. Here follows the details :

Height: 2 metres

Crown: Three coned

Probable date: 7th-9th century A. D.

Mudra: Dharmacakra.

Maitreya Sculpture at Housing colony near Leh: I have first time documented it in 1983-84 and given its brief introduction in my book 'Ladakh: The land and the People, published in 1986 by Indus Publishing Company, New Delhi.

The big bonlder has three engraved images of Buddha and Maitreyas. Here follows the details :

Boulder Height: 12 feet

Width: 09 feet

North side: Maitreya or Future Buddha

Height: 46 inches

Width: 26 inches through chest

Left hand: 23 inches

North side bolder:

Height: 49 inches

Width: 26 inches

South side:

(*a*) **Upper side:**

Image : Buddha

Asana : Meditation

Height : 26 inches

Width : 20 inches

Mudra : Meditation

Patra : Holds bowl which is used for begging alms. This patra is semi-circular in shape. It rests on his lap.

According to the Indian tradition four weeks of Buddha-hood, Tapussa and Bhallika, two merchants of Uscula in Orissa, were warned by a deity that they were approaching to Buddha. The merchants came to the Buddha and offered him rice and honey cakes. The Buddha could not accept food, whereupon, the four gods of the quarters brought him a stone bowl from which he ate the food, since then Buddha used stone bowl for begging.

(*b*) Beneath to the above image: Maitreya

Height : 32 inches

Width : 10 inches

Boulder's width at the base: 25 inches

East Side:

Boulder width: 11 inches

Height: 50 inches

Upper side image: Maitreya.

Height: 11 inches

Width: 09 inches

Beneath image: Maitreya

Height: 18 inches

Width: 22 inches

West side image:

Buddha

Height: 2 feet

Width: 6 feet (through chest)

Width: 9 feet (average)

Boulder:

Height: 45 inches (at the base)

Width: 25 inches

Dating of the above images: 9th-10th century A.D. (Fig. 5.1)

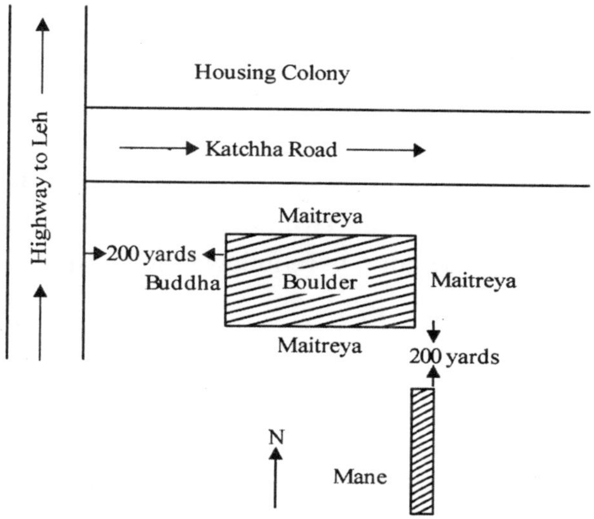

Fig. 5.1. Maitreya Sculptures at Housing Colony near Leh.

Buddha Sculpture at Changspa Near Leh: Standing Buddha with Bodhisattvas[5]. Maitreya holds vessel at his right hand. The other image Avalokitesvara[6] holds flower in his left hand and is comparatively little higher in height. Above these two flying birds Gandarvas are depicted.

Maitreya Sculpture

Location: Near Gomang chorten, about 16 km from Leh, at the left side of the road. The Maitreya image is engaved on a big boulder which has the following measurements :

Height: 62″
Width: 45″
Width at the base: 52″ } Boulder

Maritreya image

Height : 60″

Width : 40″(Through the centre of the image)

Pose : Standing.

Mudra: (i) Left hand stands free straight down above knee in Bhumisparsha.

(ii) Right hand rests near chest in Dharmacakra mudra.

Maitreya image in shey along the road side below the Shey Palace (Near Gomang Chorten): The image is engraved on a boulder, here follows the details :

Height : 46″
Width : 23″ (From center) } Maitreya image

Height : 47″
Width from centre: 29″
Width from Base: 36″ } Boulder

Posture of the image: Right hand near chest in Dharmacakra mudra.

Left hand just below near chest.

Left side flower offerings are depicted.

Buddha image in Shey village near the Shey monastery: There are four images of Buddha engraved in four directions, each has equal height and width as stated below:

Height: 4′& Width: 6″

Maitreya image in shey village along the road side below Shey palace: The image is engraved on a boulder which is broken into two pieces. Here follows the details:

Height	: 20″	Ist Part of the boulder
Width	: 22″	

Heigh	: 23″	
Width	: 28″	upper side Second part of the boulder
Width	: 25″	Base

Height	: 38″	
Width	: 18″	Maitreya image
Crown	:	Three (usually have five)

Maitreya image in Shey village along road side below Shey palace

Height	: 27″	Boulder in which Maitreya
Width	: 17″	image is engraved

Height	: 23″	Maitreya image
Width	: 12″	

Images near the Shey gonpa of Drugpa K'agyud order: During my early visits in 1998 I saw many Buddhist images here and there. On sunday 12th September 2006, I visited again and saw the same were well preserved with a covered structure, here follows the details:

From Right to Left side

1. **Chamba (or Maitreya) image:**

   Height : 49″

   Width : 20″ (From center)

   Mudra: Both hands near chest is Dharmacakra mudra

   Crown: Five

   Posture: Standing

The boulder in which the above image is engraved:

   Height : 53″

   Width : 23″ (From Center)

   Width : 23″ (From Base)

2. **Maitreya image**

   Height : 43″

   Width : 15″

   Mudra: (i) Right hand near chest in Dharmacakra Mudra

   (ii) Left hand lies near chest

   Crown: Five

   Posture : Standing

3. **Avalokitesvara image**

   Height : 22″

   Width : 20″ (From Centre)

   Hands: Four

   Right two hands : (i) Upper holds rosary

   (ii) Second stands near chest

Left two hands : (i) Upper not identified

(ii) Other rests near chest

Posture : Standing

Crown: Five

Boulder in which the above image is engraved:

Height : 32″

Width : 29″ (From Centre)

Width : 14″ (At the base)

4. Chepakmet image:[7]

Posture : Seated

Mudra: Meditation

Crown: Five [From front looks only three in number]

Height : 26″

Width : 17″

Stone in which the above image is engraved:

Height : 31″

Width : 22″

Width from base : 24″

5. Sakyamuni Buddha image:[8]

Height : 40″

Width : 14″

Posture : Standing

Mudra: (i) Right hand lies near chest in Dharmacakra mudra

(ii) Left hand stands free straight towards earth.

Stone in which the above image is engraved:

Height : 41″

Width : 19″

Width from base : 23″

6. Maitreya image :

Height : 50″

Width : 20″

Mudra: (i) Right hand lies near chest

(ii) Left hand rests below the chest

Posture: Standing

Stone on which the above image is engraved:

Height : 52″

Width : 25″

Width from base : 27″

7. Dawarpala or Gana:

Height : 13″

Width : 7″

The above image is seated at the right of the Maitreya image.

8. **Buddha:**

Height : 41″

Width : 13″

Mudra: Right hand near chest

Left hand stands free towards earth Posture: Standing

The boulder on which the image is engraved:

Height : 43″

Width : 17″

Width from base : 14″

8. Buddha image

Height : 50″

Width : 13″

Mudra: (i) Right hand rests near chest.

(ii) Left hand stands free towards earth.

Boulder on which the image is engraved.

Height : 58″

Width : 16″

Width from base : 14″

9. **Singe da image**[9]

Height : 40″

Width upper side : 13″

Width at lower part : 8″

Face : Six

Hands: Two, stands free towards earth

The stone on which the above image is engraved, broken into two pieces as :

Upper part of the boulder:

Height : 26″

Width : 15″

Lower part of the boulder:

Height : 16″

Width : 13″

In conclusion I would say the Buddhist engraved images found during research are in between 9th to 11th century A.D. Among engraved images maximum belong to Maitreya and Buddha, besides I found the carving of Avalokitesvara, Dolma, Singe da and chepakmet. The concentration of these images were collected from Shey and Leh areas.

Notes & References

1. **Hunder:** This village is near the Diskyit, the headquarter of Nubra Sub-Division of Leh district. It has two monasteries near the stream along the road.
2. **Maitreaya:** Tib. Byams-pa, Phon. Eng. Jampa "The kind one". A Mahabodhisattva and the Bodhisattva who will be the Manushi Buddha of future age. The Buddha to be who

will show the way to nirvana. He is a Bodhisativa who is equally respected by the thervadits irts and the Mahayanists. Cf. Bunce, Fredrick W: 'An Encyclopaedia of Buddhist Deities....; D.K. Print World Ltd. New Delhi; 1994: 597.

3. **Buddha:** Historically known as Gotama Buddha, in philosophical term he is known as 'The Englightened one'.
4. **Five Dhayani Buddhas (Tib. Gyelwa-rig-nga)** They are Aksobhya, Amitabha, Amoghasiddhi, Ratnasambhava and Vairocana. These five Buddhas in Meditation represent the cosmic elements. Cf. Bunce, Fredrick W. ; op. cit.:130
5. **Bodhisattvas:** The concept of the Bodhisattva Tib. byang chub sems dpa) or 'enlightenment being' is especially decisive for the character of the Mahayana. Bodhisattva after attaining enlightenment, voluntarily remains in the world in order to work, by preaching end activity, for the deliverance of all. CF. Finegan, Jack:' Tibet: A Drcamt of image, Tibet House New Delhi; 1986: 68.
6. **Avalokitesvara: (Tib spyan ras gzigs, pron chen-resik),** The 'lord who looks down with cympassion', is a manifestation of Amitabha. Cf. Finegan, Jack; op.cit: 130.
7. **Chepakmet image.** (Tib. che-dpag-med, Tshe-dpag-med, phon. Eng. tsepame' dispenser of long life', The bodhisattva of longevity who is invoked for long life, health and happiness. Face: One; arms; two, in dhyana mudra, holding an vase with elixir of life. Cf. Bunce, Fredrick W.;op. cit: 13. :
8. **Sakyamuni Buddha image:** Tib Sha-kya-thub-pa, [Phon. Eng.] Shakya Tubpa, Sa-kya-Thub-pa." the wise man of the Sakya race." Prince Siddhartha Gautama of Sakya," the Enlightened One", Cf. Bunce, Fredric W.; op. cit. 469.
9. **Singe da image:** Tib. Senge-sgda; skt. Simhanada or Simhanada Lokesvara Tib. spyan-ras-gzigs-senge-ge-syra.

   "The lord with the voice of a lion." A non-tantric form of Dhyani Bodhisattva Avalokitesvara, who is prayed to a cure of leprosy. Cf. Bunce, W. fredrick; *op. cit.:* 502.

6

Spituk Monastery

Spituk monastery is associated with big names like Atisa[1], Lotasava Rinchen bzangpo[2] and Lha Lama chang Chub Od's brother Dharmaraja Od. During Dharmaraja Od's period spituk monastery had only a small Lhakhang in Ladakh near Leh. The Lhakhang was initially built by Dharmaraja in 1050 A.D. Till the 15th century Spituk monastery did not make much progress. Only king Dragspa Bumde[3] and Lama Lhawang Lodos thought to develop the small Lhakhang into the shape to Geluk pa monastery. Consequently with the assistance of king Bumde, Lama Lhawang Lodos was able to build Dukhang, Lhakhang etc. In this connection the following storey is said:

Once king Dragspa Bumde was riding on horse and going towards Spituk. From the distance he felt that the Spituk hillock looked him as elephant. After retuning at his palace he thought: "How nice if he would be able to establish a monastery on the hillock of Spituk."

He called Lama Lhawang Lodos and said :

"Gyanle! I saw a beautifut hillock near Spituk. I want to built a monastery there. Kindly visit the hillock and inquire whether it is suitable for the monastery or not."

Lhawang Lodos visited Spituk hillock, He inspected the site, went for meditation. Later acknowledged that the place would be suitable for the monastery. Accordingly, he informed about his decision to king Bumde.

A few years ago Lama Tsong-khapa[5] sent Tang Sams Sherab Zanpo[6] and his assistant with a gift of 6 inch small

Chepakmet statue for Drags pa Bumde the same later given to king. King offered this statue to the head lama of Spituk monastery. After three years a big Buddha statue was made in the monastery, this Chepakmet statue was then placed in the temple with ritual ceremony.

During 1653-1705, Deshik Sangyas Gyatso practised Tsong khapa's doctrine. Later, he propogated Geluk pa tradition[7] in Ladakh and strengthened Spituk monastery activities. Subsequently following lamas were appointed as Deputy head lama of the monastery.

1. Duva Lozang Spaldan
2. Namkha Spalzang
3. Sonam Gyatso
4. Je Chosgyal Legpa
5. Dungrab Zorwa
6. Je Sangyas Stanpa
7. Je Dagkpa Tondup
8. Je Stanpa Gyaltsan
9. Burampa Samstan Gyatso
10. Je Rinchen Palzor
11. Tung Shesrabpa
12. Je Lozang choskyong
13. Chosji Tanpa Gyatso
14. Nyimopa Stanpa Gyaltsan
15. Lepa Chosje Tungnas
16. Tsewangpa Namkha Gyatsan
17. Tungpa Sapi
18. Citi Tasova stanpa Gyatso
19. Lepa Lozang Spaldup
20. Dakpa Gyaltsan

21. Tewang Sangyas Gyatso
22. Lepa Sonam, Samdar
23. Nawang Chogdan
24. Ishes Paljor
25. Nawang Lozang
26. Gyalsras Jigmet
27. Gyalsras jigmet Namgyal.

During 17th century Deldan Namgyal was the king of Ladakh. He had been involved in war with Galdan Tsewang[8] in1670, sent his son Nawang to Thiksey monastery for ordination, who later went to Tibet and studied in Draspang monastery. After getting Gyeses degree from the same monastery he worked as Lhopon and Khanpo, thereafter became the head lama of Thiksey monastery and returned Ladakh. He made a plan to propogate Gelukpa tradition throughout in Ladakh. And with the help of Spitukgonpa he did the same. On the line of Thiksey monastery he established the tradition to celeberate annual festival 'Gustor' in Spituk monastery. During 1785-1804 Jamspal Gyatso strenthened vinayic rules in the monastery. As a result Spituk and Thiksey monasteries progressed. In 1834– '36 Zorawar[10] invaded Ladakh his army destroyed Lamaguru monastery completeby. In order to re-establish the monastery Kushok Rangdol Nima[11] went there. He got parinirwana there, later took rebirth as first Kushok Bakula in the royal family of Zanskar at Zangla Khar. He was offered to Spituk monastery. Later became the head lama. He got Gyeses degree from Tibet and returned Ladakh. As a head of the Spituk monastery he made strict vinayic rules. During his period Sankar Karsha, Stsongde etc, monasteries got progressed. After his parinirvana his next incarnation born in Matho Kher. He also went Tibet for higher studies, got Gyeses Lharampa degree and returned Ladakh. During his period Spituk monastery got good progress. The decipline in the monastery was closely looked by him.

Spituk monastery has many temples. Here follows details:

Spituk Thok Chen Lhakhang

Before the establishment of Spituk monastery there was a khar.[12] Today we can see the ruins of this just below the old temple. The Gonkhang of the Spituk monastery was first built in 15th century A.D. by Lama Lhawang Lodos with the assistance of king Dragspa Bumde. In this temple we can see some old statues. Here follows the details :

1. Yamantaka[13] : 13' in height
2. Gonpo[14] : Six hands
3. Tamcan Chorgyal (yab–yum form)[15]
4. Paldan Lhamo[16]

Infront of the Tamcan Chorgyal the following are new statues :

(i) Neser[17]

(ii) Camsring or Camsing[18]

(iii) Namsras.[19]

Paintings in the Temple

(i)	Gonpo :	Black–Blue colour	Both paintings belong to 15th century
(ii)	Gonpo :	White colour called Gonkar	

Old Dakhang

Left side of the Gonkhang had old Dukhang. It had old mud throne and woolen chortens. Besides it had the following statues:

(i) Buddha : One storey in height

(ii) Maitreya

New Dukhang

It has four beams with glass room upper side, 35' × 8'. There are six rows on which lamas sit and offer prayers.There are almirah the left and right side of the walls in which Kagyur and Stangyur phoths are well preserved.

In the middle has two thrones of Holiness Dali Lama and Rev. Kushok Bakula. The statues of this temple are listed below :

1. Buddha: One story in height
2. Chepakme[20]
3. Co–Loketsavera[21]
4. Skudung chorten[22]
5. Cuksikzal (Avalokitesvara)[23]
6. Chamba (Maitreya)[24]
7. Dorje Jigjet (Yamantaka)[25]

Wall Paintings

The Dukhang is decorated by Buddhist wall paintings as shown below:

1. Tungshak (ie 35 Buddhas)
2. Sixteen Arhats[26]
3. Jigjet: Towards door
4. Tsong Khapa
5. Chepakmet: on the west side wall
6. Tselanamsum (Tib. tre lha rnam gsum)[27]
7. Guru Padmasambhava (Tib slo dpon padma, abyang)[28]
8. Various incarnation of Rev. Kushok Bakula towards east.

Tsang Khang (Tib. gtsang-khang)

This temple is located above Dukhang. It was built in 1988, has one precions Buddha statue brought from Nepal, must be very old. The other statue are listed below :

(i) Buddha	:	Made of caly
	:	Height –One storey about 12 feet

(ii)	Chepakmet	:	It is said that this statue was given as gift to Ladakh king Dragspa Bumde by Tsongkhapa during 15th century.
(iii)	Lama Lhawang Lotos	:	At the right side of Chepakmet.
(iv)	Maitreya	:	Right to Lhawang Lotos. Looks old statue and brought here from old Dukhang
(vi)	Tsongkhapa	:	Right to Maitreya.
	(with his two disciples	:	He was the founder of Geluka order

Jo – Khang

It was Bakula Rinpoche's rest room, called Zimshung. In 1953 one Jo–rinpoche statue made of brass, brought from Tibet. Then this temple named after as Jo-khang. It has following main status:

1.	Jo–Rinpoche	:	Centre statue
2.	Padmasmbhava Khamsum Zilon	:	Left to the centre statue
3.	Changchub Chorten[29]	:	Right to Padmasambhava
		:	Made of silver and decorated by precious stones
4.	Sixteen Arhads	:	Made of sandal wood
5.	nye ve sras chen gyat[30]		
6.	Dorje Sempa[31]	:	Holds Dorje
7.	Co-bo-je Paldan Atisa	:	Made of wood
8.	White Tara[32]	:	Right to Atisa
9	Namgyal Chorten[33]	:	Made of silver.

Thankas

Above Lhakhang has some thanks as listed below:

(i)	Panchen Rinpoche	:	13th incarnation
(ii)	Tungshak	:	Thirty five Buddhas
(iii)	Khetapala	:	Tib. Kve tra pva la
(iv)	Dolma	:	21 Tara
(v)	Paldan Lhamo	:	Tib. dpal ldan lha mo
(vi)	Camsring or Camsing	:	Tib. lcam sring

Dolma Lhakhang (Tib sgrol ma lha khang)

This Lhakhang has twenty one Dolma (Tib. rje tsun sgrol ma) statues. These are made of brass brought from Tibet. Besides it has Dukar (Tib. gdugs dkar) statue.

Thankas

Dolma Lhakhang has some small thankas as listed below:

(i)	Paldan Lhamo	:	Tib dpal ldan lha mo
(ii)	Tsongkhapa	:	Tib tsong kha pa
(iii)	Skyabje Ling rinpoche	:	Tib skyabs rje-gling rin po che

Zimsung (Tib. gzims sbug)

It is a rest room of Rinpoche, situated at the right side of Dolma Lhakhand, and has the following statues :

(i) Trongkhapa with his diciples.

(ii) Buddha

(iii) Chelanamsum : Tib. tse lha rnam gsum

(iv) Dolma

(v) Skyabje ling rinpoche

It has many religious pothis belong to Tsong-Kha teachings.

Kangyur Lhakhang (Tib. Bk'a-gyur lha- khang)

It is named after Kangyur pothis, which are properly placed in the almirah.

Statues

Kangyur lhakhang does not have many statues as:

(i) Tsongkhapa

(ii) Gonkar[34]

Thankas

(i) Bakula rinpoche

(ii) Je cun Dolma : Silver colour

: Brought from Mongolia

(iii) Opakmet[35] : Tib 'aod pag med

(vi) Dechok Khorlo Donpa[36]: Tib bde chog 'akhorlo sdom pa

(v) Macik Lamdon[37] : Tib. ma gcig lab sagron

(vi) Buddha

(vii) Jigjet

(viii) Avalokitesvara

Gonkhang

This is a old temple and has a few statues as :

(i) Sangde Zigsung[38] : Tib. gsang bde 'ajigsgsum

: Made of sandalwood

(ii) Zampal[39] : Tib dzam phal

: On the right of Sangde – Zigsung

(iii) Sugdan[40] : Tib. shugs ldan

Thankas

Gonkhang has some thankas of Dharmapalas, yidam etc. such as:

(i)	Lama Chotpa	: Tib. bla ma chod pa
(ii)	Iidam	: Tib, Yidam
(iii)	Dorje jigjet	: Tib. rdo-rje 'ajigs byed
(iv)	Choskyong	: Tib. chos skyong
(v)	Sugdan	: Tib. shugs ldan
(vi)	Tsongkhapa with his disciples	: Tib. Yab sras gsum

Kunshal Zimsung (Tib. Kun gsal–gzims chung)

Here Bakula rinpoche always stayed. It has the following statues :

(i)	Bakula Rinpoche	: Made of brass
(ii)	Avalokitesvara	: Tib. phags pa spyan rasagzigs
(iii)	Dorje Sempa	: Tib. rdo rje sems dpa
(iv)	Jamyang	: Tib. 'ajam yang
(v)	Tsongkhapa with his two main disciples	
(vi)	Dolma	
(vii)	Buddha	

Thankas

This room does not have many thankas, however, has one beautiful thanka of opakmet with silk cloth border and Bakula rinpoche photo. Besides, we can see many rituals things, which are normally used during daily prayer.

Zimsung (Tib. gzims sbug)

Here Bakula rinpoche used to go for meditation. It has some statues as listed below :

(i) Chelanamsum (Tib. tse lha rnam–gsum)

(ii) Buddha (Tib. Thub dba)

(iii) Tsongkhapa

(iv) Namsras (Tib. rnam sras)

(v) Naljorma[41] (Tib. rnal 'abyor ma)

Thankas

This room has only one thanka of camsring (Tib. lcam sring)

Branches of Spituk Gonpa

Spituk monastery has four branch gonpas viz.

(i) Spituk da cang sam stan chos ling (Tib. dpe thub grva tsang bsam gtan chos gling)

(ii) Shanka gonpa (Tib. bsam dkar gra tsang skal ldan spyi skyob gling)

(iii) Stok Gurphug (Tib. tog gur phug grva tsang)

(iv) Sabu gonpa (Tib. pa phud bkra shis dge 'aphel grva tsang

Spituk da cang sam stan chos ling or dpe thub grva tsang gtan chos gling

This gonpa was built by Lopon (Tib. slob–dpon) Lozang Gyatso (Tib. blobzang rgya mtso) in 1770 A.D. But unfortunately the old structure of this temple was destroyed. However, after repairing a new building was built in 1962. It has three rooms e.g.

(i) Dukhang : The main room or prayer hall

(ii) Zimsung : Rinpoche's rest room

(iii) Kitchen

Dukhang

The Dukhang of this monastery has 10 beams and 33′ × 31′ 9″ prayer hall. It has four rows on which lamas during prayer sit and perform rituals.

Statues

Dukhang has following statues :

(i) Tsong–Khapa : Made of Sandalwood

(ii) Buddha

(iii) Buddha } They are in Mandal

(iv) Buddha

(v) Dorje jigjet (skt-Yamantaka)

Besides it has Buddhist texts and chortens made of gold and silver

Wall Painting

Like other monasteries it has following wall paintings :

(i) Buddha

(ii) Buddhisattvas

(iii) Tus kyi khor lo (Sk. Bhava Cakra)

(iv) Idem (Dorje Jigjet)

(v) Dharma Protectors.

On the upper side of the temple has glass room with following wall paintings :

(i) Lamrim

(ii) Bakula's past life history on the left and right walls

(iii) Gyantuk chognis

(iv) Kanlop choslup (Disciple of Tsongkpapa)

(v) Phadampa

(vi) Micak

(vii) Lamdon

(viii) Dorje Phagmo

(ix) Dorje Sempa

Tsang Khang (Tib. gtsang khang)

This temple has some important thankas as listed below :

(i) Comsring : Tib. lcam sring

(ii) Panchen Rinpoche[42] : Made of nose blood

: It is precious thanka and

most of the time covered. Every year on 12 & 15 of the 2nd Tibetan month and 13 & 16 of 3rd Tibetan month opened for puiblic.

Statues in Tsang Khang

Tsang khang has some importent statues as listed below :

(i)	Camsring or Camsing	: Tib. lcam msring
(ii)	Maitreya	: Tib. rgyaba byams pa
(iii)	Gonpo	: Tib mgon po
(iv)	Dorje Jigjet	: Tib mrdo rje 'ajigs byad
		: Made of Sandal wood
(v)	Panchen Rinpoche	: Tib. Pan chen Rin-po–che.
		: Made of wood
(vi)	Buddha	: Made of brass
(vii)	Protectors	
(viii)	Buddha	: At the north side wall

Buddhist Pothis

At the left and right side of Buddha there are almiras in which Buddhist taxts e.g. Lamrim are preserved.

Besides the following thankas are hanged through wall during annual festival called 'Gustor".

(i)	Jigjet	: Tib. rdo rje 'ajigs byed
(ii)	Protectors	: Tib. Chos skyong
(iii)	Lama chotpa	: Tib. bla ma chod pa
(iv)	Mila[43]	

Zimsung (Tib. gzims chang)

It does not have many statues and thankas, however, the following are important.

1. Twenty one Dolmas
2. Buddha Statues
3. 35 Buddhas Thankas | Thankas

Sankar Monastery

The monastery also named as bsam dkar sgal ldan skyob gling. It was built in 1910. Initially it had a small temple. Later the earlier incarnation of Kushok Bakula developed it. One side has glass windows with the length of 24′ 10″. During prayer lamas of the monastery sit in four lines (i.e. seats for them is four rows).

Statues

The Dukhang has following statues :

(i) Buddha : Made of brass

(ii) Dorje Jigjet

(iii) Avalokitesvara

(iv) Head Lama throne

Thankas

It does not have many thankas. During the study tour, I saw Camsring (Tib. lcam sring) Thanka.

Wall Painting

Like other temples it has the following paintings:

1. 35 Buddhas
2. 16 Arhads
3. Protectors (Tib. chos skyong) along the door.

Cang Khang (Tib. gtsang khang)

Cang Khang has following statues

(i) Tsezing (tib. tre 'adzin)

: Height – 3′ 3″

(ii) Sakyamuni Buddha

(iv) Avalokitesvara : Height – One story

Besides it has Lama, Yidam and various Dharma Protector statues.

Dukhang Ogma (Tib. 'adu Khang' aogma)

Dukhang Ogma has the following statues :

(i) Matireya

(ii) Tsongkhapa

(iii) Padmasambhava

(iv) Jamspal (Tib. 'ajam dphal)

Ninas Khang (Tib. Bsnyen Lha Khang)

Ninas Khang has beautiful statues and walls are decorated by wall paintings. Villagers come here for prayer and lit lamps.

Statues

1. Avalokitesvara : Height – 2′
2. Padmasambhava
3. Green Tara[44]
4. Tsong Khapa
5. Chepakmet

Wall Paintings of this temple

1. 16 Arhads (Tib. brtan bcu drug)
2. Gyaltsen zee[45] (Tib. rgyal chen bji).

Dukar Lhakhang (Tib. gdugs dkar lha Khang)

In this Lhakhang the main statue is Dukar. Here follows further details:

1. Dukar (Tib. gdug dkar) : Height. 10'a"
2. Buddha : Centre statue
3. Tsongkhapa
4. Gyal trab : Diciple of Tsongkhapa
   : Right to Tsongkhapa
5 Khasdup : Disciple of Tsongkhapa
   : Left to Tsongkhapa

Zimsung (Tib. gzhims chung)

In this room Rev. Kushok Bakula used to stay.

Statues

Zimsung has a few statues as listed below:

1. Tsongkhapa
2. Gyal tsab : Disciple of Tsongkapa
   : Right side of Tsongkhapa
3. Khasdup : Disciple of Tsongkhapa
   : Left side of Tsongkhapa

   All the above statue are made of sandalwood
4. Buddha

Thankas

In this room some thankas can be seen as :

1. Tsongkhapa
2. Gyandug chognis (Tib. rgya drugm chog gnyis Eight Indian Acharya
3. Padmasambhava (Tib. slob dbon rin po che)
4. Je cun dol jang (rje btsunsgrol ljang)

5. Dolkar (Tib. sgrol dkar)

Besides it has various gifts given by VIPs.

Shar Zim sung (Tib. sharzims chung)

Zimsung has some statues such as :

1. Three Buddhas (Tib. stonpa gtso 'akhor gsum))
2. Dorje Sempa (Tib. rdo-rje sems pa)
3. Chagna Dorje (Tib. phyagna rdo rje)
4. Tsongkhapa
5. Buddha
6. Dolma

Thankas

Shar Zim sung has the following thankas:

(i) White Tara (Tib. rje btsun sgrol dkar)

(ii) Panchen paldan yishes (Tib. pan chen dpal ldan ye shes)

(iii) Avalokitesvara (Tib. spyan ras-gzigs)

Kangyur Lhakhang (Tib. bk'a-'agyur lha khang)

In this Lhakhang, Kangyur pothis are kept in almirahs of both sides walls.

Statues

This temple has a few statues as listed below :

(i) Dus sum sangyas (Tib. dus gsum-sangs rgyas) (i.e. past, present and future Buddhas)

(ii) Throne for Dalai Lama.

Gyal Khang (Tib. rgyal-khang)

It has one important thanka of Gyalpo (Tib. rgyal po), the Ishta Deva of Rev. Bakula Rinpoche. It was repaired in 1988, and always covered by a silk cloth. It is used to display for public on 29th of 10th Tibetan month.

Kilkhor Lhakhang (Tib. dkyil–'akhor lha–khang)

It has jigjet Kilkhor (Tib. rdo-rje 'ajigs byed kyi gros), which is 21 feet length and 3 feet wide.

Notes and References

1. Atisa: Tib. Jo-a-ti-sa. One of the eighty four mahasiddhas (Tib. Grub-thob), saints and miracle workers. Face one, hands: two in monastic robes, seated on lotus throne, to the right a stupa, to the left a round basket, mudra: dharmachakra: cf. Bunce, Fredrick W: An Encyclopaedia of Buddhist Deities...' D.K. Printword, New Delhi, 1994:34.
2. Lotsava Rinchen bzangpo: During 10th-11th century, under his leadership a whole school of scholars and translators arose to render from Sanskrit into Tibet not only Sutras and Tantras but also many of the numerous and extensive commentaries attached to these works Cf. Finegan, Jack: 'Tibet: A Dreamt of Image; Tibet House, New Delhi, 1986:13.
3. King Dragspa Bumde: He was the elder son of Trhitsukde, succeeded his father and ruled as the seventeenth and next to last king of the First Ladakhi Dyanasty. Cf. Finegan, Jack.; *op. cit.,* p. 169.
4. Lama Lhawang Lotos: He was the head lama of Spituk (Tib. dpe-thub) monastery founded with the help of Dragspa Bumde during 15th century A.D.
5. Tsong-khapa: Tib. rje-rin-po-che, tson-kha-pa phon. Eng. Tsongkhapa. He was the founder of Geluk-pa of Mahayana Buddhism during 14th century A.D., and considered to be a manifestation of Manjusri. Cf. Finegan, Jack; *op. cit.*
6. Cang Sems sherab zangpo: He was the disciple of Tsongkhapa, visited Ladakh on the request of his guru, met Dragspa Bumde, the king of Ladakh during 15th century latter, founded Thiksery monastery.
7. Golukpa tradition: In 1409 Tsongkhapa founded Ganden

(Tib. dga–ldan) monastery in Tibet. Later after Ganden the name of his tradition was named as Gelukpa.

8. Galdan Tsewang: He invaded Ladakh during the period of Deldan Namgyal to safe Ladakh King asked help from Aurangzeb, then the ruler of the Mughal empire.
9. Delek Namgyal: Tib. bDe-legs rnam-rgyal. He was the twenty sixth ruler in the succession from Pelgyigon.
10. Zorawar: In the extension of his power, in 1834 Gulab Singh sent his army under his commander Zorawar Singh against Ladakh.
11. Kushok Rangdol Nima: He was the earlier incanation of Kushok Bakula, was born in Zanskar.
12. Khar: It means king's palace, in Ladakh we can see many palaces, but popular among them is Leh palace, built by Singge Namgyal.
13. Yamantaka: Tib. Dorje Jigje, In Sanskrit language equivalent to vajrabhaira. His wrathful form is the manifestation of Manjusri. He is the 'Destroyer of Death', is the protector of Geluk-pa order.
14. Gonpo (six hands): Tib. mgon-po-phyag-drug-pa, one of the Dharmapala images found in the chu Fo p'u-sa-sheng Hsiang Tsan. Face: One, three eyes, fierce, flame like hair; Hands: Six vahana: Prostrate human. Cf. Bunce, Fredrick W: *op. cit.:* 464.
15. Tamcan chosgyal (yab-yum form): Various form Tamcan (or Damcan), meaning bound by vow as protective deities.
16. Paldan Lhamo: Tib. dpal ldan lha mo, "The Glorious Goddess", is one of the most important protectors of the Geluk-pa order of the Buddhism, and also known as the jewel protector.
17. Neser: Tib. No-Ser-Jo-bo-chen-poor Phying-dkar-' ba or aka-dga-' ldun-'brog-ri-i-dge-bsnyen. A Dharmapala.
18. Camsing: Tib. lcam-sring, equivalent to Beg-tse (Tib. beg-rtse). A Dharmapala or jig-rten-las-'das-pa'i-sung-ma.

19. Namsras: Pali Vesavana, Tib. r Nam-thos-sras or rgyal po rnam thos sras. A guardian king of north.
20. Chepakmet: Tib. tshe dpag med in Sanskrit equivabut to Amitayu. He is the Buddha of logavity.
21. Co-Loketsavara: He is Avalokitesvara the lord who looks down with compassion," is the manifestation of Aimitabha.
22. Skudun Chasten: This is the stupa in which concerned lama of high rank body is preserved.
23. Cuksikzal (Avalokiteovara): Tib. Chenrezi. Chak-tsong-chen-tong, Bodhisativa who once took a vow to save all living being from sufferings.
24. Chamba (Maitreya): Tib. Byams-pa, Phon. Eng. Jampa "The kind one". A Mahabodhisattva and the Bodhisattva who is equally respected by the Theravadists. He is regarded as Future Buddha.
25. Dorje Jigjet (Yamantaka): In Sanskrit language equivalent to Vajrabhairava, is the menifestation of Manjusri.
26. Sixteen Arhats: Tib. gnas-brtan, pron nepten. It is believed to have been entrusted by Sakyamuni Buddha with the continuing task of protecting the doctrine and of being present and reward virtue wherever good deels are done.
27. Tselanamsum (Tib. tse lha rnam gsum): They are :

    (1) tshe dpag med (chepakmet)

    (2) rnam rgyal ma (Pron. Namgyal ma)

    (3) grol ma (Pron. Dolma or Tara).
28. Guru Padmasambhava (Tib. slo dpon padma adyang): He was a great mystic saint from India who had tremendous miraculous powers, brought Buddhist Tantra in Tibet during 8th Century and practice. He is considered as the secondg Buddha among Tibetans.
29. Changchub chorten: In Tibetan language it may correctly spell as byan-c'ub mc'odrten and it means "chorten of illumination."
30. nye ve sras chen gyat. They as follows :

    (i) Sayi nyingpo (4)

(ii) Dipa nam sel (5)

(iii) Namkhey nying po (6)

(iv) Chamba (7)

(v) Chanrazik (3)

(vi) Jamyang (1)

(vii) Chagna dorji (2)

31. Dorje Sempa: Tib. Dro-rje-sems-dpa, rdo-rje-sems-dpah, byan-chub-rdi-rje-sems-dpah "vajra being."

32. White Tara: Tib. Dolkar. She is the manifestation of Avalikitesvara is considered compassion from as mother, depicted as one face, two hands two legs, seven eyes. The ultimat Bodhisativa of purification.

33. Namgyal chorten: It is said when Buddhe said to his disciples for his Nirvana. He agreed. Then Nanagyal chorten was built.

34. Gonkar: A form of Mahakala. He has one face, there eyes; Arms: six, Legs: Two, clour: white; vahana: Two elephants. He is depicted in Dukhang karmo of Thiksey monastery as well.

35. Opakmet: Tib. od-dpag-med, hod-dpag-med. In Sanskrit language equivalent 'Amitabha, represents the lotus energy, which transmates passion into spiritual purity. His family of emanation inclues Avalokitesvara.

36. Dechok Khorlo Donpa: Tib. Demchok Skt. equivalent to cakrasamvara or 'Samvara'. He belongs to Vajrayana or Tantra of high yoga which emphasizes on cultivating the clear light, and subdues the rudra of ego through transmutation of passion.

37. Macik Lamdon: She is Lha (or goddess) setting on lotus flower.

38. Sangde Zigsung : ?

39. Zampal ?

40. Sugdan: His Holiness said that don't prey this Lha or deity.

41. Naljorma: Tib. rdo-rje-rnal-byor-ma. Phon.Eng. Dorje Naljorma, Naro Kachoma or mkh'a spyod ma zhal tshad brgyad pa. A terrifying goddess.

42. Panchen Rinpoche: The Figth Dalai Lama had been a pupil of an aboot of Transhilunpo mwnastery Lopsang choskji Gyentsen, and in his position of authority after 1642 the Fifth Dalai Lama, to show his gratitude to his teacher, conferred upon Lopsang choskji Gyentsen the title of Pan-chen Rin-po-che.

43. Mila: Tib. Mi-la- ras-pa. One of the eithty-four mahasiddhas saints and miracle workes, a great tantric of Mahayana.

44. Green Tara: Tib Dolzang. She is the active force of compassion, the chinese wife of king Songtsen Gampo.

45. Gyaltsen Zee: Tib. rgyal chen sde bzhi, four Directional Protectors viz:

    (i) rgyalpo yul' khor srung

    (ii) Phagkye Po or Phags skyes po

    (iii) Chen Misang or phags-skyes po

    (iv) Namthae Sey or rnam thos sras.

7

Dorje Chenmo Lhakhang in Shey Village

This temple is located about 15 km from Leh near road side at Shey village[1] and belongs to Dorje chenmo, [2] the dharma protector of Lotsava Rinchen bzangpo.[3] Dorje Chenmo Lhato is also located nearby. It is under the control of Hemis monastery, the Drugpa K'agyud tradition.[4] I visited the temple on 12th Septmber 2006, found three temples viz. Dorje Chenmo Lhakhang, Lhamo Khang and Padmasambhava Lhakhang. All the temples are situated in first storey. At the ground floor I saw an old Dorje Chenmo Lhakhang. Today all the statues from this Lhakhang is shifted to the new Dorje Lhakhang. There are some old precious frescos in this dark Lhakhang (Fig. 7.1).

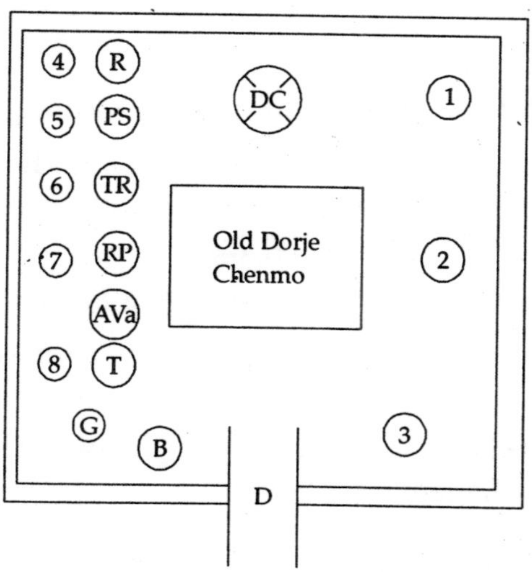

Fig. 7.1: Frescos in old Dorje Chenmo (at the ground floor of the temple)

Here follows the details :

(1) Lhamo Dudsolma:[5] : She rides on horse

(2) Lhamo Remeti[6] : She rides on horse

(3) Chakmar[7] : She ride on red

(4), (5), (6), (7), (8) } Buddhas; called Gyalva Rignga[8]

(R) : Lama Rigraspa[9]

(PS): Padmasambhava[10]

(TR) : Stag stang ras pa[11]

(RP) : Lama Rinchen Phunchok

(Ava) : Avalokitesvara[12]

(T) : Tseringma[13]

(G) : Gonkar[14]

(B) : Buddha

New Dorje Chenmo Lhakhang

After climbing through stairs I came to the first temple, known New Dorje Chenmo Lhakhang. It has one important statue of Dorje Chenmo (Fig. 7.2).

The details of other statues are listed below :

1. Dorje Chenmo: Rided on white horse weared five heads crown.
2. Lama Rigzin Tsewang Norbu: He was the teacher of Darje Chenmo.
3. Sakyamuni Buddha: Seated.

   Mudra: (i) Right hand in Bhumi sparsha

   (ii) Left hand in Meditation

Hevenly Dakinis called Rigma cu-tuk.

(i) Om baza vini dam (Tib. Om brza-vaini d'am)

(ii) Vam she

(iii) Mu rance (Tib mu rcde)

(iv) Midamge (Tib. mri dam ge)

(v) Ha se (Tib. ha sye)

(vi) La se (Tib. l'a sye)

(vii) gi ti (Tib. g'ai t'ai)

(viii) niti (Tib. ni tyi)

(ix) pu she (Tib. pu shpe)

(x) Humpe (Tib. rgh'au pe)

(xi) Di pam (Tib. d'ai pam)

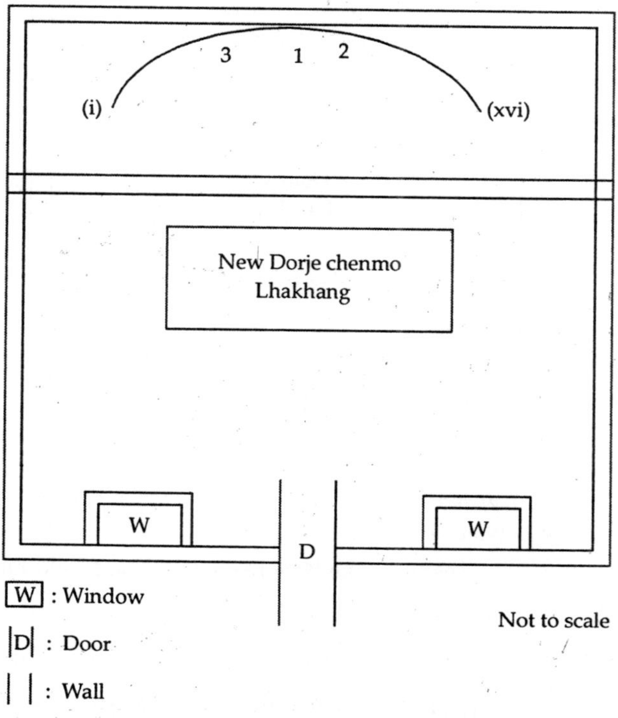

Fig. 7.2. Statues in New Dorje Chenmo Lhakhang

(xii) Gande (Tib. gndhe)

(xiii) Rupa (Tib. r'au pa)

(xiv) Ras (Tib. ra sya)

(xv) Parsa (Tib. spa dsha)

(xvi) Dama (Tib.dha rma)

The above deities/Dakinis have different postures and colours viz white, blue, red, green, yellow. All weared five heads crown called (Tib. Rig-nga), surrounded by tsa kyung vizo white, yellow etc. dragons. The statues are placed in the Glass room.

Frescos in New Dorje Chenmo Lhakhang: On the left and right walls of this temple has beautiful frescos. Here follows the details (Fig. 7.3).

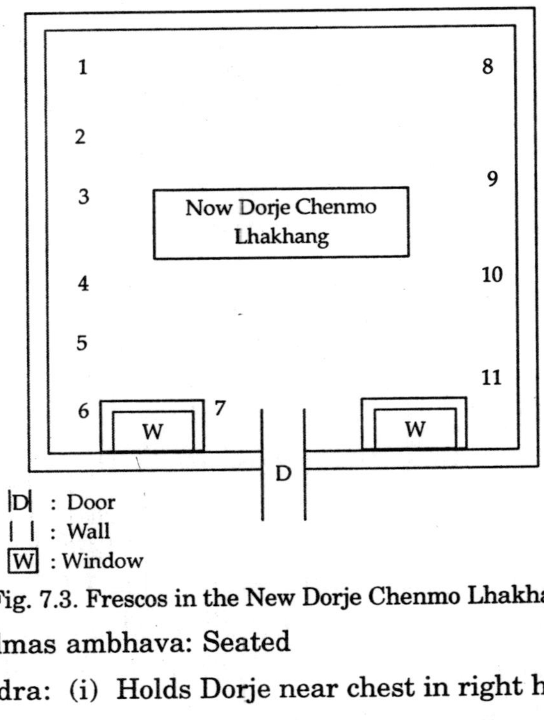

Fig. 7.3. Frescos in the New Dorje Chenmo Lhakhang

1. Padmas ambhava: Seated

   Mudra: (i) Holds Dorje near chest in right hand.

   (ii) Left hand holds skull cup in meditation mudra.

2. Buddha: Seeted

   Mudra: (i) Right hand in Bhumispersha

   : (ii) Left hand in meditation

3. Sakyamuni Buddha : Seated

   Mudra: (i) Both hands in the meditation mudra holds patra.

4. Sakyamuni Buddha: Seated

   Mudra: Meditation, hold patra at the center of the asana.

5. Buddha: Seated

   Mudra: Right hand lies near chest

6. **Dolma (Green Tara)** Colour: Green

   Mudra: (i) Right hand rest on her thigh

   (ii) Left hand rests near brest.

7. Dorje chenmo.

8. Tsewang Rigzin:

   Mudra: (i) Right hand rests near chest

   (ii) Left hand lies on thigh

9. Dudsolma[15]

10. Lhamo

11. Cakmin.[16]

Statues in Lhamo Khang of Dorje Chenmo monastery: In this temple all the statues are placed in the glass room. Here follows the details (Fig.-7.4).

1. Lhamo Sut Dusolma:[17]

   Height : 3′

   Width : 2½

2. Lhamo Remeti:

   Height : 4′

   Width : 3′

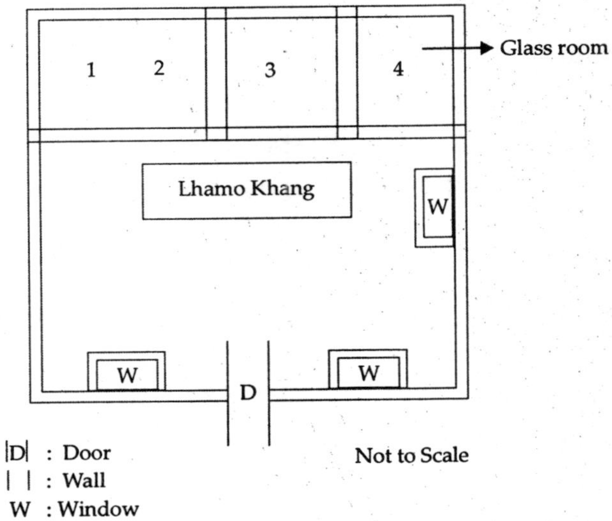

Fig. 7.4. Statues in Lhamo khang in Dorje Chenmo monastery, Shey

3. Dorje chenmo:
   Height : 1½
   Width : 1′
4. Guru Lhasig degint in yab yum form:[18]
   Height : 4½
   Width : 3′

Lhamo Khang does not have many paintings, however I saw some: Human forehead, instestines & wangpo nga paintings.

Guru Padmasambhava Lhakhang: This Lhakhang is newly built in 2001. It has Padmasambhava statue made by Spon Nawang Tsering in 2001 (Fig. 7.5).

PS : Padmasambhava

Height: 3′

Mudra: (i) Left hand holds skull cup in meditation mudra.

(ii) Right hand holds Dorje, rests on thigh.

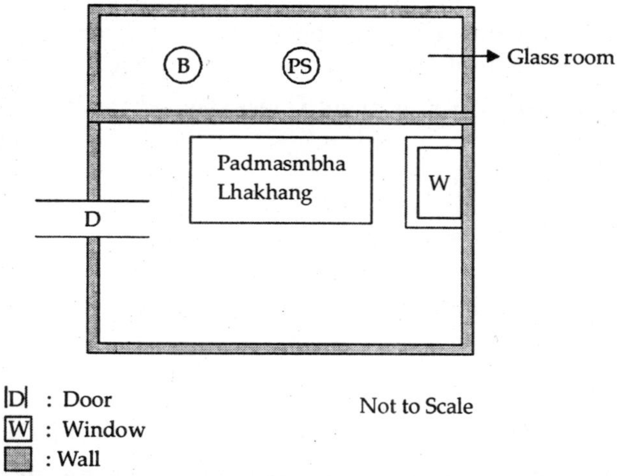

Fig. 7.5. Statues in Guru padmasambhava Lhakhang.

Buddha

B : It is at the right hand side of Padmasambhava.
Mudra: (i) Right hand in Bhumisparsha
(ii) Left hand in meditation

Notes and References

1. **Shey village:** It is situated at a distance of about 15 km from Leh along the Leh-Manali Highway on the right bank of the Indus river near the Choglamgar village.
2. **Dorje Chenmo:** It is a Lha (or personal deity) of Lotsava Rinchen bzangpo, who was a famous Buddhist scholar during 11th century A.D.
3. **Lotsava Rinehen bzangpo:** He was born in 958, was ordained at the age of thirteen and died at ninety-eighth year in 1055. During his life time he made three trips to India, translated Buddhist texts in Tibetan and constructed temples and chorten in Western Tibet.
4. **Drugpa K'agyud tradition:** Stag stang ra-pa was the supporter of Paksam Wangpo. He was responsible to spread Drug-pa K'agyud tradition in Ladakh during king Singge Namgyal, and founded famous Hemis monastery.
5. **Lhamo Dudsolma** (Tib. aka (dpal-ldan)–lha-mo-dud-sol-ma. In Sanskrit language equivalent 'Dhumavati-(Sri)-Devi aka Kamadhatvisvari or Dhumavati Devi.

6. **Lhamo Remeti** (Tib. lha-mo-remati-gsang-sgrub). A companion to dPal-ldan-dmag-zor-rgyal-mo.
7. **Chakmar:** Tib. Cag men; Choskyong of Druk-pa k'agyud order.
8. Gyalva Rignga :
   (i) Vairocana
   (ii) Akshobya
   (iii) Ratnasambhava
   (iv) Amitabha
   (v) Amoghasidhi
9. **Lama Rigraspa:** He would be a lama of Drugpa order.
10. **Padmasambhava:** The Lopon Rinpoche or Guru Rinpoche. "Lotus Born One", an Indian Tantric invited by King Trisong Detsen in the Eigth century A.D.
11. **Stag stang ras pa:** His name is derived from the Tiger nest cave in Bhutan, where he spent several years in meditation and was said to have attained the vision of all the 84 Indian Mahasiddhas.
12. **Avalokitesvara:** Tib. chenrazi "The compassinate one", literally. A mahabodhisattva and one of the most popular bodhisattvas in the world of Buddhism. The Fourth Dhyani Bodhisattva, the creator and ruler of the present age, an emanation of Dhyani Buddha Amitabha.
13. **Tseringma:** She is the goddess riding on a lion.
14. **Gonkar:** A form of Mahakala has one face fierce and three eyes, Arms: Six, Legs: Two, Colour: White.
15. **Dudsolma:** Tib. lha-mo-Dud-sol-ma, In Sanskrit language equivalent Dhumavati Devi.
16. **Cakmin:** Choskyung of Druk-pa tradition of Mahayana Buddhism.
17. **Lhamo Sut Dusolma:** She may be spelled as Lhamo Dudsolma.
18. **Guru Lhasig degint yabyum:** Tib. gu-ru lha-srin-sde-rgyad. They are eigh forms of Padmasambhava.

8

Rangdum Gonpa (Tib. rang-ldum-bshad grub zamling gyan) of Zanskar

Location: Rangdum is one of the famous monasteries in Zanskar of Kargil district, is situated at a distance of 12 km from Kargil under Panikhar block.

Historical Background: In 1726 lama Lobzang Gelek Yeshes Dakpa of Nari thang visited Ladakh. He met king Tsewang Namgyal,[1] who requested him to stay in Ladakh. During the course of his stay in his palace, Lama Lobzang gave him teachings on Buddhism. One day king requested:

"Geshes la! I listened Buddha teachings from you and benefited emensily. You have very good knowledge about Buddhism and its Philosophy. I feel happy if you establish your monastery any where in Ladakh. I'll help you."

Thereafter, lama Lobzang Gelek Yeshes Dakpa on the advise of king Tsewang Namgyal went out in search of proper place for the monastery. He arrived in Shyam area in Leh district, but didn't find suitable place for the gonpa. Finally he thought:

"There are many old monasteries in Shyam area, hence no scope for my monastery in this region as maximum lands and villages belong to them. So I should go to Zanskar."

At last after travelling couple of days in Zanskar, he reached near the hillock in Rangdum village. The hillock looked like a lion from the distance. He spent a night on the top of hillock, while sleeping he saw the following dream:

"Some villagers from Zanskar assembled near the capital of Ladakh and requested Lord Buddha to build a monastery at Rangdum, to stop evil sprit ativities and get peace and harmony in their villages."

After the above dream Lama Lobzang Gelek Yeshes Dakpa experienced an unprecedented peace of mind. He decided to establish his monastery at Rangdum village. Subsequently, to inform about his decision to Ladakh king he came Leh palace.

"Your Highness! I visited many villages in Ladakh, finally decided to build my monastery at Rangdum village in Zanskar. Therefore, I request your goodself to kindly help me by cash and kind for the construction of the above monastery."

King Tsewang Namgyal pleased to know this. In 1726 he gave Rangdum valley and nearby pasture ground to H.E. Nyari Rinpoche Lobzang Gelek Yeshes Dakpa. Later King Tsetan Namgyal and his son Tsepal Tondup Namgyal further supported him and confirming the Royal order issued by the king Tsewang Namgyal by two proclamations. As per religious conversation of king Tsewang Namgyal and spiritual Guru Lobzang Gelek Yeshes Dakpa of Tibet. The establishment of Gonpa then selected by Guru at Rangdum area is hereby deep philosophycal order issued by the kings as under:[2]

(In this) wast world, who is firm like a mountain of gold, spreads thousand rays of compassions, is the victorious king Tsewang Namgyal.

This is sent to all those monks and laymen, commonders and (all) persons, may be Chief Minister Manager, Minister, non officers village headman, horse-man Takshos, Tongspon, elders---Internal CIDs. The governors of Purik and sbalti and ministers. The monks and laymen of Lingshed, the chief Nyaraks, Youlchng, Photosar etc.. who live in my dominion of----- . The entire area of Rangdum from Spentsela pass and

----pass to the rock O-Sgon all the big and small valleys, villages, from the glacier to either side of the river the uninhabited area with its pasture, water and herb-wood, this possession and ownership all is offered to His Holiness Nyari Rimpoche supreme incarnate Lobzang Gelek Yeshes Dakpa, Pal- bzangpo by the ruler of the earth Tsewang Namgyal (live) long as the Buddha Dharma flourishes. This has been made (here) religions donation and the Government does not require------, revenue, tax of chang, animal tax, offerings, in the all sorts of taxes, which those who have hands and more (to) pay. Those mentioned above should not claim their power (not) to raise even minor dispute. On the other hand as we--- the frontier, we should make service and pay regard and (respect) as much as possible as an object of refuge for the (---) and future lives. If any one works against this mission (shall) be enquired into and if found guilty, he will be sent to (jail) so every one must know and should not make mistake (must) be complied.

Seal/Mangyul (Raja)

Thus the whole Rangdum area was donated to Lama Lobzang Gelek Yeshes Dakpa. He after sometime with the kind support of king Tsewang Namgyal started digging work for the plinth of the monastery. Fortunately during the course of digging a natural marble Buddha statue and a statue of Milarepa (Mailaraspa) were found. To acknowledge these statues Lams Lobzang became very happy and his confidence for the establishment of the monastery became more strong than earlier. In 1735 Rangdung monastery was built. After ritual ceremony it was re-named accordig to Buddhist monastic tradition 'Rang ldum bshad grub zam gling rgyan! The statues which were found during digging work also installed alongwith other statues.[3]

The monastery has some temple viz. Dukhang Gonkhang and Thub pa khang. Here follows the details :

Dukhang (Tib. 'Adu khang)

The Dukhang of the Rangdum monastery has sixteen beams. It has some statues as cited below:

1. Tsong-khapa[4]
2. Gyal tsab (Right to Tsong-khapa)[5]
3. Khasdup (Left to Tsong-khapa)[6]
4. Buddha

Thub pa khang

Thub pa khang has Buddha (Tib. thub pa sangs rgyas bcom ldan) statue.

Gonkhang (Tib. mgon Khang)

This is an old temple of the monastery was built in 1726. It has statues of Dharmpalas as listed below:

1. Dorgi Jigjet (Tib. rdo rje 'ajigs byid)[7]
2. Paldan Lhamo (Tib. dpal ldan lha mo)[8]
3. Choskyong (Tib. chos skyong)

The monastery belongs to Geluk pa sect. Nyari Rinpoche is the head of the monastery. It has seven village gonpas under its control. There are about 72 lamas who lookafter the monastic activities in Zanskar region.

To fulfil the religious needs of the following villages, monastery send pujaries :

1. Zanskar Aa ran (Tib zangs dkar a ran)
2. Akso (Tib. Ag sho)
3. Bakareche (Tib. ba dkar rtshe)
4. Skyagor (Tib. skya sgor)
5. Hamiling (Tib. Ha mi bling)

In Akso,monastery has a large area of cultivated land, maximum food and fuel requirement of the monestery is fulfilled by this.

Annual rituals in the monastery

The lamas of the monastery perform the following rituals for the welfare of the community according to Tibeatan calender. Thus, men and monastery cultural relationships are established everlasting.

1. Sangdus Dubchod (Tib. sang 'adus sgrub mchod) : Falls the 5th month of the year.
2. Decog & Dub chod (Tib. bde mchog & rgrub mchod) : The 6th month of the year
3. Yarnas : On the 10th of the 6th month and for the following fifteen days.
4. Jigjet Ki dub chod : (Tib, 'ajigs byed kyi sgrub mchod): It performs after Yarnas-Sojong.

Protective Deities: The monastery is protected by the following deities :

1. Shug-dan (Tib. rdo-rje shungs-ldan)
2. Taṇma Dorje Yu Don ma (Tib. bstan-ma rdo-rje gyu - sgron- ma): The local guardian spirit.

Past & Present Historic activities: The Rangdon monastery has a large area of pasture land about 37 km along the passage of river to the west, then towards south down Parkachik village. The area is thus varies in between 11,000 ft, to 13,624 ft. This area was initially donated to His Holiness Nyari Rinpoche by king Tsewang Namgyal of Ladakh under the condition that the whole Gonpa land would be exempted from taxation. In the year 1947– '48 after Hindustan and Pakistan partition qabalies were enconraged and supported by Pakistan, entered this area and compelled people of three villages viz. Gyalmo Stondey, Share-Tsogs and Shakhar to leave their villages. They looted their property. The Gonpa lamas however,were able to persuade and rehabilate them in their respective villages. Some years after small-pox break out in this region, again they had to leave the villages. But Gonpa lamas did not forget their duties and this time they helped them perticularly villages from Shakhar rehabitated by their efforts in 1988 – '89.[9]

In 2000, some militants entered into Rangdum monasery, on 11th July killed three innocent lamas. As a result lamas in the monastery gradually decreased to minimum number to 05 only. Therefore, totally unable to look after the routine religious obligation as to attend usual requests of the villagers nearby and the gonpa property viz, livestock and land. On the others side Gujars and Bakarwals forcibly enter with their livestock annually into the grazing land of gonpa and apprehend gonpa livestock for grazing. This serious problem nowadays gonpa authority is facing. If the State Govt. will not consider the problems of Rangdum and nearly Buddhist villages. A time may come when like Kashmir Pandits the Rangdum monastery may be destroyed and the Buddhists will have to migrate some where else. Hence, the Govt. has to the study the following judicial decisions and make all necessary measurements in order to protect the Buddhist property of villagers and Rangdum monastery as well.[10]

The Judicial decision issued by the District Court Kargil on 29-11-1985, the court has upheld the legal right of the Rangdum Gonpa on the entire area of Rangdum valley and asked the administration to restrain the Bakarwals not to interfere in the peaceful possession of the Rangdum Gonpa lands.

2. The Judicial decision issued by the High Court of J&K Srinagar on 24-01-2001, as same High court has upheld the legal right of the Rangdum Gonpa on the entire areas of Rangdum Gonpa land.

Notes and References

1. **King Tsewang Namgyal :** He was the son of Deskyong Namgyal (Tib. bde-skyong-r Nam-gyal) and ruled Ladakh for short time.
2. **Tsering Tashi:** Rangdum Gonpa; paper presented in National conference, CIBS, Leh-Ladakh 2004.
3. *Ibid.*

4. **Tsong-Khapa:** Tib-rjė-rin-po-che, Dron-kha-pa phon-Eng. Tsongkhapa. He was the founder of Geluk-pa order of Mahayana Buddhism during the 14thcentury A.D. He is considered the manifestation of Manjuṣiri, obtained the ordination of monkhood is his early age and studied Buddha's doctrine with strong interest, later went to central Tibet for further higher studies in Buddhist Phiolosphy studied Ttutra and Tantra. He learnt Madhyamika Philosophy from Randawa, composed many books on Sutra and Tantra. Cf. Batchelor Stephen:' The Tibet Guidei; Wisdom' Publication, London; 1987: 422.
5. **Gyal-tsab:** Tib. rGyal Tshab Darma Rin-chen (Pron. Gyetshab Darma Rinchhen). He was his main pupil of Tsongkhapa, thus appointed his successor and the abbot of the Ganden monastery.
6. **Khasdup:** He was the Tsongkhapa's younger pupil and his chief studends in tantric studies, often mentioned mkhas-grub-rje (Pron. khe-trup-Je) was born is 1385 and appointed about of Ganden monastery in 1431 to 1438.
7. **Dorje Jigjet:** In Sanskrit language equivalent to vajrabairava. His wrathful form is the manifestation of Manjusri. He is the suprime yoga tantra divison of the vajrayana and is the protector of Geluk-pa order, has nine faces the central face is bull's face with two horns and its complexion is dark and is the angry form. This form symbolises the ignorance which is transmuted into discrimination wisdom. Cf.. Lobzang Tsewang: 'Sakyamuni. An Echibition of Rare Thankas', CIBS, 2001: 34.
8. **Paldan Lhamo:** Tib. dpal-ldan-lha-mo.

   "The glorions Goddess", is one of the most important protectors of the Guluk-pa order of Buddhism and the guardian of Lhasa. She was given initiated by Chagna Dorje and was given the name Dorje Naljorma. Later Padmasmbhava bound her to follow the exhaustive instruction and came to Tibet with him. Cf. Ladrang Kalsang 'The Guardian dlaeities of tibet, Dharmasala Publication 2000: 17-31.
9. Tsering Tashi; *op. cit.*
10. *Ibid.*

9

Yarma-Gonpo Monastery

Location: It is situated near the base of Siacan glacier in Nubra valley of Leh district, Ladakh.

History: Yarma monastery was built by Go-tsang pa during 12th century when he was travelling in Nubra valley, came across at Tsang-sa village and suddenly saw 'Standin' on the nearby mountain. He stopped there later retreated in a nearby cave. In the mid night he felt as if one side wall of the cave started falling. He feared, but any how remained in the cave till morning. Sooafter, saw. Ishe Gonpo who had four hands appeared, a strange light surrounded to him lighted the cave. In this strange light he saw some more religious things and deities viz religious Bodhi text, Standin, Buddha, Yum Ikazati and Avalokitesvara in syambhu form. These very pious and secret statues, only high ranked lamas, Siddhas and other Holi persons can see. Khadup Gyaltsen, disciple of Gyalva Gotsangpa has written about the above images in his book, preserved in Mipham Kagyaud pothis. Kachen Lobzang Zodpa also writen about them in his book 'History of Nubra'. Today Yarma monastery has 20 lamas and functioning under Hemis. This monastery is situated infront of the above cave temple in Nubra valley of Leh district, Ladakh.[1]

Tradition: This monastery belongs to Druk-pa (or Drugpa) K'agyud tradition of Mahayana. In olden days the novices of the monestery used to go to Hemis monastery, the centre of Drukpa order in Ladakh, for primary education in Buddhism. After completing their education returned to the monastery and to do monastery works as assigned by the head lama of the Yarma Gonpa.

Branch Gonpas: The Yarma-Gonpa is one of the big monastery in Nubra valley. It has some village gonpas in which pujaris are deputed by the Yarma-gonpa management. They are listed below:

1. Tong – sted
2. Nyung – sted
3. Dung – sa
4. Khemi
5. Tsang – lung-ka
6. Sarsoma
7. Aarunuk
8. Ayi
9. Kovet
10. Tangsa
11. Murgo

} These Durgpa k'agyud gonpas are functioning under the direction of Yarma-Gonpo

Monastery administration: To lookafter monastery activities, lamas of the monastery appointed in varions posts who are responsible the assigned duties. Here follows the details

Lopon
↓
Gye – Nyen
↓
Geylong
↓
Gye – tsul
↓
Cun – zung

Table: 9.1 shows further details of the concern number of lamas in the monastery.

Children when given admission in the monastery as novices, they have to cut their hair, read & learn Buddhiist texts under the guidance of appointed senior lamas. After various gonpa examination they are promoted to Gye-tsul and about 10 years training come to the stage of Geylong. Then they are promoted further higher posts according to seniority.

Table: 9.1. Number of lamas with their respective posts

Sl. No.	*Post in the Gonpa*	*Number*
1	Lopon	01
2.	Gye-Nyen	05
3.	Geylong	06
4.	Gye-tsul	02
5.	Cun-zung	06

Temples: Like other big monasteries, Yarma Gonpo also has various temples (Lhakhangs) viz.

1. Du-khang
2. Kangyur-khang
3. Zimsung

Du-khang: It is the main prayer hall where lamas of the monastery all together offer daily prayer and read Buddhist texts.

Statues in Dukhang

Dukhang has many Buddhist statues according to Drukpa k'agyud tradition (Fig. 9.1).

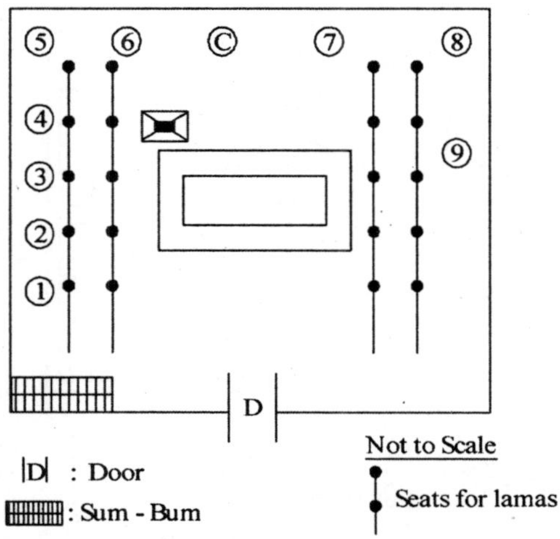

Fig. 9.1. Statues in the Dukhang of Yarma-Gonpo

① : Guru Rinpoche[2]
② : Standin Yang Sang[3]
③ : Cusikzal[4]
④ : Nang Gon
⑤ : Nang da Tulku
⑥ : Chepakmet[5]
Ⓒ : Central statue
: 4 hands Gonpo[6]
: Colour: Dark Blue
⑦ : Nam chak Gonpo
⑧ : Paldan lhamo[7]
⑨ : Stag tsang ras pa
⊠ : Dukchen Rinpoche Throne

Kangyur - Khang: This temple has kangyur and Stangyur pothis written in Tibetan language.

Statues

It does not have many statues, however Buddha statue and Cang-chub chorten can be seen (Fig. 9.2). Besides, the walls of this temple are decorated by Drugpa tradition painting.

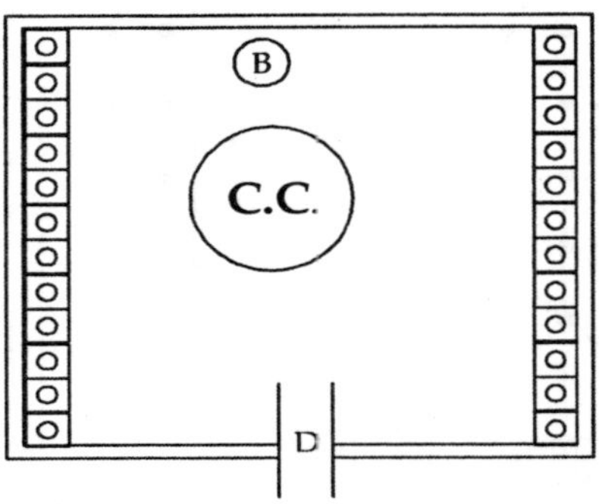

|D| : Door
(C.C) : Cang - chub chorten
▣ : Kangyur & Stangyur
(B) : Buddha statue

Fig. 9.2. Kangyur Khang in Yarma –Gonpo

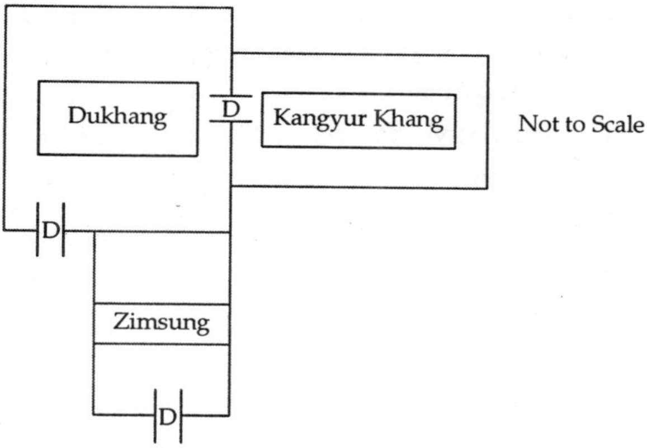

Fig. 9.3. Zimsung in Yarma Gonpo.

Zimsung: It is sitting and rest room of Rinpoche and high ranked lamas (Fig.9.3).

Conclusion: The Yarma Gonpo is one the remotest monastery in Nubra, belongs to K'agyud tradition. The Drugpa tradition monasteries are in a few number in Nubra valley.

References and Notes

1. **Jamyang Gyaltsan (ed.):** 'The History of Ladakh Monasteries'; 1989 : 182.
2. Guru Rinpoche was a great tantric saint of India. He was the manifestation of Buddha Amitabha and popularly known as second Buddha. He was invited by Tritsong Deutsen in 8th century. On his invitation Guru Rinpoche visted Tibet. Thus brought Buddhist Tantra in Tibet. In Tibet Bonchos had dominant role, people of this country were very much influenced by this tradition. Guru Rinpoche earlier did not know about them, therfore he founded Samyas monastery. But as construction of this monastery started local dietes and demons disturbed him and made serval obstruction. Guru Rinpoche then slowed them his tantric power and stopped their activities. He crushed down and bound them by oath to protect the Buddha's teachings. He

helped king Tritsong-Deutsen to build up the Samyas monastery, as well helped Acharya Santarasita to set up many blocks viz. teachings, translation and so on. He has eight forms :

1. Guru Sakya Sengey
2. Guru Padmasambhaua,
3. Guru Nyima Ozer
4. Guru Snegey Dradog
5. Guru Dorje Doloe
6. Guru Tsokey Dorje
7. Guru Padma Gyalpo
8. Guru Loden Chogsey.

In this way Guru Rinpoche through his various forms helped sentient beings. Hence, his contribution to spread Buddhism amazingly in Tibet as well in the neighbouring countries. Cf. Lobzang Tsewang: 'Sa'kyammuni: An Exihibition of Rare thankas,' CIBS, Leh - Ladakh; 2001: 26 & Shil P Guru Nawang Tsering: 'The Art of Sculpure in Ladakh. An Exhibition of Statues 2004; 2004 : 35

3. **Stamdin Yang Sang:** In Sanskrit equivant to aka Arya-Hayagrive, Krodha Yamari" The horse-necked one' A krodhadevatas and dharmapala, and a protective deity who keeps away demons. Cf. Bunce, Fredric W.: 'An Encyclopaedia of Buddhist Deties, Demigods Godlings, Saints and Dermons Vol. I, D.K. Printworld Ltd. New Delhi; 1994 : 202.

4. **Cusikzal:** A form of Avalokitesvara who once took a vow to save all sentient bengs from sufferings the prayed: "May I help all beings, and if ever I tride in this great work, may my body be shattered into thousand pieces!" First it is said, he descended into the hell realms, ascending gradually through the world hungry ghosts up to the realm of goods. From there he happened to look down and saw, he saved innumerable beings from the hall, countless more were pouring into it. This plunged him into the profounded grief and realised the magnitude of his task his head exploded into countless

pieces. His boody was reassembled by Amitabha and the Bodhisativa vajrapani into much more powerful form. Cf. S.K. Das: 'Tara: An Exhibition; 2003: 26 and Batchelor Stephen: 'The Tibet Guide', Wisdom Publication, London; 1987: 400– '01.

5. **Chepakmet:** In Sanskrit equivalent to Amitayus. He is the Buddha of long life. He appears in Sambhogakaya form of Dhyani Buddha Amitabha. Popularly known as Buddha of longevity. It is a genral Buddhist custom to portray a figure of Amitayus in red colour. But sometimes such kind of statue is also made by using golden colour with the intution of accumulating much more merits. He appears adoring with robes and various oranaments, such as earrings, neckace, bracelets anklets, long necklace and short necklace. The mantra 'Om Amarani Jivantiya Svaha' belong to him. This mantra is especially recited by the Mahayani Buddhists fot the purpose of gaining longevity. Cf. Shilp Guru Nawang Tsering; *op. cit.,* 23 and S.K. Das; *op cit.,* 23.

6. **4 Hands Gonpo:** Tib. mgon-po-phyag-bzhi-pa; in Sanskrit equivalent to caturbhuja Mahakala. He is one of the Dharmapala and has the following description: Face -one, fierce with Three eyes and flame-like hairs. Hands: Four; principal hands holds chopper and human skull- cup; right hand holds sword with flames and left holds atapatra. Legs: two; Asana: Alidhasana; colour: Blue or Black; Ornaments: Five skull crown, tiger and elephant skin as a body covering. Cf. Bunce, Fredrick W: 'An Excyclopaedia of Buddhist Deties Demigods,Godlings, Saints and Demons; Vol. I *op. cit.* 86.

7. **Paldan Lhamo:** Tib. dpal lden lha mo "The Glorions Goddess', is one of the most important protrectors of the Geluk-pa order of Buddhism and the gruardian of Lhasa. According to Indian chronicles in South India Shinji Legphe Gyalpo had a son and three daughters. The youngest daughter was Lhamo, leter was known Lhamo woebarma and became the main protrctor of Buddha Dharma. Cf. Batchelor Stenphen; *op. cit.,* 423-'24 and Ladrang kalsang:' The Guardian Deities of Tibet; Little Lhasa Pub. Dharmasala Pub:, 2000: 17-31.

10

Likir A Geluk-pa Monastery in Ladakh

Location of the Monastery

This monastery is in Likir village, Leh district of Ladakh in Jammu and Kashmir state, India.

Approach

It is 9.5 km north of Saspol and 52 kms. west of Leh. There is 2 km metalled link road from the Leh-Srinagar highway. This road turns north and winds along the hills to reach the monastic establishment.[1]

Historical Significance

According to the Chronicles of Ladakh, Likir monastery was built in the time of Lhachen Gyalpo[2] the father of Lhachen Utpala[3] in the middle of eleventh centruy A.D. while an inscription in the monastery names both the king and monk Duwang choje[4] the founders. In this regards historians say the following story:

During Lhachen Gyalpo period there was only a temple of Kadampa tradition.[5] After sometime siddha Lama Duwang Choje visited this temple. King Lhachan Gyalpo was a religious person, also came to Likir to listen choje carefully. King was very much impressed by his teachings later offered the site to Lama Duwang choje who blessed the site. There after some lamas started to stay there for meditation

Local beliefs

When Lama Duwang choje came out from the cave after

meditation. King Lhachen Gyalpo requested: "Guruji Pranam ! How nice it would be, if you establish a monastery in Likir village!"

"I'll Think."

After sometime Lama Duwang choje went to Namsras Photang, he performed rituals and threw wheat seeds in all directions. At the end before shooting arrow into the sky he said:

> "The arrow will decide the place of monastery". He shote the arrow into the sky, it striked the place where the present Likir monastery is established. The mountain from where Lama Duwang choje shot arrow is known Suri. After sometime a god (or Lha) appeared in the form of bird, he took the arrow and brought it to Photang. Subsequently, choje Lama went to the place where arrow striked the place, and purified the place by performing rituals. Later with the support of king Lhachen Gyalpo he built a temple on a stupa shaped mountain.[6] In the passage of time he built a Dukhang for 100 lamas. Thereafter, another Dukhang 'Chorten Dukhang' was built. It was decorated by Buddhist statues and paintings. In the meantime king asked nearby villagers to donate children to the monastery. Later it became tradition and villagers started to donate one child from each family to the monastery, thereafter lama population started increasing. Subsequently in 1040 A.D. chosje implemented rules and ragulation of Kandampa tradition in the monastery.

Auspicious Signes

Likir had the following auspicious signes under which the monastery was constructed.

1. There is Glacier at the north, which shows the vicitory sign of Dharmpalas.

2. At the west red mountain is the indication for longivity of Buddha Shashan at the south a big white stone looks like pass and infront of this some pictures look like 16 Arhats. This indicate that Likir would become a popular monastery.

Inscription: Tibetan text

Skyabs gnas thub mthog / 'a khor lo stom ba nas/ dlung b'ai sil gyi/ gnang ltar bk'a gyabs kyi/ rten 'abril las/ gsang ltar rgyal b'ai/ dkyil skor ris med sar/ klu dkar dgra kun sna lcog 'de.

Roman Transliteration

Skyab nas thup chok khorlo Dam pa nas,-Lang pa sel gi nang tar ka gyab kyi sten del las sang star gyal ve kilkor rismet sar, lu kar da kun na co de.

Translation

This place has all characteristics as required for Yidam Caksamvara's religious place. At the place where monastery has been established belong to Devraj jokpo (or Nagraj) . The monastery is constructed on the head of Nagraj and Likir village lies on its body.

Name of the monastery: Likir monastery derived from Lhukyil (Tib. klu-'khyil) ie. Lhu =Naga and 'Khyil = a place. Thus the site of the Likir monastery was encircled by the bodies of the two great serpent spirits, the naga-rajas Nanpa and Taksako. As a result the monastery widely known as Lhukyil, which later corrupted to Likir.

Introduction of Geluk pa order: 400 years later after the establishment of Likir Gonpa. Geluk-pa tradition[7] adopted by the monastery by the inspiration of Lhawang lodos during 15th Century. He was the disciple of Khasdupje[8] came in Ladakh from Central Tibet and was a well knpwn Buddhist scholar of Buddhist Sutra and Tantra. He at first arrived Nubra then went to Likir. In Likir monastery he saw a few lamas of Kadampa sect, they were not looking the monastery well. Lama Lhawang felt sorry and met king. He requested:

Maharaj: "I felt pitty to see the poor condition of Likir monastery. There are only a few kadampa lamas in the monastery, and mostly stay in villages. Therefore, kindly preserve the monastic culture."

Ladakh king Lodos Chogdan listened him carefully and in order, to strengthen the monastic activities he passed an order under which nearby villagers of the Likir monastery had to donate one child to the monastery to become lama. By 1442, lama population in the monastery had been incresase considerbly. Later Lama Lhawang Lodos preached them and converted kadampa tradition into Geluk-pa, and gave new name 'Galden Targyasling' to the monastery. To protect the gonpa's property he gave the responsibility to Dharmpala, Shetapcan. Besides he implimented a tradition to send lamas to Sangpul in Tibet for higher studies in Buddhist philosophy. This tradition came to an end when Tibet was occupied by China in 1959.

The Relation between Likir and Sangphu Monasteries :

Sangphu monastery is located in Dok cho side in Tibet. It was established by Atisa's disciple Nong Lonava lek pe shesrab in 1073 A.D. on the advice of his master. Atisa kept all powers secret before the construction of this monastery. The monastery by vertue of this secret powers called Sangphu. Initially 500 lamas were attached to this, later in view of its popularity througout in Tibet and its adjoining countries, 11 more related monasteries were established. Sangphu monastery belonged to Lama Lhawang Lodos and protector Re-thap-chen. When Lama Lhawang lodos converted Likir monastery into Geluk-pa order, lamas from

Likir monastery started going to Sangphu monastery in Tibet for higher studies. Likir monastery in those days supplied ration (i.e. wheat or barley) to Sangphu for their lamas.

The protector of Likir monastery: It is said that 'choskyong chenma seyi thap can' was the protector deity of Nong lotsava Lek pesesrab, who was a Tibetan , lama and great scholar of Buddhist philosophy during 1059 to 1109. At the age of 17 years he went to Lek pe shesrab and studied Buddhist philosophy under his guidance for one year. There after via Ladakh he came in India, studied Buddhist Philosophy and Tantra for 17 years. In 1092, at the age of 35 years he returned Tibet. Later he translated many Buddhist philosophy and Tantra pothis from Sanskrit to Tibetan. It is said that once he had been preachings 10,000 people at a time. He had 108 discipes. He got parinirvana at the age of 52.

Lineage of Geluk-pa order: Here follows the lineage of Geluk-pa-order under which Likir monastery function :

Gyalwa khyab dak dorje chenpo

↓

Nyam len cin labas

↓

Cok ki tulku chenpo

↓

Jamyang Sang Zang tho camba Gonpo

↓

(Gyalthen choskyut teaching given to thupstan yongsi Takpo)

↓

Tsongkhapa Lobzang takpe pal

↓

Gyalve Gyalchab Darma Rinchen

↓

Kheyasdup Gelek palzag

↓

Thustok vangcuk lekpa gyalchan

↓

Khence dagnit lotos coskyoung

↓

Thupstan salzat choskyi Gyaltsan

↓

Manthos thangpo pa vaste

↓

Jamyang cangpa Dongyut

↓

Galden thi-pa

↓

Statues in Thekcen Choskyi Cuglakhang Chenpo (Dukhang) of Likir monastery

In this Dukhang Buddha and Bodhisatitvas statues are made of by Ladakhi artists. Here follows the details.

C : Sakyamuni Buddha with

Sariputra and Maudgalyajana

1: Sangyas of sung (Past Buddha)

2: Maitreya (Future Buddha)

3: Tsongkhapa with his main

disciples Gyalsab je and khasdupje

4. Zamgon Lozang Takspe

5. Chang Chub Chorten

6. Dungsten

7: Namgyal Chorten

Details of statues in Dukhang

Sakyamuni Buddha: (Tib. Sh' a kya thub pa),[9]

: Made of cley

: Height: About 12′

Sangyas Ot sung: In Tibetan language equivalent snags rgyas 'aod-srung.

: Made of clay

: Height: About 12'

Maitreya (Future Buddha): Tib. sangs rgyas byam pa

: Made of clay

: Height: About 12′

Changchub chorten:[10]

: Made of gold and silver

Silver chorten:

: Height: About 12′

: Made of silver

Dugsten: This chorten is built in the memory of skechen tampa (Tib. skyes chen dam pa)

Rig nas ter gyi pe zod chung la khang (Tib. rig gnas gter gyi dpe mo dzad gtsug la khang)

Locatioin: It is in the first floor of the monastery; called Pe zod khang or 'Ba-khang'. On the occasion of Dos-mo-che festival, lamas dress up here, after wearing masks of different deities they come down to chamra for cham.

This temple is used by lamas for Sum-Bum reading. It was repaired in 1949 (Fig. 10.2).

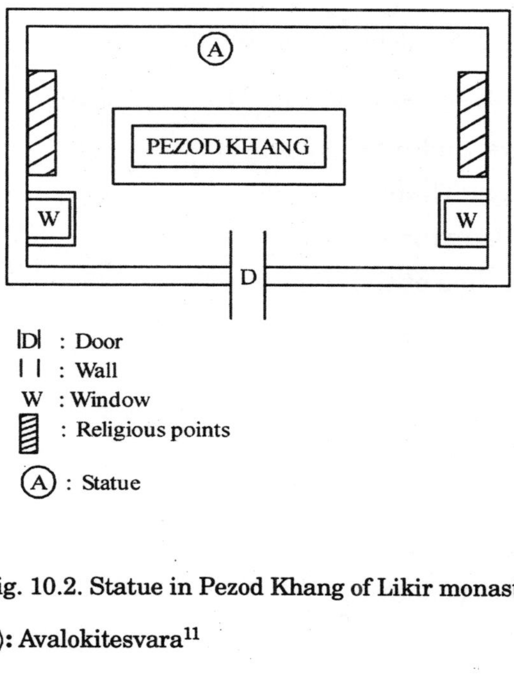

Fig. 10.2. Statue in Pezod Khang of Likir monastery.

Statue: (A): Avalokitesvara[11]

This Dukhang has only one statue of Avalokitesvara about 12 feet in height. It was made by a Ladakhi artist.

Wall paintings: The walls of the Dukhang is beautifully decorated by Buddha and Boddhisttva paintings (Fig.10.3).

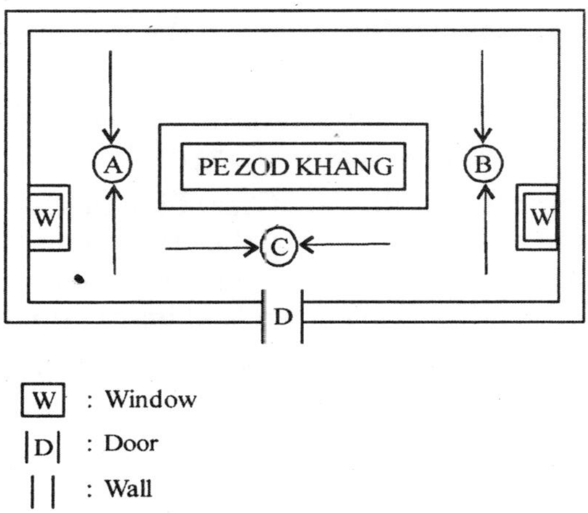

Fig. 10.3. Wall paintings in Pe zod Khang of Likir monasteuy.

Painting on Ⓐ side wall of the Dukhang:

Thirty five Buddhas:

1. Sakya Thuba
2. Dorje nyinpo rab tu zomba
3. Rin chen ot tho
4. Lhu wang gi gyal po
5. Pa ve de
6. Pal gyes
7. Rin chen mela
8. Rin chen la od
9. Thung va ton yot
10. Ti ma met pa
11. Rin chen la va

12. Pal jin
13. Changs pa
14. Changs pa jin
15. Chu lha la
16. Chu lhaila la
17. Pal zang
18. Candan pal zang
19. Zi zit tha yas
20. Ot pal
21. Nyanan met pe pal
22. Shet met kye bu
23. Me tok pal
24. Chang pe ot ze nam pa rol non pa knen pa
25. Pad me od zer snam par rol vas non par khen pa
26. Nor pal
27. Tan pe pal
28. Chang pal shin tu yongs dags
29. Van poi log gyi gyal chan gyi gyal po
30. Shin tu nam pa non pe pal
31. Yal las skin tu nan pa gya va
32. Nam par non pe shegs pe pal
33. Kun nas sna va kot pe pal
34. Rin chen pad mos nam par non
35. Rin vang gi gyal po.

Paintings on Ⓑ side wall of the Dukhang:

Sixteen Arhats:

1. Yan lag jung
2. Ma pham pa

3. Nag na nas
4. Dus dan
5. Dorje moi bu
6. Zang po
7. Ser beu
8. Bhara dhaza can
9. Ba kula
10. Da can zin
12. Bha ra dha za son nyun len
13. Lam stan
14. Lhui de
15. Bed ced
16. Mi ched pa

Paintings on the © side wall:

Gyaltsen Zee:

1. Yul khor sung
2. Can mi zang
3. Phags skyes po
4. Nam thos sras

Zims Chung (Tib. Zims chung)

In Bodhi language it is equivalent to 'Zims chung bsam tan ni 'aod khil'. It looks as Rabsal (Tib. rab gsal)[12] from the distance, as it has many big windows, normally high ranked lamas stay here. It is decorated by khorlo in the middle and two dear either sides on the front faced roof.

Statues: It has the following statues :

1. Jo shakya nam sum (Tib. Jo s'akya rnam gsum). The main statue made of sandal wood.

2. Panchen Paldan Ishes (Tib. Pan-chen dpal ldan ye shes)[13]
3. Gyalsab je (Tib. rgyal chabs rje): Main disciple of Tsong khapa.
4. Tsongkhapa (Tib. Tsong kha pa): The founder of Geluk pa tradion of Mahayana Buddhism
5. Khasdub je (Tib. mkhas grub rje): The other main disciple of Tsang Kha pa.
6. Dalai Lama Thupstan Gyatso (Tib. rgyal bthub bstan rgya mtso):[14] This is important an old statue, brought from Tibet.

Thankas

I did not get time to count all thankas of this Dukhang, however, saw many thankas of Boodhisattvas and gurus. Some of them were very old and brought from Tibet.

Thrones

Zims chung has thrones of high ranked lamas e.g.

1. His Holiness Dalai Lama
2. His Holiness Nari Rinpoche, the head of Likir monastery

In 1950, it was repaired. We can see many worshipping objects 'Sol cog (Tib. gsol cog),. They are well placed before the statues on a table 'tsok -tse', comparatively small table than the usual.

Zim chung dod gu nos dub khil

The above Zims chung is literatelly called 'Zims chung 'aod rgu dnos grub' akhyil, situated at the east of the main monastery building.

Statues

It has following statues:

1. Tsongkhapa (Tib. Tsong kha pa)
2. Gyalsab je (Tib. rgyal chab rje)
3. Khasdub je (tib. mkhas grub rje)

Tsongkhapa is the main statue and placed at the centre of the temple.

Pothis

Zims chung dod gu has many pothis of religious interest.

Throne

It has Nari Rinpoche throne, infront of this many worshipping objects are placed on a small table 'tsok-tse'.

This Zims chung was repaired in 1972.

Zims Chung Sam phel vang gi gyal

In Tibetan language we may pronounce it as 'Zims thung bsam 'aphel abang gi rgyal,. It is located at the north of the main monastery.

Statues

Zims Chung Sam phel vang has some Buddhist statues as listed below:

1. Padmasambhava
2. Avalokitesvara (Tib. spyan ras gzigs)

   : The main statue.
3. Buddha (Tib. Thub va).

Chorten

It has one golden Namgyal chorten.

Thankas

Like other Zims chungs it has many thankas of Bodhisattvas.

The worshipping objects are placed before the statues. During especial festival Nari Rinpoche stays here.

It was repaired in 1950.

Zims Chung Namgyal thik pe chok

This Zims Chung is equivalent to ' Zims chung rnam rgyal thig b'a mohog.

Statues

There are twenty one Dolma (Tara) statues brought from the plains of India. They are equal Shape, size and colour. According to Dolma prayer pothi they are named as:

1. While Tarā of Atisa' (Atisa') - krama sita (Tib. Jo-lugs sgrol dkar)
2. White Tārā of Bari, Bari lugs Sita Tara (Tib. rgrol dkar Ba-riai-lugs)
3. White Tārā of Gn̄an Gn̄an-lugs Sita Tarā)Tib. Gnan-lugs sgron dkar)
4. Whita Tārā of Vanarata Vanaratna-Varnama Sita Tara (Tib. Nags rin-lugs-kyi sgrol dkar)
5. White Saravati, Sita Saravati (Tib. dbyanis can ma dkar mo)
6. Sadanga Tara of Gn̄an (Tib. Gnan gol yan lag drug pa)
7. Ka dams lha ji nam gi dolma (Tib. bka gdams lha bjiai nam gi sgrol ma)
8. Green Tara of the great Pandita Sakyasri from Kashmir, Kas,mira-mhapandita-krama Syama Tara (Tib. Sgrol ljan kha chen pan chen lugs)
9. Green Tara; s'yāma Tara (Tib. sgrol-ljan̄)
10. Red Tara of th Sakya sect, Sakya-lugs rakta tara (Tib. sgrol ma dmar mo sa lugs)
11. Wealth-bestowing Tara, Dhamada Tara (Tib. sgrol ma nor sbyin ma)
12. Yellow Tara, Pitā Tara ("Tib sgrol ser mo, gtso-bkhor-gsum)
13. Pavicatmike Tara (Tib. sgol ma, lha lria)
14. Pratsara (Tib. so-sor brari ma)
15. Marici (Tib. a'od ger can ma)
16. White Tara of great pandita Sakyasri from Kashmir, Kas'mira-mhāpandita Krama Sita Tara (Tib. sgrol dkar kha che pan̄ chen lugs)

17. Varada Tara (Tib. dbañ mchog ster bai sgrol ma)
18. Khdiravani Tara (Tib. Sen ldeñ nags kyi sgrol ma)
19. San's Kusunita Tara (Tib. sgrol ma rab rgyas ma)
20. Duhkha sadhana Tara (Tib. sgrol ma sdug bsrial bsreg ma)
21. Skuha sādhana Tara (Tib. sgrol ma bde sgrub ma)

I mey be wrong to spell all the Dolmas. In fact I have seen the same form, size and mudra of the twenty one Dolmas. In may opinion the Dolma may be worshipped in twenty one ways.

Besides it has Je geleks taskpa (Tib. rje dge legs grakpa) statue.

Buddhist Pothis

It has many pothis, written in Bodhi language by Buddhist scholars (or Pandits), Lotsavas and learned lamas.

Worshipping objects

There are many worshipping objects viz. Damru, Tilbe, Dorje etc.

This Zims chung can be used by scholar lamas, Rinpoches and VIPs. It was repaired in 1984.

Dorje thek pe gyut ki Cuglakhang

Cuglakhang is pronounced as' do rje theg p'ai rgyud kyi gtug lag khang'. Here lamas of the monastery gather on the eve of 'Dup chot' ritual ceremony. On this occasion they make mandala by small pables, and colour them according to central deity of mandala.

Paintings in the Cuglakhang

Paintings on the west side wall :

1. Sangva duspa lhaguat (Tib. dpal gsangs ba'adus p'ai bla rgyud[15]

2. Zo nog domsum (Tib. Zo rngog' abrom gsium[16]
3. Mela (Tib. Mi la)[17]
4. Je yab sras sum (Tib. rje yab sras gsum)[18]

Paintings on the North side Wall

Sangde Zuk sum (Tib. gsang bde' ajug gsum)

1. Sana duspa mandala (Kalacakra)
2. de-chok[19]
3. Jigjet (Yamantaka)[20]

Besides it has Likir monastery main protector 'Sethapa' (Tib. bse khrab-pa).

Paintings on the east side Wall:

1. Gyentuk chog nis (Tib. rgyan drug mchog gnyisj.[21] In Sanskrit equivalent to Indian Acharyas.
2. Chela Nam sum (Tib. tse lha rnam gsum):
   (i) Chepakmet - Left side
   (ii) Green Tara - Right side
   (iii) Namgyal ma - Centre
3. Rigsum gonpo (Tib. rigs gsim mgonpo)
   (i) Cenrazik (Avalokitesvara) -white
   (ii) Manjusri (Left - Red)
   (iii) Chagdor (Right - Blue)

In addition it has the painting of Lama Lhawang Lodos (Tib. lha dbang blo gros)

Paintings on the South side wall: This wall has paintings of protectors as listed below:

(1) Setapa[22]
(2) Gonpo

(3) Paldan Lhamo[23]

(4) Gonkar[24]

(5) Yamantaka

(6) Yamraj[25]

(7) Four hands Mahakala[26]

(8) Six hands Mahakala[27]

Paintings on the wall out side along the door

Gyaltsen Zee:

(i) Yul khor sung (Tib. Yul - akhor srung)

(ii) Can mi zang (Tib. spyan -mi bzang)

(iii) Phagsskyes po (Tib. Phags-skyes po)

(iv) nam thos sras (Tib. r nam thos sras)

This cuglakhang sometimes is known Gonkhang. It was constructed at the place where in olden days king of Ladakh had its palace; however, repaired in 1982.

Statues in the Cuglakhang.

The cuglakhang has the following statues (Fig. 10.4)

(1) Setapa

(2) Padan Lhamo

(3) Namsras

Besides in the glass almirah there are some statues as cited below:

(i) Jigjet

(ii) Gonpo chagtuk: At centre

(iii) Chorgyal

(iv) At the khor Gonpo chagtuk

(v) Zambeyang[28]

(vi) Ka gyud kyi lama.

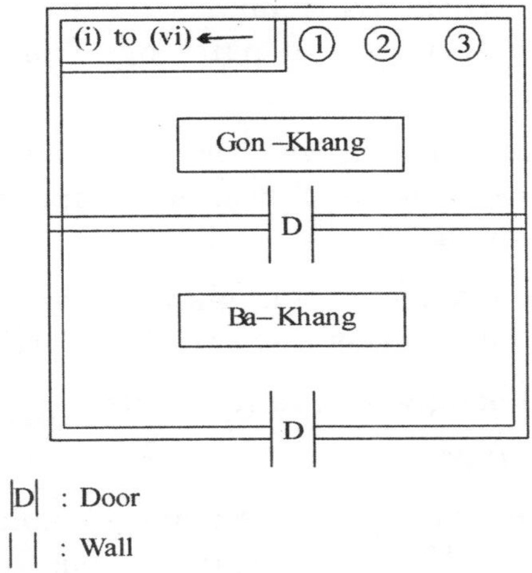

Fig. 10.4. Statues in Cuglakhang (or Gon-Khang).

Phur Ding Rol po Ishes Jalyas khang (Tib. 'aphur lding rol p'ai ye shes kyi gzhal yas khang)

This temple has the following main statues :

1. Jigjet (Tib. 'ajigs byed)
2. Gonpo chag tuk (Tib. mgon po phyag-drug)
3. Damcan (Tib. dam can chos rgyal)
4. Paldan Lhamo (Tib. dpal ldan lha-mo
5. Gyalpo chenpo namsras (Tib. rgyal po chen po rnam thos sras)
6. Gyal chen shugdan (Tib. rgyal chen shugs ldan)
7. Setapa (Tib. bse khra pa): Made of sandal wood

Thankas

This Lhakhang has many thankas of Buddha and Bodhisattvas, Setapa (Tib. bse khra pa) is the main precious one.

It is said that earlier 'Sukdan' statue was also placed in this Lhakhang. It was considered the protector of Geluk order, had two statues made of sandal wood and clay, and had painting. When His Holinesss Dalai Lama advised to replace these statues and paintings from the temple. Nowadays we do not see the same.

In olden days during war bow, arrows, small guns and swords were uses. Some of such old weapons were earlier place in this temple.

'Lho-tor' is made of butter, placed in this temple inside the glass almirah, some of them are 10-12 years old.

This Lha-khang was repaired in 1983.

Dolma Lhakhang

In Bodhi language it is pronounced 'aphrin las myur skyob sgroma lha khang. It has twenty one Tara statues of equal shape, size, colour and mudra.

Thankas

Dolma Lhakhang has eight Indian Acharya thankas as shown below :

1. Phags pa thog med dang (Tib. aphags-pa thog med dang)
2. Phags pa lu dub (Tib. aphags pa klu sgrab)
3. Phags pa chogs lad (Tib phags pa-phyogs glad)
4. Phags pa lon tan od (Tib. phags pa lon tan aod
5. Phags pa
6. Phags pa thos dag (Tib. phags pa thos dags)
7. Phags pa lha (Tib. phags pa lha)
8. Phags pa sha kya od (phags pa sha-kya aod).

It was repaired in 1983.

Khas cun zang po Lhawang Dorje Khang (Tib. mkhas btsun bzang po Lha abang chos rje khang)

This temple was used by Lama Lhawang Dorje, the founder of Likir monastery. Later a re-named as Lhawang Dorje Lhakhang.

Statues of this Temple

Lhawang Dorje Lhakhang has the following statues:

(1) Chorje Lama Lhawang (Tib. chosje- bla ma lha dbang)
(2) Nari Rinpoche
(3) Nari Rinpoche
(4) Nari Rinpoche
(5) Kalcakra[30]
(6) De-chok (Skt. Cakrasamvara),[31] and
(7) Yamantaka

Three earlier incanation of Nari Rinpoche, the head of Likir monastery

All the above statues are old. Besides there are many small statues.

Thankas

The temple has some thankas as listed below:

1. Tsongkhapa with his disciples viz. Khasdupje and Gyaltsabje: This is the main thanka.
2. Buddha: This thanka is a big one and exhibited during Dosmoche festival.

Worshiping Objects

Here follows some worshipping objects placed in the Lhawang Dorje Lhakhang.

1. Dorje (vajra or thunderbolt)
2. Tilbu (Ghanta)
3. Rolmo
4. Sil-nyane
5. Tung (Sankha)
6. Daru
7. Perkhang.

Old Dukhang

In old Dukhang we can see old ritual objects, thankas etc. It was repaired in 1987.

Lama Tradition

Till 15th century A.D. Likir, had only a small temple under Kadampa order. Lama Lhawang Lodos later renovated the temple and established Gelukpa tradition. Since them Likir monastey is functioning under this tradition. However, time and again Sang phu (Tib. gsang phu) monastery of Tibet. (now under China) used to depute Chosje lamas for the preservation and development of Gelukpa tradition in this monastery.

Here follows the details :

Chosje Lopon Singhe gyatso

↓

Chosje Paljor Zangpo

↓

Chosje Tungpa Lozang Lhawang

↓

Chosje Legs me

↓

Chosje Lobzang

↓

Chosje Chags tug

↓

Chosje Lozang Chosdup

↓

Chosje Choglak Namgyal

↓

Chosje Shesrab choszang

↓

Chosje Lozang Delegs

↓

Chosje Shesrab Lungriks

↓

Chosje Shesrab gyatso

↓

Chosje Sonam Namgyal

↓

Chosje Tungpa Sonam Phunchog Chosphel

↓

Chosje Chos Palzang

↓

Lozang Tsering Chosphel

In the 11th Rabjung or in 1638 A.D. Tungpa Shesrab gyatso started a tradition to send lamas from Likir monastery to Sera, Despung and Gadan monasteries in Tibet for higher studies in Buddhist philosophy. About 36 lamas from Ladakh every year were sent to Tibet till late sixties for higher studies in Tibet. In 1959 Tibet was occupied by China, this tradition was stopped. Nowadays lamas from this monastery go to South India in Tibetan monastries for higher studies. This time about two hundred lamas are studying in different Tibetan monasteries in South India.

Monastic Tradition

The monastic tradition in the monastery is almost same as was introduced by Nari Choktul Jey Geleks Ishes Takpa. Here follows the details:

Nari Choktul Jey Geleks Ishes Takpa

↓

Lobzang Jigmet Tanbe Gyaltsen

↓

Nawang Tsulthim Stenbe Gyaltsen

↓

Khasdup Stanzin Choskyi Nima

↓

Lodzang Khasdup Stanzin Gyatso

↓

Nari Stanzin Chosgyal

The monastic tradition in the monastery is based upon Tashilhumpo. Initially 36 lamas out of 110 lamas were sent to Tashilhumpo for higher studies.

Administration

Nari Rinpoche is the head lama of the monastery. Lamas appointed in the responsible posts at the monastery according to their seniority to keep the strict discipline.

Nari Rimpoche mostly live in Dharmshal in Himachal Pradesh. He time to time visit Ladakh and look after the gonpa administration. Till today he has 13 incarnation. Table 10.1 shows the details:

Table 10.1. The details of Nari Rinpoche incarnations

Sl. No.	*Name*	*Village*	*Lived in years*	*King of Ladakh*	*Teacher*
1	*2*	*3*	*4*	*5*	*6*
1.	Dolzing Takpa Gyaltsen	Pot ustod Tangs	63	Dragspa Bumde	Tsongkhapa
2.	Panchen Sonam Takspa	Pot ce tang	60	Lotos chogdan & Kunga Namgyal	Gedum Gyatso
3.	Sonam Ishes Wangpo	Stot lung lamber	40	Lhachen Lhawang Namgyal	Sonam Gyatso

1	*2*	*3*	*4*	*5*	*6*
4.	Sonam Geleks Wangpo	Olkha Zala	38	Lhachen Tsewang Namgyal & Jamyang Namgyal	Yontan Gyatse
5.	Tulku Takpa Gyaltsen	Skyet song kangs	38	Singge Namgyal	Panchen Dozang Choskyi Gyaltsen
6.	Zabs Tung tan be gyaltsen	Zang lokher	43	Deldan Namgyal	Changyangs Gyatso
7.	Tulku Lozang Tasis	Konphey-chak	37	Delek Namgyal	Kalzang Gyatso
8.	Gey Geleks Ishes Trakpa	Takspo sung	63	Lhachen Nima Namgyal & Deshkyoung Namgyal	Jamyang Gyatso
9.	Lobzang Tanbe Gyaltsen	Potala Lhaezol	88	Phanchok Namgyal & Tsewang Namgyal	Lung toks Gyatso
10.	Nawang Tsulthim Gyatso	Lhandan	24	Tsetan Namgyal & Tondup Namgyal	Tsulthim Gyatso
11.	Khasdup stenzin Choskyi Nima	Lhandan	40	Jigmet kunga Namgyal & Tondup Namgyal	Khasdup Gyatso
12.	Khasdup Stenzin Gyatso	Sunkyu Lhanden	63	Dadul Namgyal	Thupsten Gyatso
13.	Stanzin Chosgyal Gyalve Yabji	Present Rinpoche	–	–	–

Source: Janyang Gyaltsen (ed.):

Some Important Religions Objects in the Likir Monastery

There are some very impotrant statues, thankas and masks in the monastery. Here follows the details:

1. **Tsongkhapa statue:** According to the lama of the monastery, there is one Tsong Khapa statue, which is syambhu and can talk.
2. **Yamantaka statue:** It is a ferocious form of Manjusri. Once it omitted blood, the lamas them performed rituals. Later the statue stopped omiting.

   It is said that long ago some lamas in the monastery did not follow vinaya rules, To see indisciplined lamas Yamantaka statue showed its anger. But they did not change there behaviour. The statue again expressed its anger and omitted blood from its mouth in a very fierce way. To see the blood the concerned lamas frightened and obeyed monastic rules and regulation.
3. **Lama Lochen Shesrab (Tib. bla ma lo che shes rab) statue:** This statue also has religious importance, hold patra.
4. **Panchen Paldan Ishey mask (Tib. pan-chen dpal ldan ye shes kyis phyag nas):** This natural mask, called Syambhu. It is said once Panchen Paldan Ishey asked his mask" where do you want to go?" It did not reply. Panchen Paldan Ishey again asked:

   "Do you want to go to Ladakh?"

   The mask moved its head affermative. Later it was taken to Likir monastery. This mask is bigger than the ordinary one, and looks dangerious.
5. **Thankas:** There are many thankas in the monastery. Some of them listed below:

   (i) Je Yabsras Sum: It is a big thanka and usually exhibited during Dosmotse festival. This thanka has centre figure of Tsongkhapa, his two main disciples Gyal tsab and Khasdup as shown below:

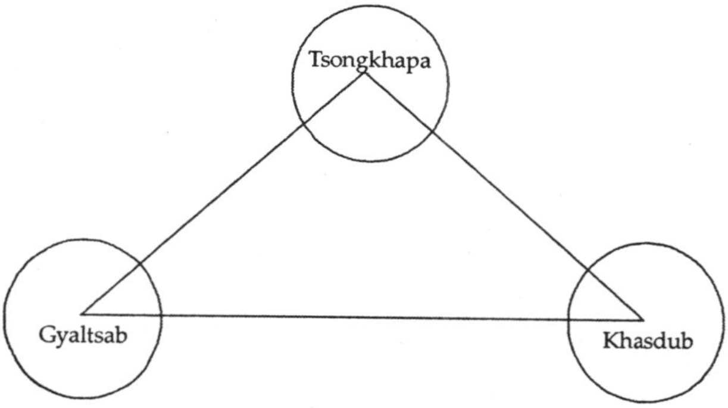

(ii) Arhats: This thanka is made of stone colour paintings.

(iii) Eighty four thankas of 84 siddhas.

(iv) Thirteen thankas of earlier incanations of His Holiness Dalai Lama.

(v) Eight thankas of eight great Indian panditas

(vi) Various thankas of Bodhisattvas and Dharma protectors.

Branch Gonpas of Likir Monastery

The monastery has dominancy in Shyam and Purig side of Ladakh. It has maximum branches. To fulfil the religious demands of laymen, Likir monastery deputs lamas (as pujari) to its branches. Sometimes two lama pujaris are deputed according to population. Here follows the details :

1. Hanu
2. Nurla
3. Ang
4. Saspoche
5. Hemi
6. Hemi Sukpachan
7. Leh Colony
8. Mangyu

} One lama pujari

9. Timasgam
10. Saspol
11. Bazgo
12. Alchi
13. Wakha
14. Sargol
15. Mulbec
16. Sapi

Lama who performs as 'Komnyer' used to perform ritual works at the concern gonpa. He is also responsible to lookafter gonpa property. Normally 'Komnyer' has two years tenure, but on special case his tenure may be inceresed for three years or more.

Here follows some branch gonpas of Likir monastery.

Saspol Gonpa

It is also known as 'gon-mla-phuk' was established earlier to Likir monastery. The old structure of this gonpa is ruined. An old Dukhang of this structure can be seen in a cave. It is said that Madhyantika came here and sat for meditation. In 11th century A.D. Lotsava Rinchen bzangpo decorated it by wall paintings viz. vairocana and other five Dhyani Buddha. Later he meditated for some time. Sabsequently it beaome the tradition which continued till 19th century A.D. Lama of the Likir monastery under the tradition retreated every year according to their turn.

Gon-mla-phuk gonpa was constructed during 1030-'40. It was not only popular in Ladakh, well known in Tibet. The Tibet Government 'Devazang' then annually sent tea, barley skyab Khadaks (Zaldar), chakdam etc. to this gonpa.

Alchi

It was constructied during 1010-'20 by Lotsave Rinchen bzangpo with the help of 32 Kashmiri artists.

Alchi choskor has Avalokitesvara, Lotsava Rinchen Zangpo etc. are important statues. Besides, it has many chortens thankas, ritual objects etc. It was repaired during 1500-1560. Likir monastery deputes one pujari lama .

Mangyu

Mangyu gonpa is constructed by Lotsava Rinchen bzangpo during 11th century A.D. The wall paintings in this gonpa also made by Kashmiri artists. It has three Buddha statues made of Sandal wood. The clay statues of Manjusri and Avalokitesvara are of about 12 feet high.

The gonpa has thankas brought from Tibet; 12 Bum and Panchen Paldan Ieshey pothis, one stone chorten and many ritual objects. One pujari lama is deputed from Likir monastery to lookafter this.

Tingmasgam Gonpa

This gonpa was constructed during 1420-'40 when Dragspa Bumde was the king of Ladakh. It is about 45 km from Likir monastery. Two lamas are deputed by the same monastery to lookafter this. It has one big Mitreya statue of about 12 feet in height, Brass Avalokitesvara, marbale Avalokitesvara, clay Avalokitesvara Buddha etc.

Among thnakas- Yamantaka, Head lama of Gelukpa, 35 Buddhas, Avalokitesvara etc. are important. Beside it has wall paintings of Buddhist deities, Kangyur and Stangyur pothi

Yong thar dod cams chosling

It was earlier looked by Tingmasgam villagers. In 1976, was taken up by Likir minastery, since then it is functioning under the same monastery, has about 12 feet high Maitretya and many small Buddhist statues.

It is about 64 km from Likir monastery towards east, has 12 Bum pothis and one wooden chorten.

Bago chosling

It was built by Lotsava Rinchen bzangpo in 11th century A.D. In 1759 Kachen Lozang Rabgyas refounded according to Geluk pa tradition. It was decorated by beautiful wall paintings in 1910.

It has followings Buddhist thankas: Maitreya, Avalokitesvara, 35 Buddhas, Mahakala, Paldan lhamo etc., and has one Namgyal chorten. It is situated 30 km from Likir monastery at the east.

Negon Gephel Tharpaling

It was established in 1860 A.D. has 12 feet high Maitreya statue made of clay, thug je chempo (i.e. Buddha) Tadin, 16 Bum pothis, Namgyal chorten, and many ritual objects. In 1957 Lama Lozang Tsulthim repaired it with the help of villagers. Besides it has wall paintings of Bodhisattvas, lamas etc.

Saspol gonpa (Sa-ce Rin chen Gang)

This gonpa was fonded by Lotsava Rinchen bzangpo during the pereiod of king lhachen Trakpa, Unfortunately the old Lhakhang destroyed by rain. We may acknowledge some old paintings on the ruined walls. It was refounded under Gelukpa tradition with the help of Likir monastery, after 15th century A.D.

It has 12 feet high Avalokitesvara (Tib. Cuksikzal) Tsongkhapa and Rigsum gonpo statues. Among popular thankas are-21 Dolmas (Taras), Zigjet, Dukar etc.

This gonpa is about 24 km far from Likir. One lama pujari is deputed by Likir monastery who lookafter the monastic activities. It has Kudum, Gyalpo, Namgyal and Chang Chub Chortens. Besides, we can see 12 Bum pothis and ritual objects.

Sapol cam chen chos kholing

It is a Lhakhang in a Saspol cave, has 12 feet high Maitreya statue. On the walls we may see paintings of 35 Buddhas, 16 Arhats and protectors. Besides, Jung du pothis chortents and ritual objects are worth seeing.

In 1980 it was burned. later re-established under the direction of Likir monastery, and deputed one lama pujari to lookafter the gonpa.

Chams Khang Thod ling

This temple is 16 km far from Likir monastery in the east. Lamas come here for meditation, Therefore, popularly known as Chamkhang. It has Avalokitesvara and other Buddhist statues, some of them made by stone. On walls we can see the paintings of Lamas, Yidams and Bodhisattavas. To lookafter this temple one lama is deputed by the Likir monastery.

Nurla Tashidezongling gonpa

This gonpa was constructed during Sonam Zoldan's period, when he donated the same to the earlier incarnation of Lozang Stanzin Gyatso. It has 12 feet high cuksikzal statue made of clay. Besides, has lamas, Yidam, Choskyong, Camsing and thankas. In addition Namgyal chorten and some religious texts, have culture importance.

Hanu Ogma Tashis Thonjes gon

In 18th century A.D. Tang Wangpa Tsulthim Jungnas of Tashilunpo monastery[32] visited Ladakh. Later, went to Hanu for meditation. Thereafter he built a monastery with the help of villagers.

Statues

The monastery has following popular statues :

1. Camba Choskor (i.e. Maitreya,[33]
2. Tsongkhapa[34]
3. Avalokitesvara

It has Bodhisattva thankas, 16 Bum pothis, and 8 kind chortems. One Lama from Lirkir monastery is deputed here to lookafter this. It is about 100 km far from Likir monastery.

Hesuk Tashis Gepheling

In 18th century Lama Tsulthim Nima went to Hemishulpacan for meditation, after sometime got parinirvana. Later his body ash was placed in a big Avalokitesvara statue.

In 1820 Lama Tsulthim Sonam donated the above site to Likir monastery. The administrative authority of this monastery thereafter founded a new gonpa on the above Mane Khang Known Tashis Gepheling. It has Buddha, Maitreya, Manjusri etc. Buddhist statues. One can see thankas 35 Buddhas, Je yabdras sum Bodhisattva and Dharma protections.

The gonpa is about 55 km far from Likir, one lama Pujari is deputed from the Likir to the lookafter this. It has 108 Kangyur pothis, Mani pharcin and ritual objects which are useful for religious activities.

Mulbe Gadan Lha che

The gonpa is located in Mulbe village near a mountain. It was built by Lotsava Rinchen bzangpo in the 11th century A.D. The wall painting of this gonpa is made by Kashmiri artists. Here folows the details:

1. Sakyamani Buddha: Centre fresco.
2. Manjusri:[35] Right to Centre
3. Avalokitesvara: Left to Center
4. Mandala: Jigjet las cuksum (i.e. a mandala of 13 deities)
5. Kunderik mandla
6. Vairocana Mandala

It has some chortens of religious importance.

Malbe Gaden Gonpa

This gonpa was established by Yontan Gyaltsan in 16th centuery, later it came under Likir monastery, has following main statues:

1. Agu Tungpa Dorje
2. Gyalva Dorje Chang (skt. Vajrasattva)
3. Tamcan chosgyal
4. Various lamas of Geluk pa tradition
5. Bodhisattvas.

Besides the gonpa has some thankas of various Buddhist deities, Bodhisattvas ect. and ritual objects. It is about 110 km far from Likir monastery.

Wakha Namgyal Toling gon

The gonpa was constructed on a mountain in Wakha village by Nari Rinpoche Tungpa. Rinpoche mostly retreated in Shargol. However, seldomly visited Walkha, his parents lived in Wakha, whenevar they visited to the above gonpa to see:, Rinpoche felt happy. Thereafter, the gonpa named after as Toling, 'To' means 'Happy' 'Ling' means Picnic'.

Statues

This gonpa has following statues:

1. Buddha
2. Avalokitesvara
3. Tsongkhapa
4. Some small Buddhist statues.

Thankas

It has following populor thankas:

1. Jigjet
2. Dharma Protectors
3. Buddha with Manjusri, Avalokitesvara and Vajrapani
4. Dorje Jigjet
5. Buddha
6. Bodhisattvas
7. Lamas of Gelukpa order.

Pothis

It has some Buddhist texts such as:

1. Kangyur pothis
2. 16 Bum pothis
3. Beser Galden Choj zung
4. Zungdus

The gonpa has De-she-gyat and Boddhisattvas paintings on the walls. One lama Pujari is deputed by Likir monastery, who lookafter the gonpa and perform daily prayer.

Shargol Galden Dup Phuk ling (Tib. shar rgol dgal lden sgrub phug gling)

The gonpa is situated in Shargol village, across the Wakha river on right side of the Leh-Srinagar Highway.

Statues

It has Tungpa Dawa or Agu Tungpa and twenty one Dolma statues of sandalwood.

Thankas

1. Avalokitesvara
2. Buddha life his

Wall paintings

1. Tsongkhapa
2. Gyaltsab
3. Khasdub
4. Lamas of Geluk pa tradition
5. Bodhisattvas
6. Avalokitesvara
7. Manjusri
8. Vajrapani[36]
9. Gonpo Chagtuk

10. Mahakali (Probaly Paldan Lhamo)
11. Se tapa (Tib. Se khra pa)

Besides, it has 12 Bum pothis, ritual objects, chortens and other religious objects necessary for religious ceremonies. It is under the control of Likir monastery. One lama is deputed by the same momastery to perform daily religious prayer.

C̄ang chub chos ling (Tib. byan- chub-chos-ling)

This temple is in Shargol, constructed by a Likir monastery lama Ser chumgpa infront of the Tung-pa chorten. It has one big co Sakyamuni Buddha (Tib. Zo bo shakya muni) statue of about 12 feet in height.

Saphi chos ling gon (Tib. sa spyi chos gling dgon

The gnpa is situated in a Saphi village in Kargil district, along the Leh - Srinagar highway. It is about 140 km from Likir monastery, was constructed during 19th century with the the help of Sa-pi villagers.

Statues

1. Avalokitesvara (Thousand hands and eyes). It is the main statue.
2. Tsongkhapa (Tib. rgyava Tsong-kha-pa)
3. Avalokitesvara : Hands: six
   : Tib. can ras gzik phyag drug

Thankas

1. Avaalokitesvara
2. Amitaba

Buddhist texts

1. Kangyur pothis (108 volumes)
2. Dode Skalzang (Tib. mdo sde skal bzang)
3. Zong dus (Tib.gzung bdus)
4. Padma thang jig (Tib. padma thang jig)

Leh Ladang stans ling (Tib. gle bla brang bsti gnas gling)

It is situated in Leh, was constructed by the first incarnation of Nari Rinpoche Khasdup Stanzin gyatso (Tib. mkhas grub bstan azin rgya mcho) During 1915-'20.

Tashis Phel gyal ling (Tib. bkris aphel rgyas gling)

It was constructed in 1984 at housing colony, has Buddha and Bodhisattva statues according to Geluk-pa order. Two Lamas deputed as pujaries by Likir monastery who lookafter the gonpa and offer daily prayer. Besides, it has some chortens, e.g. namgyal chorten made of wood.

In brief the branch gonpas of Likir monastery can be shown in the following table (10.2)

Table 10.2. Brief description of branch gonpas of Likir monastery

Name of gonpa / village	*Date of establishment*	*Name of fouder*
1	*2*	*3*
Gon mila phuk /Saspol	—	dacum Nima Gon
Alchi	1010–1020	Lotsava Rinchen Zangpo
Mangyu	1017–1020	Lotsava Rinchen Zangpo
Timasgang	1420–1440	Dragspa Bum
Thajod camling/Ang	1430–1440	Chosgyal Dragspa Bum
Stargacan/Basgo	1710–1720	Lhacen Nima Namgyal
Chosphel Ling/Basgo	1759–1760	Kachen Lozang Rabgyas
Gephe Therpa ling/Neye	1858–66	Upal Yulchi
Rinchen gang/Sarce.	1010–1020	Lotsava Rinchen Zanngpo
Chanchen choskorling/ Saspol	1020–1035	Lotsava Rinchen Zanppo
Chamskhang therdotling Saspol	1820-1835	Lama Mela Nispa
Tashi De Zong Gon/Nurla	1921–1930	Sonam Zoldan
Tashis Thong Jes/Hanu Gonog	1800–1803	Cangspa Thsulthims Zungnas
Gepheling/Hesuk	1915–20	Tung Ogyen Pa

1	*2*	*3*
Gelden ce/ Mulbec	1765–70	Nari Tungpa Dava
Gyal Toling Gon/Wakha.	1760–65	Nari Tungpa Dava
Gyał Tashi Gang/ Wakha	1010–20	Lotsava Rinchen Zangpo
Galden Duphukling/Sargol	1770–75	Naris Tungpa Dava
Chosling Gon/Saci	1850–60	Ulas cul ci
Lavang Satens/Leh	1940–42	Ulas cul ci
Tashis phel Lagyaling/ Leh	1983–85	Ulas cul ci
Galden Targyasling/Lukhil	1070–78	Chosje Lama Lawang

Uchos (Tib. dbu-chos) lhan chogs of Likir monastery

'Uchos' means 'Religious geathering' derives by two words 'dbu' and 'chos' meaning thereby 'Main' and 'Religious works'. Thus under 'Uchos' Likir monastery conducts a general meeting in which all lamas from the branch monasteries as well lamas from the Likir monastery take part. In the 'Uchos' all the important decisions are taken which are related for the preservation and permotion of the Geluk pa tradition.

Members of the 'Uchos' have good knowledge of Buddhism as well as religious activities of the Likir monastery and its branch gonpas.Generally lamas for'Uchos' are unanimously appointed. Hence, only those lamas are appointed for the General Body of the monastery who are honest hardworker and good scholar of Gelukpa tradition. 'Uchos' is just like a Administrative Body of the monastery, lookafter the monastic activities. It has following posts;

1. **Lama Thi Zin (Tib. bla ma Kri azin):** The highest post in Uchos is 'Lama Thi zin'. He is responsible to lookafter adminstration in the Likir monastery and assign duty to the lamas according to seniority.
2. **Uzat (Tib. dbu-mzad):** To start ritual or any kind of worship, the presence of Uzat is essintial. He is

responsible to start worship. Later according to his voice or instruction, rithem of sound and speed of worship is followed by other lamas.

3. **Geskos (Tib. dge-bskos):** He is responsible to keep discipline in the monastery, especially during ritual ceremonies his role is important. If any lama disobey his instructions, he gives punishment In case the concern lama does not obey his orders, he refers his name to 'Uchos' for his expalsion from the Bhikshu Sangha of the mastery.

4. **Nerpa (Tib. gner-pa):** He lookafter cash and kind of Likir monastery. During 'Tu-chot' 'Tong-go' (Tib. gton-sgo) etc. He makes necessay arrangements for Manza :

   Likir monastery gives its land on rent to villagers for cultivation who in return give wheat to monastery according to the terms and condition. The same later is distributed to lamas who reside in the monastery permanently. In 1984, I visited the above monastery, then Nerpa informed me that this year he distributed total received wheat among lamas at the rate 200 kg/lama, called Duphogs (Tib. abru-phogs). Likir monastery administrative authority appoints four 'Nerpa' for one year. In case disput occurs in any branch gonpa of Likir, The gonpa authority sents one 'Nerpa' to settle the same. In normal practice Nari Rinpoche's repersentative do this job.

   The property of branch gonpa of the Likir is looked by the concern 'Kon-ner'. Therefore,Nerpa lookafter the cash and kind of Likir monastery only.

5. **Tung-yik:** He is like a clerk of the Likir monastery,and responsible to write letters according to the direction of higher authority of the monastery.

   Lamas in the monastery has only religious duty, they are not allowed to leave the monastery without permission. If any lama wants to go out, he has to take permission from the Nirpa. In monastic tradition it is called 'Gong-pa' (Tib-dgong-pa.) Nowadays two 'Nirpa' stay in the Likir Labrang in Leh. Hence, for 'Gong-pa lama of the momastery has to come to 'Likir monastery'. In olden days four 'Nirpa' were lived in "Likir Labrang' Two of them looked the discipline of the monastery others were collected the wheat from tenents, now only two 'Nirpa' collect the same . Later on its annual function they distribute the same to the listed lamas of the monastery.

In case any lama of the monastery leaves the monastery without permission or he disobey monastic rules, e.g. drives car, scooter etc. He may be punished under 'Sas' (Tib. shas) monastic rules and regulation.

6. **Ludang :** He is the repersentative of Nari Rinpoche, is responsible to see monastic discipline within and outside the Likir monastery. Besides, he lookafter monastery properly.
7. **Dup-chot:** It is responsible to lookafter religious cermonies. In the lama meeting, two lamas are selected as 'Nirpa' They go out for 'Marca' (means to collect donation). On the occasion of Mandala rituals they arrange all neccssary things. Normally lamas of the monastery make Sangva-Duspa' 'Dechok' and 'Jigjet' mandala by small stone particles.
8. **Chosda:** It is a lama committee appointed by the senior lamas of the monastery. This committee is responsible to see welfare activities and keep donation records.

In conclusion Likir monastery has many temples in its campus and branch gonpas in Shyam side, popularly known Lower Ladakh. The main building was constructed during 15th century under the Geluk pa tradition. Later all the old gonpas of 11th centuries were taken under the control of Geluk pa order.

Notes & References

1. **Finegan, Jack: Tibet:** A Dreamt of Image',Tibet House & Willey Eastern Ltd. New Delhi; 1986: 192 and Sharm, Janhwij: 'Architectural Heritage—Ladakh', the Indian National Trust for Art and Cultural Haritage in association with Har-Anand Publication. Pvt. Ltd.; New Delhi; 2003:50.
2. **Lhachen Gyalpo:** Tib. Lha chen rgyal po (pron. Lhachen Gyalpo). He was the fifth king in the first Ladakh dynasty. The Likir monastery was built in his time and was the centre of a brotherhood monks, while from one hundred to five hundred recluses lived at he lakes near. mount Kailasa and were provided by the king with the necessaries of life. C.f. Finegan, Jack.; *op. cit.,* 166.
3. **Lhachen Utpala:** Tib. Lha chen utpala, his sanskrit name Utpala indicates that he had close cultural relations with India. He was the sixth king in the succession from Pelgyigon, and probably ruled in the second half of the eleventh century A.D He was one of the strongest kings of Ladakh kingdom that he invaded Nunti (i.e. Kulu, south of Zanskar and including Lahul and Spiti) where the king of that district bound himself by an oath to pay traibute to the king of Ladakh, "so long as the glaciers of Tise (i.e. Mount Kailash) do not melt away, nor the lake Ma-pham (i.e Manasarovara) dry up. Besides he also subjugated blo (Pron. Lo, modern Mustang, now in Nepal), Purang, and several localities in Baltistan. All of these territories then paid an annual tribute and their represontatives came to be king's *darbar* in this connection. Thus viewing to the above facts we understand that Ladakh during king Lhachen Utpala's period was having strong power in Western Tibet Cf. finegan, Jack; *op.cit.,* 166-'67.
4. **Duwang choje:** Tib. Lha dbang chos rje. He was the great champion of meditation. He blessed the site and in 1065 Likir monastery was built. According to the local scholars Duwang choje was the close relative of king Lhachen Gyalpo. During his lifetime not more than sixty "meditaives ascetis" resided permanently at Peting, but

they formed the nuceus of the kadampa, with Peting containing as its main monastery. Drom, is said taught the Doctrine with reference to the Four Noble Truths and although he was very learned in the Tantras as well as the Sutras, he kept Vajrayanic doctrine secret and did not teach it extensively. It was however, because the school believed and preached that the individual should practice the entire teaching of the Buddha (Sutra & Tantra) that they were called the Kadampa. Thus the components of the name bka' gdams (Pron Kadam) may be understood in the sense that bka' (Pron. Ka) or "speech" signifies the words of the Buddha, and gdams (Pron. dam) means the "teaching" of all of those words. Cf. finegan, Jack; *op. cit.,* 99.

According to Ladakh Chronicle Ladakh king Lhachen Gyalpo offered Samstanling site to Lama Lhawang Choje for meditation, and took the full responsibility to supply food or other necessity things.

5. **Kadampa Tradition:** Kadam–pa derive from Atisa, and his **Bodhipathapradipa.** The actual foundation of this tradition was the work of 'Brom ston rgyal ba', byung gnas (Pron. Dromton Gyelvie Jungne) or Brom (pron. Drom) for short (1005–1064), the Tibetan lay disciple (**Upasaka,** Tibetan dge bsnyen, Pron. genyen) who, when Atisa had worked in Western Tibet for three years and was about to return to India, persuaded him instead to come on to central Tibet, where Atisa worked for the remainder of his life. In 1054 when Atisa was approaching death at sNye Thang (Pron. Nethang) near Lhasa, he said to Drom as his closest diciple "you should build a small monastery, and I shall entrust my teaching to you, keep it!" Drom replied. "In genral, I am unfit to do it and in particular, I am only and **Upasaka** unable to perform great works. Atisa said: "Do the work according to my instructions! I shall bless you. Do no despair!" In obedience to the command of his master, Drom first built a monastery at Nethang and then in 1056 a monastery at Rwa sgrengs (pron. Reting), 90 km. North of Lhasa, where he lived and taught for nine years.
6. **Geluk-pa Tradition:** It was founded by Tsongkhapa, was called New Kadam-pa from its strictness in monastic discipline it was re-named as Geluk pa tradition. Cf. Finegan, Jack.; *op.cit.,* 101.

8. **Khasdup je (Tib. mkhas grub rje).** Pron khe trup je). He was the main disciple of Tsongkhapa later became the abbot of Ganden from 1431 to 1438.
9. **Sakyamuni Buddha (Tib. sh'akya thubpa):** The Enlightened one. In 6th centrry B.C. descended to the world to show the right path to the future beings. After attaining enlightenment at Bodhgaya, turned the three wheel of Dharma in Varanasi, Vaisali and Grdrakupa.
10. **Chengchub chorten:** In Tibetan language spell as' byan c'ub chorten', means "chorten of illumination".
11. **Avalikitesvara:** Tib. chenrezi. He has many froms. In Ladakh I saw two forms viz. (i) Four Armed Avalokitesvara and (ii) Thousand Armed Avalokitesvara.
12. **Rabsal (Tib. rab-gsal):** It look like Glass room.
13. **Panchen Paldan Ishes (Tib. Pan chen dpal ldan ye shes):** He may also called in Tibetan language as blo bzang dpal ldan ye shes or Pelden Yeshe, his period was 1738-1780.
14. **Dalai Lama Thupstan Gyatso (Tib. rgyal bthub bstan rgya mtso):** He was the 13th Dalai Lama ruled Tibet before 1933, was born in 1876.
15. **Sangva duspa lhagyut (Tib. dpal gsangs ba 'adus p'ai bla rgyud):** In short the main deity belongs to sangva duspa or 'Sangdu'. He belongs to Yoga Tantra or father Tantra and emphasized on the development of the illusory body.
16. **Zo nog domsum (Tib. zo rngog abrom gsum):** They are cited below:
    (i) jo bo dpal ldan As ti sha
    (ii) rnog lath' ai shes rab
    (iii) 'abrom ston rgyal b'ai' adyung gnas
17. **Mela (Tib. Mi la):** Tib. Mi-la-ras-pa. One of eighty four mahasiddhas saints and miracle workers. A great tantric of Mahayana.
18. **Je yab sras sum (Tib. rje yab sras gsum):** They are as follows:
    (i) rje tsong kha pa
    (ii) rgyal tshab dar ma rin chen
    (iii) mkhas grub dge dpal bzang

19. **de-chok:** Tib Demchok, Skt. equivalent 'cakrasamvara'. He belongs to vajrayana or Tantra of hightest yoga which emphasises on cultivating the clear light and usually pronouce as 'Samvara'.
20. **Jigjet (Yamantaka):** A wrathful form is the manifestation of Manjusri. He is the Destroyer of Death', belongs to the supreme yoga tantra division of the vajrayana and is the protector of Geluk-pa order of Mahayana Buddhism.
21. **Gyentuk chognis (Tib. rgyan drug mchog gnyis):** They are as follows :
    (i) Kru sgrub
    (ii) thog med
    (iii) aphags pa lha
    (iv) dbyig gnyen
    (v) phyogs glang
    (vi) chos grags
    (vii) yon tan od
    (viii) sh'akya od
22. **Setapa:** Tib. hphags-ma-gdugs-dkar, gdugs-dkar-can-me. Phon. Eng. Dukar chemma. Skt. sitapatra. A form of Dhyani Bodhisativa Avaloiktesvara; depicted with eleven faces and twelve hands.
23. **Paldan Lhamo:** Tib. dpal ldan lha mo. A most important protectors of Geluk-pa order.
24. **Gonkar:** A form of Mahakala, has one face, three eyes in white colour.
25. **Yamraj:** He is the Dharmapala , in Tibetan language equivalent 'gshin-rje, is the god of the dead.
26. **Four hands Mahakala:** Tib. mGon-po-phag-bzhi-pa, He is one of the Dharmapala has one fierce face with three eyes; four hands, two legs, blue or black in colour and five skull crown.
27. **Six hands Mahakala:** Tib. dpal mgon phyag drug. Pron. Pelgon chak-druk, the "great black" one appears as Buddhist fom of the Hindu Siva, Cf. Finegan Jack : Tibet: a Dremat of Image, *op. cit.,* 133.
28. **Zambeyang** or 'Jan-dbyangs, Pron. Janyang "Charming Splendor" is the god of wisdom.

29. **Damcan (Tib. dam can chos rgyal):** The dam-can meaning bound by vow, is considered as protective deity of Buddhism.

30. **Kalcakra:** Tib. dpal-dus-kyi-hkhor-lo, Das-'k' or, Phon Eng. Palduchi Khorlo, 'Dukhor'. The wheel of time ' A Yidam and a terrifying god-form emanation of Aksobhya.

31. **De-chok (skt. cakrasamvara):** He is usually stands on the body of Rudra and his consort vajravarahi (Tib. Dorje Pagmo). Together symbolise the union of emptiness and bliss. some say Samvara embrace with his consort represent intelligence and emergy; together symbolise the union of the wisdom of nirvana and samsara.

32. **Tashilunpo monastery :** It is located on the side of Dubu Mountain west of Xigaze, was founded by Genduntrup, Tsongkhapa's nephew and disciple, who become (retroactively) the First Dalai Lama. Later the fifth Dalai Lama conferred upon his former teacher the abbot of the monastery. Lopsang choskyi Gyentsen the title of Panchen, for whom Trashilunpo remained the official residence. Cf. Finegan, Jack; *op. cit.,* 154.

33. **Camba Choskor (i.e. Maitreya):** Tib. Byams-pa, phom. Eng. Jampa "The kind one". A Mahabodjisattva and the Boddhisattva who will be the Manushi Buddha of futrue age. The Buddha to be who will show the way to nirvana. He is equally respected by the Thervadists.

34. **Tsongkhapa;** tib rje-rim-po-che, tson-khe-pa. Phon. Eng. Tsongkhapa, was the founder of Geluk-pa order of Mahayanea Buddhism during the 14th century A.D., and considered to be a manifestation of Manjusri. c.f. Batchelor stephen: The Tibet Guide; Wisdom Pub., London; 1987: 422.

35. **Manjusri:** Tib.' Jan-dbyangs. Pron Jamyang," charming Splendor", is shown is yellow, white red, blue and black forms; beautifully handsome young bodhisattva and god of wisdom.

36. **Vajrapani:** Tib. Phyag na rdo-rje: holder of the thunderbolt diamond scepter" is manifestation of Akshobhya and is usually shown as dark blue in colour with a crown of skulls and holding the dorje, and sometimes with a snake (naga). c.f. Finegan, Jack; *op. cit.,* 130.

11

Royal Palaces in Ladakh

Leh Palace: This is the best known building of nine stories, was completed in about three years. It was built by Singge Namgyal probaby in 1630, has two distinctive features :

1. Timber porch
2. Stone-work

Timber porch of this building is facing east direction. Normally in all big buildings such as monasteries and historical building, we can mark this style of timber porch.

The porch has a mixture of "Mediterranean Classical" and Tibetan decorative motifs. Which is unique in Ladakh. The style of timber porching though belongs to Tibetan character, it was originally came from India. In India such style of timber porching is almost extint, however, preserved in Ladakh.[1]

Stone work: The stone work at Leh place is excellent. It is the earliest detable example.[2]

Shey Palace: The Shey Palace was built in the late 1640. The building was surrounded by big walls for safty. In the walls many holes were made, probably through these Ladakh soldiers could shoot arrows or similar weapons to the enimies. Today palace is renovated by Archeological Department, Govternment of India, New. Delhi. But the surrounding walls are in ruined condition.[3]

Basgo Fort: This fort is in ruined condition. The date of this fort may be in between 1560 A.D.—1590 A.D. and situated above the Maitreya monastery building.[4]

Temisgam Palace: It was built by king Dragspa Bum who resided in the Lower Ladakh. His brother Dragspa Bumde was the king of Ladakh during 15th century. The Temisgam Palace was also built in the same century.[5]

To-yos-khar: Lhachen Palgyigon was the first king of Ladakh who made Shey as his capital. He had two sons viz. Lhachen Dogon and Lhachen Chosgon. After Lhachen Dogon, Lhachen Dasgspalde ruled Ladakh for about 25 years from 1050 to 1075. During his period Lotsava Rinchen bzangpo visited Ladakh. He built many viharas, chortens and decorated the choskhors by wall paintings. Toyos-Khar also built during the same period in the following reasons:[6]

1. During 10-11th century Lotsava Rinchen bzangpo had been decorating Mangyu, Alchi and Sumba temples by beautiful Buddhist mural paintaings, with the help of skilled 32 artists, To see the auspicious work Lhachen Dagesplde ordered his Ministers to build To-yos khar in Saspol village, about 65 km from Leh, at an altitude 11,000 ft. from the sea level. Later on the request of Ladakh king Lotsava Rinchen bzangpo probably started his works from Saspol. We can see the ruins of 108 stupas, three temples and wall paintings on the walls of cave temples. These were the ready plateform for paintings, whereas Alchi choskhor, they had to build the structure.

2. The ruins of the above place speaks itself about ancient building structure, however it is difficult to trace out the correct date of its cunstruction. The Lhato in which Royal lha tse-lha-mo resided indicates that the above palace was built during 10-11th century A.D. Tsering Sonam happned to visit the above site and measured the width and height of the palace; walls width 36″ to 39″ and height 27′ to 50′. The palace had 2½ kanal area. There were 25 to 30 rooms in the palace.

3. Royal main land (Tib. ma-zig) is located just below the palace. Today it is under Rizong gonpa and lookafter by concerned Labrang.
4. In all the Royal places, there is a tradition to perform folk dance. This dance had special significance with turning left side. The same tradition still in practise during new year Losar festival.
5. In olden days all palaces were covered by boundary walls. Here too we can see four boundary walls. Inside the boundary villagers were lived safely. Tsering Sonam pointed out sixty such familis (Tib. Ko-ram-co rgyat) who were having in their houses inside the boundery walls. Some families are listed below :

   (i) Da-kyajur pa

   (ii) Canpa

   (iii) Compa

   (iv) Go-rong-pa

   (v) Pa-tuk-pa

   (vi) Kha-tse-pa

   (vii)' Pa-tuk-pa

Bugzal, which was donated by Pa-tuk-pa family to Rizong monastery is still preserved. Later the land of the said family come under the possession to To-yon-pa. Comopa, Canpa and Go-rong-pa land area was more than Mane gyatsa family. This land later came under Chagzot pa Tsering stan pa. Saspol lies near trade route, therefore invaders often attacked. Consequently, the palace was several times damaged.

Today whole Saspol village is under Gelukpa order, Drug-pa k'agyud holds a small portion of land. The land belongs to To-yos Khar. was donated to Stag-stang-ras pa by king Singge-Namgyal, as he was the **Raj Guru** of Ladakh kingdom.

Conclusion: In conclusion it seems me that Ladakh kings built their palaces under defensive plan, whenever enemy came closer to one palace, king and his Ministers shifted to another palace and passed instraction to the concerned authorites. In this way they safed their life.

References

1. Neil Howal: 'Royal Fortresses of Ladakh', Archeology Today, May 1987, 29-35.
2. *Ibid.*
3. *Ibid.*
4. *Ibid.*
5. *Ibid.*
6. Tsering Sonam 'Saspol: A ancient historic village' paper presented in the All India Seminar, CIBS, Leh-Ladakh; 2004.

12

Sengge Namgyal : A Great Protector of Ladakhi Buddhist Culture

Sengge Namgyal was the son of king Jamyang Namgyal and muslim queen Gyal Khatun. He had inherited the warlike spirit of his grandfather, Ali Mir. From his childhood he was very strong, clever at wrestling running, jumping, shooting with bow and arrow as well as matchlock and riding. He was a skill administrator during his regime Ladakh got tremendus progress. All his ministers did their works skillfully according to his orders.[1]

He lived mostly at Shey place. The palace was earlier destroyed by Baltis, Therfore, he wanted to ranovate the same. But on the advise of his great guru lama Stag-tsang-ras-pa[2] he decided to construct a new palace in Leh town. Later he ordered his ministers to construct Leh palace. During 17th century A.D. many villagers for this precious work were engaged to support voluntarily. The work was difficult and needed lot of money. King then decided to extend the boundaries of Ladakh kingdom to get cash and kind money from the neighbouring country. He invaded 'Guge'. This time he re-conquer the earlier lost province for his kingdom, and carried away ponies, yaks, goats, and sheep even so far as from the north solpes of Kailas. Later he declared war against the central provinces.[3]

After returning Leh, Sengge Namgyal once again payed his attention for unfinished grand building enterprise (i.e. of Leh palace). The nine storeyed building took three years. This time queen Skalzang Dolma also gave her full contribution. On her advise king built one **Chotkhang.** He installed Buddhist statues made of gold and silver metals, besides decorated walls by beautiful frecos according to Drugpa k'agyud order. And placed Kangyur. Stangyur pothis at one side almirah in the temple. The wall paintings was done under the direction of Spon Namkha Spalgon of Sabu village. [4]

In 1622 Sengge Namgyal built another remarkable building in the Maitrey monastery at Basgo, above the ruins of the ancient fort. It still contains the statue of Maitreya of clay, copper and gilt, as big as he would be in his eightieth year, three stories high. It took two years. Queen Gyal Khatun donate 312 tola gold and 3.5 kg. precious things for this. The Basgo building and Maitrey a statue works completed on 15th of 9th Tibetan month in 1623. Later king invited 100 lamas, 80 artists and 200 VIPs for Rabnas ceremony. On this occasion **Khorlo Damba** was celeberated. From this day Basgo monastery started to celeberate annual festival, which later became tradition. Subsequently, he built 700 metre long Mani wall and two Namgyal chortens both of its ends.[5]

In 1625 Baltis started to disturb Ladakh border, as a result Ladakh king declared war against Baltis of Skardu **Co.** Ladakh army entered Skardu defeated Baltis. King Alikhan and Cung Ali Muhammad were killed. Ladakh army entered upto Tibet, captured some parts of Tibet, later returned Ladakh with good amount of cash and kind from Tibet, and donated some portion from this to his guru Stag-tsang-ras-pa (Table 12.1).

Table 12.1. Donation received from King Sengge Namgyal in 1625

Sl. No.	*Item*	*Amount / quantity*
1	*2*	*3*
1.	Ponies	100
2.	Yaks	100
3.	Sheep	1000

1	*2*	*3*
4.	Gold	300 gm.
5.	Grain	3000 loads
6.	String of pearls	01
7.	String of coral beads	01
8.	String of turquoise beads	01
9.	Coats of mail	15
10.	Pieces of sild	25
11.	Pieces of broacade	10
12.	Pieces of gauze	25
13.	Pieces of broad gauze for scarfs of blessing	25

Source: France, A.M.: A History of western Tibet' Reprinted Asian Educational Services, 1995 : 100.

King Sangge Namgyal favoured Buddhism, with his Guru Stag-tsang-ras-pa, strengthened Drugpa k'agyad tradition in Ladakh by establishing Hemis, Chemre, Trashigang and Hanle monasteries. Besides, he founded a small gonpa at Nyoma. Queen Skalzang Dolma also helped him for this religious work she imported Buddhist texts from Zanskar and ordered lamas to write Buddhist pothis by gold ink. In those days Hemis was the main center of Stag tsang ras pa, therefore, it became the centre monastery of Drugpa k'agyud order. Later by his kind blessing Hemis started 'Hemi stesu' thereafter it become tradition.[7]

Sengge Namgyal built a long Mani-wall at Lingshed and a famous wooden bridge across the Indus at Alchi. He went for war with Purig and Baltistan, capture Purig and put them under his control.[8] Soon after he again went for war, and reached up to Ngamring;[9] but at Shir karmo[10] his army could not able to cross the Chatra river and defeated. He returned Hanley.[11]

In the middle of 17th century A.D. Sokpa army invaded Ladakh. To defend his kingdom Sengge Namgyal with his force went Guge. But at Wangle he fell ill, stayed there for one month, later died on 22 November 1642.[12]

Nots and References

1. Francke, A.H. : A History of Western Tibet', Reprinted Asian Educational Services, 1995 : 96.
2. Stag-tsang-ras-pa: He via Sarchu came Leh. However, after staying 4 years in Serda Bangpo house in Gya returned Tibet. After sometime came Ladakh with his 10 disciples. At Tise he was welcomed by Chosje Muzin. When king Sengge Namgyal came to know about his visit, immediately sent a deligation of Ministers & VIPs for his welcome at Nyoma. Later King himself went Marshilang with his ministers to welcome him. Stag-tsang-ras-pa thereafter went to Gotsang and installed many buddhist statues. In 1624 at Vamle and in 1626 he made Mani Tungcur. In 1630 he founded Hemis monastery near Gotsang cave. At the death of king Sengge Namgyal he performed this cremation by Buddhist tradition in Leh. After sometime queen Skalzang Dolma expressed his desires to visit mount Kailash. Stag-tsang ras pa did not allow her by saying that queen's health would not be suitable for long journey. But Queen went to Zanskar. As she arrived in Zanskar, fell seriously ill, later died. Her dead body brought to Shey palace. Stag-tsang-ras pa cremated her with Buddhist ritual tradition. Thereafter he started preaching, in 1651 he got parinisvana. Cf. Phunsog : Ladakh.
3. Francke, A. H.; *op. cit.,* 98-99.
4. Sonam Phunsog : Ladakh; 132-33.
5. *Ibid.*
6. Francke, A.H.; *op. cit.,* & Sonam Phunsog : *op. cit*
7. Francke, A.H.; *op. cit.,* & 100 & Sonam Phunsog; *op. cit.*
8. Francke, A.H.; *op. cit.,* 100.
9. Ngamring: It is seven marches from shigartse Cf. Francke, A.H.; *op. cit.,* 99.

10. Shirikarm : This place is situated on the right bank of the Charta River Cf. francke, A.H.: *op. cit.,* 9.
11. Francke, A.H.; *op. cit.,* 99. According to K. Marx, the difficulty of crossing the Charta River may to some extent account for the defeat of the Ladakh army. It was agreed that the frontier should remain as before, and Sengge Namgyal's dominion should include all the country up to Chatra River.
12. Sonam Phunsog; *op. cit.*

13

Pt. Rahul Sanskrityayan's Views about Ladakhi Culture

Rahul Sanskrityayan, a great scholar of Sanskrit, Pali and Hindi. He was a thinker, linguist and a prolific writer, popularly known as Mahapandit. His first hand knowledge about Ladakh and its people not only give a deep insight information about culture but also provide clues to various archaeological findings.

There are number of Indian travellers who came in Ladakh. To name few notable Indians are Col. Sazan Singh and Dr. Prem Singh Jina. Col. Sazan Singh's journey was based on his hunting expeditions during 1955. On the other hand Dr. Jina visited in all parts of Ladakh except Zanskar region. He is the eye opener of morden Ladakh, has written 28 books on Ladakh. His writings belong to Ladakhi Art, culture and religion including tourism.

Rahul's observations, calculation and experiences showed his capacity to communicate his information in classical way. He chose Hindi as an effective vehicle of communication. He visited Himalayas more than ten times between 1926 and 1956, traveled mostly on foot, on horseback and sometines in public transport whenever available, visited Ladakh during 1933, and written his travel diary, Yatra ke Panne.

Rahul was a great writer, wrote more than hundred books including novels, travelogues, treatises on religion culture, archaeology and above all about the people. Most of his writings were devoted to Himalayas, depicting in them the topography, life style, their customs, beliefs and superstitions.

He was always keen to write orginal. His contribution based on travels in Himalayas was unique. His works relating to Himalayas mostly on Himachal Pradesh, Kumaun, Garhwal, Nepal, Tibet, Darjeeling & Ladakh. His detailed and meticulons writing plan and instant recording of his memories, travels, events and observations in his diaries enabled him to utilize the materials in his works.[1]

Rahul not only loved Himalayas, its snow-clad mountains and cool climate, but the people of this region. He made friends and mixed with them tried to know their life -style, custom, tradition, History and Culture. He prefered to make friendship with old people so that he could know their old traditional culture. In his works he used their folktales, lores, belief, festival, religion and life style.[2]

He used to visite the villages in Himalayas where he could find old sites. In Ladakh after crossing Zojila, as he came to Dras valley, took interest in Dards custom and writes:

> "Dards are similar to shins. As I crossed Zoji-la saw many Dards, were giving kheer to their horses which was strange."[3]

His imagination was true as Dards migrated into Ladakh via Gilgit, settled down in Dah-Hanu, Garkon, Derchik, Dras etc. In oldern days Gilgit was under the influence of Buddhism, therfore, their ancestors were also Buddhists. During 14th century Dards of Dras were influenced by Islam, when Hamdani propogated Islam in this region. However, Dards of Dah, Hanu, Garkon, Derchik etc. followed Drigung pa k'agyud tradition of Buddhism.

Rahulji considered Kargil as a place of Baltis, but he did not mention about their migration. The chronicles of Central

Asian History tells us that they migrated to central Tibet in 4th–5th B.C. from Tangur. Thereafter, settled down in various groups along the banks of Indus, Shyok and Singar rivers. In Sherian language they were called 'Po – lo – Po' and in Tibetan 'sbalti'[4].

Baltis of Kargil used to go Indian Hills e.g. Nainital, Shimla, Mussorie, Manali etc., for labour job, sometimes they were employed by businessmen, with them visited Tibet Yarkand etc. However, returned before winters. Younghusband says:

> "Baltis are good load carrier, because in their country – Baltistan and its neighoburing countries there are no good roads, so they carry their loads on their backs upto long distances."

Baltis have strong and hard body, they could do difficult work easily. Rahul says:

> "The ancestors of Holiyal village migrated from Gilgit. This village is situated 4 km away from the main road."[5]

In1982 I visited above village. One old person informed me that their ancestors were migrated from Gilgit, but treated lower cast and not allowed to establish their relations with Baltis of Kargil.

After Kargil Rahul came to Shergol. It was the first Buddhist village in Srinagar – Leh route. Commenting on this he says:

> "Earlier before there was no muslim, now (1933) more than 50 per cent Muslim population. This is only possible with sexual thrust. Muslims married Ladakhi Buddhist girls. This tradition helps to increase Muslim population very fast. If this trend will continue after 100 years whole Shergol village will be a Muslim village."[6]

I visited Shergol village in 1982, thereafter in 1992 and found Rahul pradiction right as more than 60 per cent population of this village belong to Muslim community.

When Rahul arrived at Mulbek he saw huge rock carving on big rock and recognised it as Avalokitesvara. I saw this 50 feet high statue.It is Maitreya of Gandhara art, as on his head chorten is made. But from its four hands one may consider it as Avalokitesvara. Normally huge rock images belong to Maitraya Buddha.

About Alchi monastery he said: "Alchi is situated near Saspol. It was constructed by Losava Rinchen bzang po in 11th century, In this Choskor there are three Bodhisattva temples. Inside of these have strange (paintings)."[7]

In 5th July 1933 Rahul stayed in Leh. In those days Buddhists were planning to form a Buddhist society. Commenting on education system of Leh people, he says:

> "... local people are sending a letter to Kashmir Government after their signatures, requesting for scholarship, Bothi language in Primary school, Sanskrit teacher in Leh school and for the appointment of Tibetan teachers from outside."[8]

Ladakhis were then not well educated Rahul says: "There are only two educated persons in Leh. One who can translate English to Tibetan language and other is teacher in Leh Middle school."

In my knowledge these two persons were Yusuf Gergan and E. Joldan. Yusuf Gergan was a good scholar, he had written, one book in Bodhi language on 'Ladakh History', the other person Joldan was also a good scholar, I met him in 1983, he presented me a book writen in English entitled 'Harvest festival of Ladakh' it had a collection of papers on Gelam Kesar Harvest festival of Dah Hanu area etc. E. Jolden was a simple and honest person. Today Leh Degree college is named after him.

After taking rest at Leh, he marched for Shey. It was the capital of Ladakh kingdom till 16th Century. The ruins of Shey palace still can be seen, He says:

> "The old capital of Ladakh was Shey, when Leh became the capital, the importance of Shey palace remained the same, as at the birth of each prince of the kingdom all

the royal family members used to go to Shey place and celeberate his birth cermony. The maximum part of the palace is destroyed, walls are still there. There is 20 – 25 hands high Buddha statue in a temple near the palace. To see the upper portion of the statue, we have to go upper storey. There are beautiful frescos on the walls at upper storey, but they are hardly seen because all walls of the temple have become black by lamps smoke. At the ground floor there are Kangyur and Stangyur pothis."[9]

About one more temple in the village, he says:

"There is one more Lhakhang in the village. It has some old statues. The **pujari** of this temple is **Lhapa.** Lhapa is the person who can go into trance stage. At present he is a young boy of 25 years. The temple is small and has statues in the middle of decorative artificial flowers and plants. Inside village there are many ruined sites. It is said that when Ladakh was a independent country, many houses of this village were under king palace .... Here lives Shey lonpo, had high rank is Ladakh Kingdom. Lambardar of this village belongs to the Lonpo family. There are some popalar tress as a result some greenery can be seen."[10]

Later travelling about 5 km. he arrived Thikey monastery, which belongs to Geluk pa order. He remarks:

"In Ladakh Thikse, Rizong and Likir are the main Geluk pa order monasteries. Likir does not have incarnated lama. The rest have Rinpoches. In Ladakh they are called Kushok. Likir monastery is the oldest one, established in 11th century. Thiksey monastery has good land area, some small gonpas are under its control. The monastery has about one hundred lamas and many temples. One beautiful statue was brought here from a Khangsar house.

Regarding conversion in Ladakh he says:

> "One respected khangsar family in Thiksey is converted to Muslim. Muslims are doing their conversion very well. If this trend will continue, I hope in the coming one hundred years there will be hardly any Buddhist in this village."[12]

There is one old Choskor near Thiksey. It was built in 11th century by Lotsava Rinhen Zangpo. Rahul visited this and made the following remarks :

> "This Choskhor was built by Lotsava Rinchen Zangpo.It was constructed on plain, had boundary wall, in the middle 100 temples, chortens and rooms for monks were constructed. some chortens and walls of the temples are still existed in ruin condition. In the end of 16th century Skardo king Ali Mir invaded Ladakh and destroyed all the monasteries on his way to Ladakh. This Choskhor was also destroyed by his army. There are some old chortens at Nyerma, which are beautifuly decorated by old paintings from inside. The paintings also destroyed. Besides, I found one stamp written in Sankrit language."[13]

Later via Upshi (11,900 ft.) Rahul came to Meru. Here he found some ruins of old settlements. He says :

> "Upshi is a small village. Later I came to Meru. There is a proverb about this village that — Among palaces, Khalatse is the oldest one, and among villages, Meru tse is the oldest."

On way to Teri, he found many stupas and even a ruined temple. According to Rahul these were built before 11th century. As before 11th century mostely all the Buddhist temples were construted on plains. However, the Teri chorten is one of the 84,000 Asoka chortens. Travelling further in Chang – Thang region he found a place where Padmasambhava performed *yagacar kriya*. At the border of old Ladakh and Kulu he found some inscriptions, but did not tell about them in details. While visiting Par-sev, he found an empty place, but was used for trading. He remarks.

"Par–Sev is a long and empty place. During spring season a big trade fair is conducted here, in which traders from Kulu, Lahul, Spiti, Ladakh, Zanskar and Tibet come togather and display their merchandise viz. wheat, barley, sheep, goats, wool, hores, donkeys and exchange them according to their requirements."[14]

In conclusion Rahul Sankrityayan was a prolific writer, thinker and a great traveller, was fascinated and attracted by Himalayas to the extend that of one time he decided to find a permanent abode for the rest of his life in the lap of Himalayas, and finally find a home at Herncliff Mussorie. He wrote about himself:[15]

"At one time, I was a Sanyasi, then become Aryasamaji, and Buddhist Bhikshu afterwards, I became Marxist even having immense faith in Buddha."[16]

Notes and References

1. Bisotra; Rattan lal : Rahul Sanstritayan: the man of the Himalayas; In: Himalaya Today, Vol. V, No. 3, Issue No. 15, Oct.-Dec. 1994: 22.
2. *Ibid.*
3. Rahul Sankrityayan: 'Yatras Ke Panne; Kitab Mahal, 1933: 240-50.
4. *Ibid.*
5. *Ibid.*, 260.
6. *Ibid.*, 262.
7. *Ibid.*, 264.
8. *Ibid.*, 266-75.
9. *Ibid.*, 290.
10. *Ibid.*
11. *Ibid.*, 294.
12. *Ibid.*
13. *Ibid.*
14. *Ibid.*, 305.
15. Bisotra, Rattan Lal; *op. cit.,* 23.
16. *Ibid.*

14

Tibetan Inscription near Dorje Chenmo Chokhang Shey

Text

Shel gyis blon pos khar dpon/
grongs dpon bcas kyi gcas/
gon par gzhon gsum rnams la springs pa/
shel pho brang gi mngun gyi/
gstag 'abum ster can
lha bnga chen mo/
bong zem tsun gyis sma tsams nang gzhug su/
ngang pa ngur pa chu bya la slogs srog
chags shog thog kyi rigs rnams thar
pa gling du che thar la gnang ba yin cing/
khyad par du byang db'adi log cig gis
rtags gzhib zan ngan rtag rgyu khag che yin 'abum pa nas/
da chos zla dang 'po'ai ches 'adi nas
gzung su nang mi rtsi b'ai las byas pa byung tse/
Thub chen du rgyam chod dang dar chen/
grong du gser srang gang re rtsis thogs med
gtsang 'abum zhus nas slar yang
bk'a shog gyis brtan tsig 'adi don
la ji srid bskal p'ai par nas dgos gin/
shing by'ai zla ba dang po'ai tses nam gang la bris/

Roman Transliteration

shel gi lon pos khar pon/
dongs pon cas kyi cas/
gon par zhon sum nams la tins pa/
shel pho tang gi dun gyi/
stag/
bum ster can/
lha bang chen mo/
bong zem tsun gyis sam tsams nang zhug su/
nang pa ngur pa chu ca la sogs srog
chags shog thog kyi rigs nams thar pa
ling du tse thar la nang va yin cing/
Khyad par du cang tiab di log cig gis stags
zhib zan ngan stag gyu khag che yin dug pa nas/
da chog za dang pove tses di nas zung/
su nang mi tsi ve las cas pa jung tse/
thub chen du gyam chod dang dar chen/
dong du ser srang gang re tsis
thogs med tseng bum zhus nas lar
yang ka shog gyis tan tsig di don la
ji srid skal pe par nas gos yin/
shing ce za va dang pove tses nam gang la dis.

Translation

(This order was written in the wood bird year) for Shey Ministers, Kharpon,[1] Dongs – pon[2] and lamas of the (Shey monastery).[3]

(All people who are living in between Shey Palace[4] and) Chenmo Bongzun are warned not to kill ducks, water living beings and other (related) animals. Specially the (migratory) water birds who migrate from the north (to the Shey lake). On the basis (of their migration to Shey) we can understand about the good and bad season of the year. Therefore, (those who kill these important migrated birds) from the first day of the Ist Tibetan month will be punished. They will have to lit one hundred lamps before the Shey Place Buddha statue, to hoist **dar chen**, to donate gold coin. (All the people of the village) will have to follow in the following years.

(The order) is writen on 23rd (Amavasiya) of the 1st Tibetan month.

Notes and References

1. **Kharpon:** He who was looking after the palace of Shey.
2. **Dongs–pon:** Tib grong-dpon, he who lookafter the activities of Shey villagers.
3. **Shey monastery:** It is the Shey palace monastery, has two temples, one was built by Sengge Namgyal, other was built by his Baltistan wife. Cf. Finegan, Jack: 'Tibet: A Dreamt of Image' Tibet House, Delhi, 1986: 20.
4. **Shey palace:** Shey is about 15 km from Leh, situated on the right bank of the Indus river. It was the ancient capital of Ladakh and has old king palace.

PART–II

15

Ruthok Lhundup Chosling Gonpa

Friday morning on 18th April 2008, I decided to visit Ruthok Lhundup Chosling gonpa, situated at Choglamsar, 8 km from Leh, at the right side of Indus river, near SOS camp. In order to study the gonpa, I thought to take the help of chomo Sanghe Chosdon, a student of Central Institute of Buddhist Studies, Choglamsar, Leh-Ladakh. Her house was near to the gonpa.

"Nomole!"

"Who is there?"

"Guruji."

"Julley, please come."

"chomo, I want to see the Ruthok Lhundup chosling gonpa, do you know some one there?"

"I don't know, but I'll accompany you, hope your work will be done."

"Thank you."

" Guruji, don't stand outside, sit here and have a cup of tea. I'll chang my dress and soon join you."

She went to her room.

× × × × × ×

At 9.30 A.M. I accompanied her and very soon reached Ruthok Lhundup gonpa.

Sanghe Chosdon met a lama there, told him about my planning. The lama went to the Lhopon, the head Lama of the monastery for permission. Lhopon was a Tibetan lama, glad to see me and allowed to see the monastery.

This monastery has only one Dukhang in which Buddha, Bodhisattva statues and thankas are preserved. It does not have wall paintings as usually we see in other big monasteries. It is a branch gonpa of Sara monastery of Karnataka, which was established by Tibetan Refugees after 1959. Lhopon also deputed by the Sara gonpa welfare society. At present Ruthok Lhundup chosling has seven lamas and one cook, he is also lama. The details is given below.

At the centre His Holiness Dalai Lama photograph is placed on his throne. His right hand in Bhumispharsa, left hand holds pothi and placed in his lap, wears yellow cap and red Lama dress of Gelukpa tradition. On the left and right side of the throne has many Buddhist statues. The details is listed below.

Statues on the left of H.H. Dalai Lama Throne in the glass almirah

1. Buddha:

   Arms : Two

   Mudra : Meditation

   Asana : Meditation

   Height : 1′

   Widht : 6″

   Material used : Clay

2. Buddha

   Asms : Two

   Mudra : Meditation

   Asana : Meditation

   Height : 1′

   Width : 6″

   Material used : cley

3. Padmasambhava[1]

Posture	:	Seated
Height	:	6″
Width	:	4″
Arms	:	Two; left hand holds skull cup, right hand holds dorje, rests on his knee.

4. Jamyang[2]

Arms: Two; holds flame sword

Posture	:	Seated
Height	:	6″
Width	:	4″

5. Sakyamani Buddha[3]

Arms	:	Two
Mudra	:	Bhumisparsha
Asana	:	Meditation

6. Avalokitesvara [4]

Arms	:	Four
Mudra	:	Two main hands are in namaskar mudra
Height	:	6″
Width	:	4″

7. Padmasambhava

Pasture	:	Seated
Mudra	:	Left hand holds skull cup, right hand holds dorje, rests on his knee

8. Paldan Lhamo [5]

Arms	:	Two
Posture	:	Seated on horse

Vasana	:	Horse
Height	:	1′
Width	:	6″

Statues on the right of H.H. Dalai Lama throne in the glass almirah

9. Tshe - dpag-med[6]

Arms	:	Two
Mudra	:	Meditation, holds patra of longivity in his lap
Asana	:	Meditation
Material	:	Brass

10. Namgyal ma[7]

Posture	:	Seated
Meterial	:	Brass

11. Dolma[8]

Posture	:	Seated
Arms	:	Two

12. Dolma

Posture	:	Seated
Arms	:	Two

13. Dolma

Posture	:	Seated
Arms	:	Two

14. Dolma

Posture	:	Seated
Arms	:	Two

(13–14) Placed infront of Tshe–dpag-med.

15. Padmasambhava

Arms	:	Two	Ahead of Tshe-dpag-med
Posture	:	Seated	
Height	:	6″	
Width	:	4″	

Statues in the next almirah

16. Tsongkhapa[9]	:	Centre
17. Gyaltsabje[10]	:	Disciple of Tsongkhapa at his right
18. Khasdupje[11]	:	Disciple of Tsongkhapa at his left
19. Chagna dorje	:	Ahead of Tsongkhapa
20. Tsongkhapa	:	Ahead of Tsongkhapa Sl. No. 16
21. Gyaltsabje	:	At the right of Sl. No. 20
22. Khasdupje	:	At the left of Sl. No 20
23. Padmasambhava	:	Ahead of the Sl. No. 16

× × × × ×

Ruthok Lhundup chosling gonpa has some precious thanksas, here follows the deatils:

On the right side wall towards door

1. Jetsun champa[12]

Hands	:	One
Hands	:	Two; right hand holds cakra on padma, left hand holds patra on padma.
Mudra	:	Dharmacakra
Asana	:	Dhyana
Head dress	:	Ring nga crown with stupa
Height	:	6′
Width	:	4′

2. Sakyamuni Buddha

Arms	:	Two
Mudra	:	Right hand in Bhunnisparsha, left hand holds patra in Dhyana mudra
Asan	:	Meditation
		His two main disciples Sari Putra and Maudgalyayana are depicted on his right and left side.
Mandala	:	Sixteen arhats
Height	:	6′
Width	:	4′

3. Guru Rinpoche[13]

Arms	:	Two
Mudra	:	Left hand holds kapala
Mandala	:	

(i) Below at the eright corner: Guru Dorje Dolot[14]

(ii) At the left corner, Singe Dadok

(iii) Right in the middle, Mandarva[16]

(iv) Ishey chosgyal[17], left in the middle

(v) Opakmed[18]

On the top at the centre, holds patra at his lap, both hands in meditation, red body, Dhyana asana.

4. Green tara[19]

Arms	:	Two
Head dress	:	Five leaves crown
Body	:	Green
Mandala	:	

(i) Gyal zhun

(ii) Chagna Dorje

(iii) Twenty one Dolmas

5. Jigjet[20]

Mandala : His 13 froms

This thanka has His Holiness Dalai Lama signature at its back

6. Tandin Yabyum[21]

Mandala : Nine forms of Avalokitesvara

7. Tungkhor Yabyum[22]

8. Sakyamuni Buddha with Sari and Maudgalyayana

Mandala : Various forms of Buddha

9. Tandin

Without yum

10. Paldan-Lhamo

Mandala :

(i) Tsering ma

(ii) Do-sung ma

(iii) Thing gi shal sang ma

(iv) Lob- sang ma

(v) Din sang ma

11. Tungkhor yabyum: A terrifying deity

12. Bhava Cakra (or wheel of life)

This gonpa has four pillars, seats for lamas in four rows. Ling reinpoche during his visit presented 20-25 Buddha Thankas, 1′×1′ in size. the image of Buddha is similar as the Buddha statue in Bodhgaya in yellow colour, are hanged through ceiling. Besides, on the outside door some photos of various Rinpoches are hanged viz.

(i) His Holiness Dalai Lama

(ii) Gya Karmapa

(iii) Sras Rinpoche

(iv) Ling Rinpoche

(v) His Holiness Dalai Lama

(vi) Panchen Lama

(vii) Sakya Kunga Rinpoche

At the right and left of the His Holiness Dalai Lama's throne many Kangyur and Stangyur pothis are placed in shelves.

The following Fig. 15.1 shows further details :

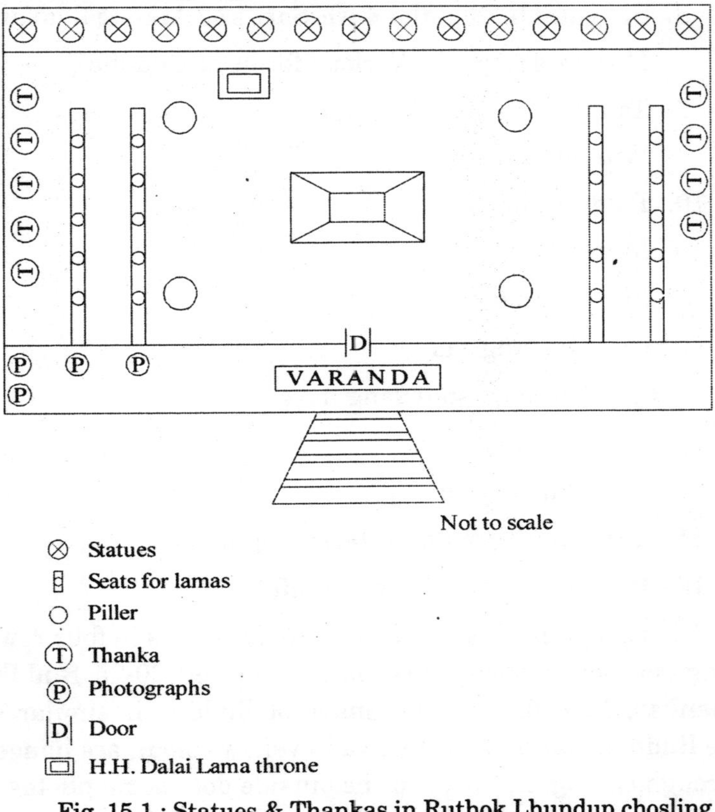

Fig. 15.1 : Statues & Thankas in Ruthok Lhundup chosling Gonpa

In conclusion Ruthok Lhundup Chosling though a small gonpa, has maximum Tibetan lamas, but any lama wether from Ladakh or other parts of India may come here depending upon the meeting of Sara gonpa welfare society. Karnataka. This monastery belong to Gelukpa tradition. Lamas of this monastery often go to the houses of Tibetan Refugees for ritual purposes. At the end I thanked Chomo Sanghe Chosdon for her kind co-operation.

Nots and References

1. **Padmasambhava:** He is the manifestation of Amitabha, propogated Tantric teaching of Mahayana Buddhism in Tibet during eighth century A.D. He assisted Trisong Deutsen, king of Tibet of that period and built Samye monastery.
2. **Jamyang (Skt. arya Manjusri).** He is the embodiment of the wisdom of all the Buddhas. One of the chief disciples of Sakyamuni Buddha and descended human world as a Boddha and desconded human world as Bodhisattva for the welfare of all living beings. He is the deity of wisdom.
3. **Sakyamuni Buddha:** In 6th century B.C. he descended to the world for the welfare of living beings and to show the right path of nirvana. He got enlightenment under the Bodhi tree in Bodhgaya.
4. **Avalokitesvara:** He is the chief Bodhisattva of Mahayana Buddhism and considered as Bodhisattva of compassion.
5. **Padan Lhamo:** The Glorious Goddess, is one of the most important protectors of Gelukpa (or Gllugs pa) order of Mahayana Buddhism and the guardian of Lhasa
6. **Tshe-dpag-med (Buddha Amitayus):** He is the Buddha of longevity.
7. **Namgyalma:** She is the deity of longevity, has white colour and possesses eight arms and three faces bearing three eyes in each face.
8. **Dolma (Skt. Tara):** She ferries us in the ocean of sumsara and is regarded as the menifestation of Avalokitesvara.
9. **Tsongkhapa:** He was the founder of Gelukpa tradition of Mahayana and regarded as the incarnation of Manjus'ri.
10. **Gyaltsabje:** He is the chief disciple of Tsongkhapa

11. **Khasdupje:** He is the chief disciple of Tsongkhapa
12. **Jetsun champa:** Loving one
13. **Guru Rinpoche:** He is Tantric master and has eight manifestation viz.
    (i) Guru Sakya Senge
    (ii) Guru Padmasambhana
    (iii) Guru Ngima Ozer
    (iv) Guru Senge Dradok
    (v) Guru Dorje Doloe
    (vi) Guru Tsokye Dorje
    (vii) Guru Padma Gyalpo
    (viii) Guru Loden Chokse
14. **Dorje Doloe:** He tamed the evil spirits by means of his transcendental power.
15. **Senge Dradok:** He defeated the non-Buddhists in an open debate in Nalanda.
16. **Mandarva:** Consort of Padmasambhava
17. **Ishey Chosgyal (or Eshy Tsogyal):** Consort of Padmasambhava
18. **Opakmed:** Buddha Amitabha, he is the Buddha of infite light, is known is teh fourth of the Dhyani Buddha family, The embodiment of compassion. He resides in the heaven known as Sukhavati situated in the western quarter of heaven.
19. **Green Tara:** She is the green form, is the active force of compassion.
20. **Jigjet (Skt. Vajrabhairava):** He is the wrathful form of Manjusri, has nine faces, sixteen hands and thirty four legs.
21. **Tandin Yabyum** (Tib. rta-mgrin or rta-mgrim-rgyal-pa), in Sanskrit equivlant to aka Arya-Hanyagriva. He is a wrathful emanation of Avalokitesvara in Yabyyum form embraces shakti.
22. **Diikhor yabyum (Tib. dpal dus kyi hkhor-lo, Dus-k'ir).** A terrifying god form emanation of Dhyani Buddha Aksobhya, yum (consort) vishvamati.
23. **Bhava cakra (wheel of life):** The portrait represents the cyclic existence of Samsara.

16

Karma Dupgyud Choeling Gonpa

On 24th April, 2008, Thursday evening I alongwith Chomo Sanghe Chosdon[1] visited Karma Dupgyud Choeling gonpa. It is situated 9 km from Leh and opposit to His Holiness Dalai Lama Photang[2] in Choglamsar. The location of the monastery can be shown in the following Fig.16.1.

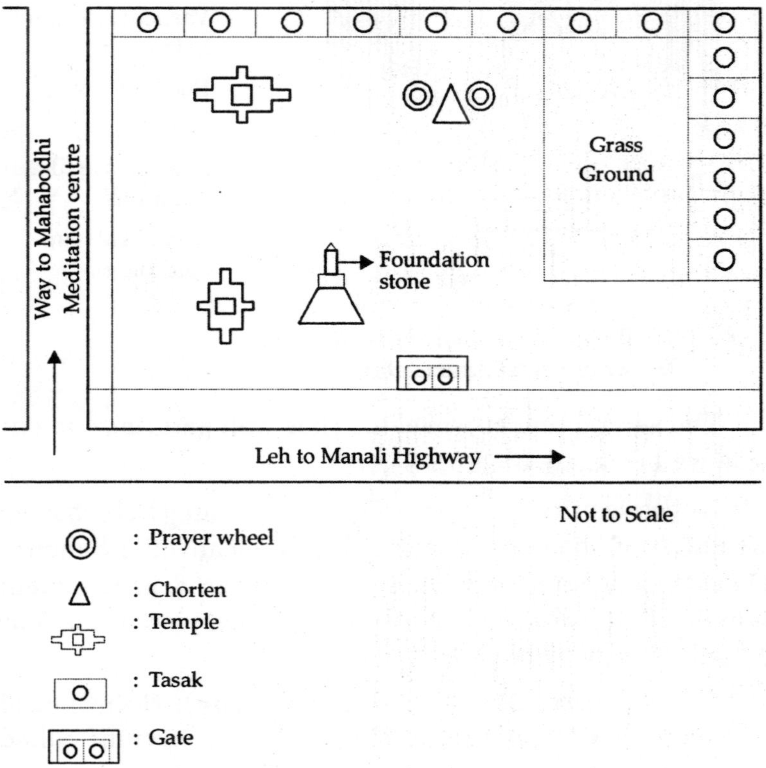

Fig. 16.1. Karma Dupgyud choeling gonpa.

When I visited the monastery, maximum lamas were busy in prayer, reading Tibetan Pothis with loud tune, in certain interval beat drums. One lama of this monastery known to Sanghey Chosdon. She went to seach him. I went right side of the temple to see the prayer wheels. One side wall of two prayer wheels were decorated by beautiful mural paintings (Fig. 16.2.)

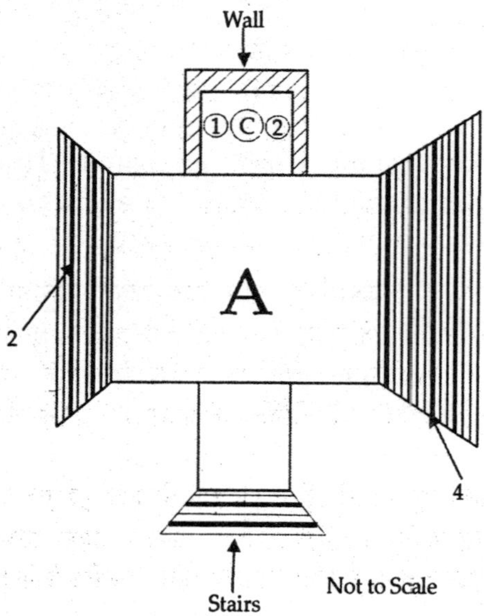

Ⓐ : Prayer wheel

Ⓒ : Dorje Chang
Body : Blue
Asana : Dhyana

① : Tilopa
Mudra : Right hand in Varada; left hand holds fish
Body : white

② : Naropa
Mudra : Vartika, left hand holds skull cup near heart

Fig 16.2. Prayer wheel near the temple of Dupgyud choeling monastery

The second prayer wheel also has wall paintings on one side wall (Fig. 16. 3)

In between two prayer wheel, one Changchub chorten was built of about 7′ in height. In the meanwhile Sanghey Chosdon appeared with a lama, we entered in the main temple of the monastery. Like other monastery it has four lokpalas on the outside wall viz.

1. **Dhritarashtra (Yul khor bsrung):** Guardian of the east and king of the celestial musicians called

(C)Marpa[3] : Both arms in Bhumirparsa
Body : White
Asana : Dhyana

(1) Milaraspa[4]
Body : White
Mudra : Right hand rests on his knee

(2) Dakpo Rinpoche (Head of the Karma K'agyud)[5]
Head dress : Red Hat
Mudra : Meditation holds patra in his lap
Asana : Dhyana
Dress : Red zanggos and Red shantap.

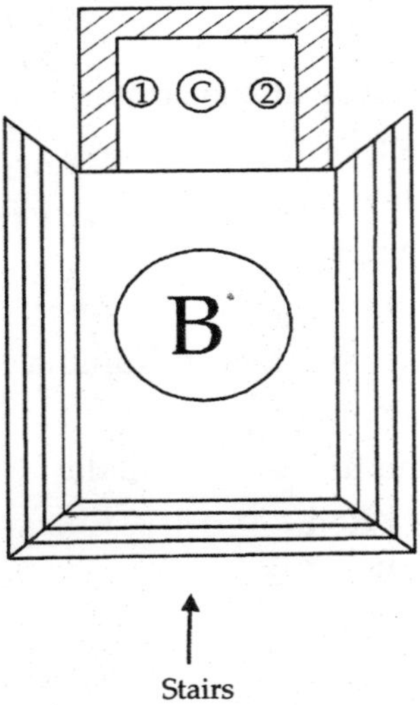

Fig. 16.3 : Prayer wheel near the temple.

gandharvas (Tib. driza), is white colour and holds a stringed instrument.

2. **Virudhaka (Phags skyes po),** Guardian of the south and king of the dalignant spirits called **Kumbhanda** (Tibetan grul bum, pron. trulpum), is dark blue colour and holds a sword (khadga)
3. **Vaisravana (Tib. r Nam thos sras Pron. Nam those) or Kubera, Guardian of North and king of the Yakshas,** is yellow in colour, holds a banner of victory (Dhvaja) and mongoose (nakula)
4. **Virupksha (Tib. Mig mi bzan),** Guardian of the west and king of the serpent deities (nagas Tib. klu), is red in colour and holds a serpent in his right hand and a jewel.

The Dukhang of the monastery has no wall paintings, has six pillers, four rows for lamas, at the end of each row has nga (Musical drum). At the corner has mandala, two main thrones of His Holiness Dalai Lama and 17th Gyalva

Karmapa. Besides, I saw many statues along the wall infront of the door. Here follows the details :

1. Gonpo Bernak[6]	:	Right side at the corner Arms : Two.
2. Paldan Lhamo[7]	:	Sri Devi Arms : Two Vahana : Horse Asana : Seated on Vahana.
3. Tandin[8]		Arms : Two Garments : Dharmapala Body : Red
4. Tseringma[9]	:	Long live Tara Arms : Two

All the above faces of the statues are covered, however, are opened on an especial occasion.

At the back of the above statues along the wall infront of the door (in the glass almirah)

1. **Right side at the corner:** Chotpes of butter. They are the symbol of Gonpa Bernak (two arms gonpo), Paldan Lhamo etc. At the lower shelf ahead to chotpe, Paldan lhamo is rided on horse, one feet height, and width. Further details is shown in the following Fig. 16.4.

Statues along the (A) side wall in glass almirah

1. Opakmed[10]	:	Center statue
Arms	:	Two
Mudra	:	Bodh hands in meditiaton, holds a patra in his lap
Asana	:	Meditation
Height	:	6′
Width	:	4′
Material	:	clay

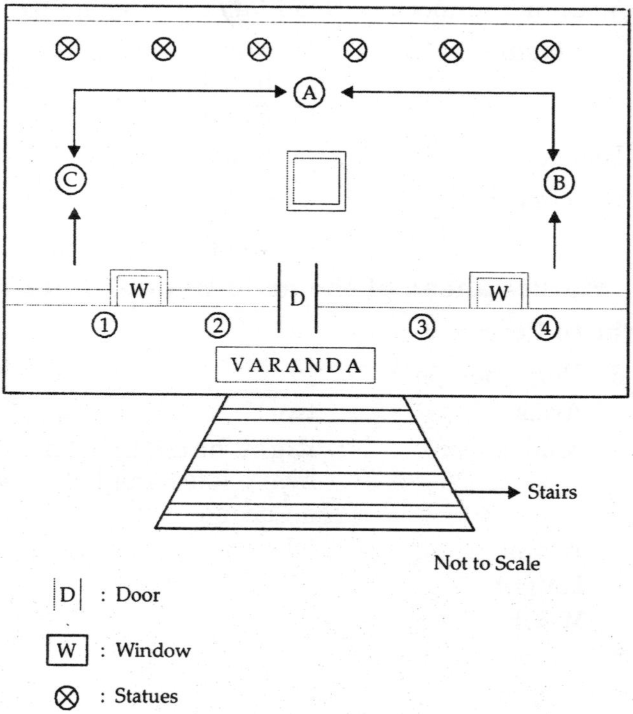

Fig. 16.4 Main temple of Dupgyud Choeling monastry

2. Avalokitesvara[11] : Right to centre statue
   Arms : Four
   Mudra : Two main hands in namaskar
   Asana : Meditation
   Garments : Bodhisattva
   Form : Tantric
3. Dorje chang[12] : Right to the centre statue
   Arms : Two
   Mudra : Vajrahumkara, holds dorje and bell near his heart.

Left to the centre statue

4. Guru Rinpoche[13]

5. Chime Rinpoche, Head lama of k'agyud pa,

Mudra	:	Right hand in Dharmacakra, left hand holds pothis in Dhyana.
Head dress	:	Red Hat
Garments:		(*i*) Zanggos : Red
		(*ii*) Shantab : Red

Statues ahead of the main Buddhist Statues

Right to Left:

6. Dorje Sempa[14]

Arms	:	two
Mudra	:	Right hand holds Dorje near heart, left hand holds bell, rests on asana
Asana	:	Dhyana
Height	:	2′
Width	:	6″

7. Padmasambhava

Height	:	1′
Width	:	6″

8. Avalokitesvara

Form	:	Tantric
Arms	:	Four
Mudra	:	Two main arms in Namaskar mudra

9. Dorje Sempa

Arms	:	Two
Mudra	:	Right hand holds Dorje near heart, left hand holds bell, rests on asana
Asana	:	Dhyana

10. Sakyamuni Buddha

Arms	:	Two
Mudra	:	Right hand in Bhumisparsha, left in meditation

Left to the main statue

There are many small Buddhist statues preserved in the wooden glass almirah.

In the Upper Shelf Right to Left

11. Milaraspa
    - Arms : Two
    - Garments : (*i*) Zanjgos : White
      (*ii*) Shantab : White
    - Asana : Meditation
12. Marpa
    - Arms : Two
    - Mudra : Both hands in Bhumisparsha
    - Asana : Meditation
13. Tilopa[15] :
    - Arms : Two
    - Asana : Meditation
14. Chagna Dorje[16]
    - Arms : Two
    - Body : Blue
15. Padmasambhava
    - Arms : two
    - Mudra : Holds skull cup
16. Chagdor[17]
    - Arms : Two, holds skull cup and vajra
    - Body : Blue
17. Karmapa lama
    - Arms : Two
    - Asana : Meditation
    - Ganments : (*i*) Zanggos Lama dress
      (*ii*) Shantab
18. Chagdor
    - Arms : Two, holds skull cup and vajra
19. Karmapa lama
    - Arms : Two
    - Asana : Meditation
    - Garments : Lama dress

In the lower shelf Right to left

20. Avalokitesvara

Height	:	3′
Width	:	1′

21. Sakyamuni Buddha

Arms	:	Two
Asana	:	Meditation
Garments	:	Right hand in Bhumisparsha, left holds partra in his lap
Height	:	3′
Width	:	1′

22. Padmasambhava

Arms	:	Two; holds skull cup

23. Buddha

Ahead of the above almirah one kudun chorten Chimet Rinpoch ringcell. I saw some beautiful thankas hanging along the wall through the ceiling, here follows the details

Along the (B) wall

1. Milaraspa
   With silk cloth frame height 4′
   Width 3′
2. Karma Pakshi
   Height 4′ With silk cloth frame
   Width 3′
3. Milaraspa
   Height 4′ With silk cloth frame
   Width 3′

Along the (C) wall

4. Kundu Kunzang yab–yum
5. Ist karmapa
6. Paldan Lhamo
7. Gonpo chagzee[18]

8.	Opakmed	Meditation mudra, holds patra in his lap
9.	Opakmed	
10.	Buddha	
	Mudra	: Right hand in teaching, left hand in meditation.

11.
12.
13.
14.
15.
16.
17.
18.
19.
20.
21.
22.
23.
24.
25.
26.
26.

Sixteen thankas of 16 Arhats, they are the member of Buddhist order who advanced the path of nirvana and were subject to no more redirths. Their duty on earth is to preserve and preach the law of the Buddha. They are Angaji, Ajita, Vanavasin, Kalika, Vajriputa, Bhadra, Kanakavatsa, Kankabharadvaja, Bakula, Rahula, Cudapanthaka, Pindolabharadvaja, Panthaka, Nagasena, Gopaka and Abheda.

After completing my research work on Karma Dupgyud choeling gonpa, I thanked lama who assisted me in the monastery. Then I along with Chomo Sanghe Chosdon returned Chojlamsar.

Notes and References

1. Chomo Sanghe Chosdon : Student of Central Institute of Buddhist studies, choglamsar, Leh-Ladakh.
2. His Holiness Dalai Lama Photang :His Holiness Dalai Lama during his visit to Ladakh stays in Photang.

3. Marpa (Tib. Mar pa chos kyi blo gros Pron.

   Marpa chliokyi Lodro). He after earlier study with Drokmi came as a pupil to Naropa, who was then a great mahasiddha and teaching at Phullahari. In all Marpa visited India three times and stayed with Naropa more than sixteen years, under whom he studied the Guhyasamaja Tantra, the Hevajra Tantra, and the essence of all Mahamudra." Cf. Finegan, Jack : Tibet : A Dreamt of Image',Tibet House, New Delhi; 1986: 91

4. Milaraspa (or Milarepa): He was the disciple of Marpa. Under Marpa he studied and was subjected to severe discipline, including the labour of building and repeatedly rebuilding the nine story stone tower of Sras mkhar dgu thog. He was encouraged by Marpa's wife. Later, learned that in his absence his widowed mother and family had been enslaved by an evil uncle, and he went and took revenge by magical means. After that he turned to the life of a wandering yogin, and lived in many solitary places. By virtue of the inner mystic heat, he was able to endure the coldest weather in only cotton clothing , hence his familiar name, Milarepa,' The cotton clad Mila." Dwelling at Mount Kailasa and lake Manasarovara, which were holy places of the Bon-po, he overcame them in magic contests and took possession in the name of Buddhism. Cf. Finegan, Jack; op. cit.: 92.

5. Dakpo Rinpoche (Tib. Dwags po lha rje). He was the reincarnation of king Songten Gampo, thus called & Gam po pa. He was the disciple of Milarepa and received the initiation of a vajra-guru, and was ordained as a fully qualified teacher of Tantra.

6. Gonpo Bernak : A Dharmapala, a deity who has two sides to his character: death and the giver of richer. As a wrathful god, destroys the enemies of Buddhist teachings Cf. Bunce, W. Fredrick: An Encyclopaedia of Buddhist Deities Demigods, Godlings, Saints and Demons; Vol. I, D.k. Printworld Ltd., New Delhi, 1994: 307.

7. Paldan Lhamo : Tib. lpal ldan lha moi 'The glorious Goddess', is one of the most important protectors of he Gelukpa order of Buddhism. She is also the jewel protector, extremely aggressive and was the custodian of

religious properties. She was initiated by chagna Dorje and was initiated by Chagna Dorje and was given the name Dorje Naljorma. Later Padmasmbhava bound her to follow the exhaustive instruction and came to Tibet with him. Cf. Ladrang Kalsang:' The Guardian Deities of Tibet,' Little Lhasa Publication ., 2000: 17- 31.

8. Tandin : Tib, rta-mgrin or rta-mgrin-rgyal-pa Phon. Tamdin, in Sanskrit equivant to aka Arya - Hayagriva 'The horse necked.

9. Tsering ma : Tib. bkra-sis tshe-ring ma, one of the goddess in Lha-mo's train or one of the sister of five long life.

10. Opakmed (tib. od-dpag me , Pron. Opame). infinite light shown as red in colour, the hands in the position of meditation and holding a blue alms bowl. Cf. Finegan, Jack; op.cit. 129-'30.

11 Avalokitesvara : (Tib. spyan ras gzigs) He is a manifestation of Amitabha (Tib. Od dpag me). Here he is known Sadaksari.

12. Dorje chang : Buddha with crossed arms holding dorje and bell.

13. Guru Rinpoche : Guru Padmasmnbhava, was a manifestation of Amitabha (Tib. Od dpag me)

14. Dorje Sempa (Tib. rdo-rje sem-dpa skt. vajrasattva): He is a Buddhist tantric deity.

15. Tilopa : He was a famous Bengali Mahasiddha.

16. Chagna Dorje : Tib. phyag na rdo - rje Skt. vajrapani. He is a manifestation of Akshobhya.

17. Chagdor : Tib. phyag na rdo-rje or phyag - dor Skt. vajrapani, bearer of the thunderbolt.

18. Gonpo Chagzee : Tib. mgon-po phyag bzhi pa, Skt. equivalent to Caturbhuja Mahakala. He is one of the Dharmapala has one face, fierce with three eyes and flame like hair; four hands, principal hands hold chopper and human skull cup right hand holds sword with flames and left holds atapatra; two legs in Aldharasana; blue-black body; has five skull crown, tiger and elephant skin as a body covering. Cf. Bunce, Fredrick.W.; op. cit.: 86.

17

H.E. Chosje Togdan Rinpoche : A Head Lama of Ladakh and his Photang

H.E. Chosje Togdan Rinpoche is a spiritual leader of Drigung Kagyud order. In olden days Drigung Thil, the head monastery of Drigung kagyud tradition, situated in Tibet, used to appoint chosjes to its branch monasteries viz. Mount Kailash, Tsari, Lachi, Ladakh etc. As the Togdan Rinpoche earlier incarnation belonged to Ladakh, therefore, his successive incarnation thereafter appointed Chosje from Ladakh.

Togdan Rinpoche is the incarnation of great Indian Maha Siddha Hungchen Kara. It is said that Siddha Hungchen kara later incarnated as Kongbo Togdan Tulku, was disciple of H.H Drigung Terton Rinchen Phuntsog (1509 – 1557). Thereafter, his successive six incarnation were born in Tibet. Thus seven incarnation of Indian Maha Siddha Hungchen Kara were Tibetan Tulkus. 8th and present 9th incarnations belong to Ladakh. The present incarnation is Konchok Stanzin Thubstan Stanpai Gyaltsan was born in a poor Ladakhi Buddhist family in 1938. His father Konchok belonged to Durbuk village, situated 110 km. from Leh. He lost his mother Skalzang Dolma just after two hour old. He was, therefore, lookafter by his aunt. When he was only one and half years old, started to show miracles. His footprint on a boulder near Durbuk can be seen.

At the age of five years previous Skaybgon Chetsang Rinpoche, Shiwe Lodros recognized him as the incarnation of Togdan Rinpoche. In 1943, he was enthroned as chosje Togdan rinpoche in Shachukul Monastery, located near his birth place. He received traditional education under Kagyud order. In 1950 with his teacher Gergan Sonam visited Drigung monastery in Tibet. Later he received higher education is Mahayana Buddhist philosophy under various spiritual masters. He studied Buddhist philosophy in Drigung Nyima Changra, a philosophical college and due to his sharp knowledge became popular within a short time. In 1960, Tibet was occupied by China, thus returned Ladakh with his tutor and other Ladakhi lamas. Since than, he has been carrying out his responsibilitics and looking the administration and welfare works of fifty Drigung monasteries in Ladakh.

As being religious head of Kagyud tradition, Rinpoche holds special transmission of dgongs gchil, Yamantaka, Phowa and Dharmapalas of Drigung Kagyud. In addition he holds the transmission of Rinchen gter mzod of Ningmapa tradition. In 1967, Rinpoche arranged Rinchen gter mzod. empowerment at Tso Padma, Rewalser. On this occasion H.H Dudjom Rinpoche gave this empowerment to a great assembly consisting 30 Tulkus and several thousand people. Later H.H. Dudjom Rinpoche initiated him as his successor for imparting this great empowerment of Rinchen gter mzod. Thereafter, Rinpoche discovered several sacred 'hidden places" and revealed some mind treasured texts. His collected works comprise one volume of short commentary of dgong gchig.

Today Togdan Rinpoche is the only spiritual leader who holds all kinds of oral and empowerment transmission of Drigung pa tradition. He has given several empowerment and oral transmission to the present H.H chetsang Rinpoche on Rigzin Chostaks works. In 1974, he invited Khyunka Rinpoche to Ladakh, who later started meditation centre at Chushul. The same later moved to Lamayuru. In 1981 Atitse monastery was repaired, Rinpoche then established a school for young monks there.

In 1978, he supervised a spectacular reception ceremony in honour of His Holiness Drigung Skyabgon Chetsang Rinpoche at Leh. In this ceremony monks from phyang, Lamayuru and Shachukul monasteries participated in large number. Thereafter, H.H Chetsang Rinpoche and H.E. Togdan Rinpoche together worked for strengthening Drigung kagyud tradition in Ladakh. In 1979, 800th Anniversary of Drigung Thil monastery was celeberated at Phyang monastery under the supervision of both above said spiritual leaders. In 1985 His Holiness Chungtsang Rinpoche also visited Ladakh. Then H.E. Togdan Rinpoche became President of All India Gonpa Society. He remained at the post for four years (1972 to 1975), during this period he attended world Buddhist Conferences in Taiwan, Spain, Germany, Switzerland and France.

As in 1959, H.E. Togdan Rinpoche returned Ladakh, felt the need to strengthen religious and social welfare activities. Therefore, he toured entire villages in Ladakh and delivered religious sermons for propogation of Buddhist's teachings, thus made the pepole to know Buddhism more clearly. In those days Ladakh did not have good education facilities, only a few students could go to Srinagar and Jammu for higher studies. Rinpoche made all efforts to send students to above places for education.

In Ladakh Lamayuru, Phyang and Shachukul are the big monasteries of Drigung Kagyud tradition, besides 47 smaller gonpas of this tradition are functioning in various villages. H.E. Togdan Rinpoche visited these gonpas and strengthened the monastic activities under the patter of Tibet.

In 2000 and 2001 Rinpoche was one of the main presenters of several precious oral transmissions of Drigung Kagyud tradition in Drigung Kagyud institute. He gave oral transmission of many biographies of holy beings of the past consisting of forty text in total. On 12th December 2002 on wards for more than two monthes, he offered the oral transmission of one hundred volumes of Buddha's precepts in auspicions presence of H.H Drigung Kaybgon Chetsang Rinpoche, Taglung Shabdrung Rinpoche, other tulkus and khenpos, an assembly of more than 400 monks, nuns and lay people. The ceremony duly concluded on 19th February 2003.

In 1967 the political situation of Ladakh turned towards a new direction, which led to form Ladakh Action Committee and made agitation against the Government. to fulfil various demands of Ladakh region. Togdon Rinpoche then unanimously elected as the chairman of the Ladakh Action Committee. Under his auspices the state Government. accepted 10 demands. Thereafter, Rinpoche became a known political leader. To know his political importance in Ladakh region, Chief Minister of J&K state Sh. Syed Mir Qasim appointed him as Vice–chairman of Ladakh Development Board for four years. During this period Rinpoche executed many developmental schemes; prominent among them were: Durbuk canal, Alchi Bridge, High School at Temisgam and many lower level schools, Medical Aid Centres etc.

In 1973 under the leadership of Sher - e- Kashmir Sheikh Mohd Abdullah took a new turn in state politics, to strengthen National Conference party in Ladakh, Rinpoche was appointed President of National Conference for Ladakh region. He remained as head of the party till 1989 in Leh. Later he was nominated as MLC in the J&K Assembly and then elevated as Minister of State for Ladakh Affairs and Planning in the Cabinet of Chief Minister, Dr. Farooq Abdullah.

As Minister of state for Ladakh Affairs and Planning H.E. Togdan Rinpoche has taken various steps for speediest development of Ladakh. He has tried his best to enhance budgetary grant for Ladakh region and also the concerted efforts of Assembly members of the Ladakh constituency, the Budget of Leh district has gone up from Rs. 23.00 crores in 1996 to Rs. 32.00 crores for the financial year 1997. He has supplemented the request of the people of Ladakh for opening of Kailash Yatra, which would give a new boost to Tourism in Ladakh.

In this way since 1960 Rinpoche has been selflessly serving for the people of Ladakh at the capacity of various positions in the State Government until recently when he resigned from his post as Ministry of State for Ladakh affairs and planning, which he held for the last six years. He submitted his resignation keeping in view the sentiments and aspirations of the people of Ladakh who are demanding Union Territory status for the province. Thus on 19th September, 2003, after submitting his resignation to the Government. he retired from his political life.

Photang Urgyan Dorje Choszong Saboo Dakhar (or Photang of H.E. Chorje Togdan Rinpoche)

The name of Photang is derived from the nearby hillock, which looks like the hat of Padmasambhava. The translation of the photang may be spelled as Vajra Dharma Palace'

The Photang is situated about 8 km near Saboo village. It has many beautiful thanka paintings and statues (Fig. 17.1).

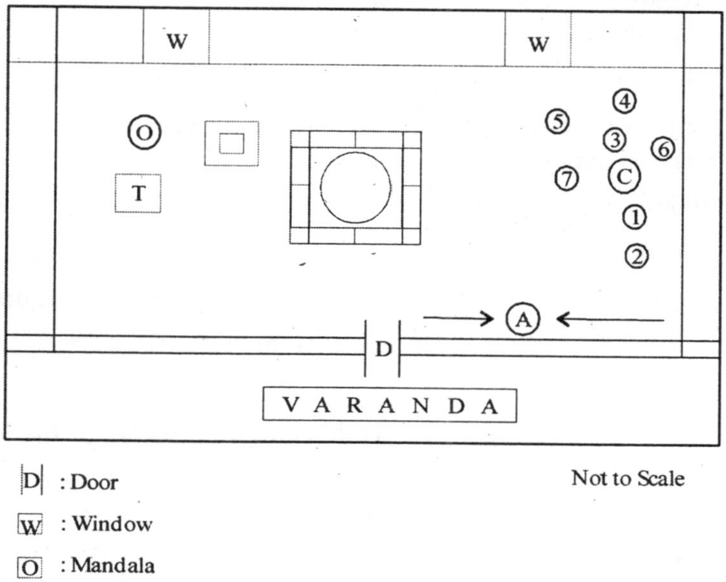

Fig. 17.1 Statues in Photang Urgyan Dorje Choszong

(1) to (7) : Statues

(0) : Chorten

(T) : Togdan Rinpoche. Throne

: His Holiness Dalai Lama Thsone

: Wall

(c) : Padmasambhava

Arms : Two

Symbol : Dorje an skull cup

Mudra : (*i*) Right hand holds dorje, rests on his knee.

(*ii*) Left in meditation mudra, holds skull cup.

(*iii*) At his left armpet holds magic stick.

Asana : Meditation

Head dress : Hat with Dorje at the top centre.

Height : 6′

Width : 4′

Position : centre statue of the temple.

Statues in the glass almirah at the left on the centre statue:

1. Sakyamuni Buddha

Arms : Two

Mudra : (*i*) Right hand in Bhumisparsha

(*ii*) Left in meditation

Symbol : Patra

(*i*) Holds patra in his lap at his left hand

Asana : Meditation

Height : 5′

Width : 4’

2. Skyova Jigstengompo[1]

Arms : Two

Head dress : Red hat , upper wide
Mudra : (*i*) Right hand in Bhumispaasha
(*ii*) Left in meditation
Asana : Meditation
Garments : (*i*) Zang gos: Red
(*ii*) Shantab: Red
Height : 5′
Width : 4′

Right side of the Centre statue in glass almisah

3. Denzung Rinpoche (Tib. ngden' abyung Rin-po-che)

Arms : Two
Mudra : (*i*) Right hand karana mudra
(*ii*) Left holds bell
(*iii*) Right hand holds dorje
Asana : Meditation
Height : 5′
Width : 4′

4. Thogla Devi (Protector of North): She is the protector of Togdan Rinpoche as well as His Holiness Dalai Lama.

Vahana : Yellow horse; riding on horse
Symbol : (*i*) Right hand holds stick (cakyu)
(*ii*) Left holds flag
Ornaments: Bodhisattva
Height : 3′
Width : 3′

5. Apchi Choskyi Dolma

Vahana : Blue horse
: Riding on horse
Symbol : Damaru and skull cup
(*i*) Right hand holds damaru
(*ii*) Left holds skull cup
Ornaments : Bodhisattva

6.	Samvara	:	Tib. Demchok Skt. equivalent to Cakrasamvara.[2] He stands on the body of Rudra and his consort vajravarahi (Tib. Dorje Pagmo). Together they symbolise the union of emptiness and bliss.
	Face	:	Four; yellow, blue, green and red, which represent four Buddha families.
	Hands	:	Twelve — His main hands hold vajra and bell; represent non-duality — His other hands holds a skullcup, a snare, the head of Brahma, a tantric staff, an elephant knife, a flying knife, a trident and a drum.
	Skin	:	Tiger and elephant skin shawl, which symbolizes the fearlessness.
	Legs	:	Two, trampling Bhairava and his consort.
	Consort	:	Vajravarahi is red and has two arms and one face. She holds skullcup and curve knife
	Body	:	Blue, symbolises the cosmic Dharma dhatu of space which is deviod of all the qualities.
	Ornaments	:	Bone garland and a necklace of fifty on / fifty two heads / freshly severede heads. He wears the crescent moon in his top knot of the hair.
	Posture	:	Dance posture having transmuted passion into Karmic energy; or vajrahumkara mudra.
	Asana	:	Aradhaparyankasana.

7. Dharmapala : 4 hands Gonpo

Arms : Four

— Right first hand holds sword

— Second holds dorje near heart

— Left first hand holds trishul

— Second holds skull cup near heart

Body : Dark blue

Asana : Standing ;Pratyalidhasana

Below the statues Sl. No 4, 5, 6, and 7 Chotpa (Lostor) made of butter are placed. They represents the offering to (i) Cakrasamvara, Vajrayogini, Apchi Choskyi Dolma (or Dharma Tara)

Along the wall infront of the main door

8. Changchub chorten[3]

Material used: Silver

Height: 5'

Width : 4'

9. Throne for His Holiness Dalai Lama

10. Throne for Togdan Rinpoche

Statues along the wall (A) towards door

11. Sakyamuni Buddha

Metal : Brass

Height : 3′

Width : 2′

Arms : Two

Mudra : (*i*) Right hand in Bhumisparsha

(*ii*) Left in Meditation

Asana : Meditation

12. Buddha (chamba)[5]

Hands : Two

Mudra : (*i*) Right hand in Vartika

(*ii*) Left hand in Meditation

Asana Meditation

Height : 3′

Width : 2′

This statue was presented to Togdan Rinpoche on the eve of Sindhu Darshan in 2001.

13. Tsongkhapa yabsras sum[6]

1. Tsongkhapa: Centre 1′×6″

Arms : Two

Mudra : Dharmacakra

Asana : Meditation

2. Gyaltsabje: Deciple of Tsongkhapa, 8″×6″

Mudra : (*i*) Right hand in Vitarka

(*ii*) Left in meditation

asana : Meditation

(3) Khasdupje: Desciple of Tsongkhapa, 8″×6″

Mudra : (*i*) Right hand in Vitarka

(*ii*) Left in meditation

Asana : Meditation

14. Nawang Namgyal : A Drugpa lama

Head dress : Red hat

Arms : Two

Mudra : (*i*) Right hand in Bhumisparsha

(*ii*) Left in meditation

(*iii*) Right hand holds patra

Height : 6″

Width : 4″

Asana : Meditation

In upper shelf of the almirah

15. Dolma : White Tara[7]

    Asama : Meditation

16. Tshe-dpag-med[8]; 1×6″

    Arms : Two

    Mudra : Meditation

    Symblo : Holds long life patra in his lap

    Asana : Meditation

17. Namgyalma[9]

    Arms : Eight

    Faces : Three faces

    Asana : Meditation

    Height : 1′

    Widht : 6″

18. Padmasamphava[10]

    Arms : Two

    (*i*) Right hand holds dorje, rests on his knee

    (*ii*) Left holds Kapala

    Asana : Meditation

    Height : 1½

    Width : 6″

19. Jamyang[11]

    Arms : Two

    (*i*) Right hand holds sword

    (*ii*) Left in vitarka, holds pothi on Padma

    Asana : Meditation

    Height : 1′

    Width : 6″

20. Vajrapani

Arms	:	Two
		(*i*) Right hand holds vajra, stretched up
		(*ii*) Left in Karana mudra
Asana	:	Standing; Pratyalidhasana

21. Avalokitesvara:

Group	:	Tantric
Arms	:	Four
		— Two main arms in namaskar mudra
		— Right first holds rosary lifted up
		— Left holds padma lifted up
Asana	:	Meditation
Height	:	1′
Width	:	6″

Statues in the same almirah at lower shelf

22. Sakyamuni Buddha

Arms	:	Two
Mudra	:	(*i*) Right hand in Bhumisparsh
		(*ii*) Left in Meditation
Asana	:	Mesditation
Height	:	6″
Width	:	4″

23. Padmasambhava (6″×4″)

Arms	:	Two
Mudra	:	(*i*) Right hand in Abhaya mudra
		(*ii*) Left holds Kapala in meditation mudra
Armpit	:	Holds Khatvanga

Head dress	:	conical hat
Height	:	6”
Width	:	4”
Asana	:	Meditation
Metal	:	Brass

24. Padmasambhava (6″×4″):

Arms	:	Two (*i*) Right hand holds sun (*ii*) Left in Kanana mudra
Asana	:	Meditation
Head dress	:	Rignga; hair pulled and tied up, has beard
Ornaments	:	Bodhisattva
Height	:	6″
Width	:	4″
Metal	:	Brass

25. Padmasambhana (6″×4″)

Arms	:	Two (*i*) Right hand holds damaru (*ii*) Left holds patra
Asana	:	Meditation
Ornaments	:	Bodhisattva
Head dress	:	Rignga
Metal	:	Brass

26. Ishey Chosgyal (6″×4″)

Asana	:	Two
Mudra	:	(*i*) Left hand holds parta of Jewels to offer Padmasambhava (*ii*) Right in Karana mudra
Head dress	:	Rignga (Leafed crown)
Asana	:	Meditation
Metal	:	Brass

27. Mandarva (6″×4″)

Arms	:	Two
Mudra	:	Dharmacakra

Asana : Dhyana
Head dress : One leafed crown
Ornaments : Bodhisattva
Metal : Brass

28. Padmasambhava in Yab-yum form (6″×4″)

Mudra : Vajrahumkara
: (*i*) Holds dorje and bell near his heart
Arms: Two (*i*) Left hand holds patra
(*ii*) Right holds dorje
Asana : 'Yab' embraced 'Yam' in Dhyanasana

29. Padmasambhava (6″×4″)

Arms : Two
(*i*) Right hand holds damaru
(*ii*) Left holds patra in his lap
Mudra : Left hand in meditation
Head dress : Five leafed crown
Ornaments : Bodhisattva
Asana : Lalitasana (or Dolma style)

30. Padmasambhava (6″×4″)

Arms : Two
— Right hand holds dorje
— Left in karana mudra
Eyes : Three
Group : Tantric
Psture : Standing

31. Padmasambhava(6″×4″)

Eyes : Three, without hat

Group : Tantric

Symbol and Mudra; (*i*) Right hand holds **Phurba**

(*ii*) Left in Karana murdra

Posture : Standing

Metal : Brass

Both sides of the above glass almirah has Kangyur pothis of about 30 volumes. Besides, along the wall other side of the door also have 94 pothis of Kangyur.

× × ×

I visited Photang Urgyan Dorje Choszong, Saboo Dakhar at morning 11.30 A.M. alongwith Lama Jigmet of Deskyit Gonpa. It was Sunday, Togdan Rinpoche also arrived from Stok. He quickely informed me about thankas, hanged along the ceiling in Namling. Here follows the details :

Towards main statue

1. Dorje chang[12]

Body : Blue

Arms : Two

Asana : Meditation

Height : 6′

Width ; 5′

2. Cakrasamvara (Yab-yum)[13]

(*i*) Yab : Blue

(*ii*) Yum : Red

Posture : Standing

Mandala: At the top of the Thanka

(*i*) Buddha

(*ii*) Tilopa

(*iii*) Naropa

(*iv*) Marpa
(*v*) Milaraspa
(*vi*) Phagmogrupa
(*vii*) Gambopa
(*viii*) Skyova jigten Gompo

At the right and left of the centre fresco;

(*i*) Yellow Neljorma
(*ii*) Red Naljorma — Left side
(*iii*) Green Naljorma
(*iv*) Blue Naljorma — Right side

At the botton of the Cakrasamvara

(*i*) Gonpo: Four hands
Right hand holds sword — Right side
(*ii*) Apchi choskyi Dolma — Left side

3. Skyova Jigsten Gonpo: Centre fresco
Mudra: Dharmacakra; without hat
Mandala; At the bottom

(*i*) Drigung pa lama
(*ii*) Position: Right side of the centre fresco
(*ii*) Cakrasamvara
(*iii*) Apchi choskyi dolma
Position: Left to the centre fresco

Vahana; Blue horse; she is riding on her vahana
Height : 5′
Width : 4′

4. Apchi choskyi Dolma
Asana : Seated on blue horse
Mandala: Four hands Gonpo; holds sword in his one arm
Height : 5′
Width : 4′

Thankas hanging through ceiling towards door

Right to Left :

5. Namgyal ma

Body: white

Mandala

(*i*) Vajrapani:[13] At the bottom of the thanka

(*ii*) Two hands gonpo: Upper at the right and left of the centre fresco

6. Lokpala : Vaishravana[14]

Symbol : (*i*) Holds Dhavaj in his right hand

(*ii*) Mongoose in his left

(*iii*) In the mandala has Apchi choskyi Dolma, Tshe-dpag-med etc.

7. Vajrapani (Tib. phyag rdor)

Body : Light blue

Symblo : Holds vajra in his right hand stretched up right.

8. Padmasambhana (5′×4′)

Tib. slob dpon pdma 'abyung gnas

Mudra symbol: Right hand holds dorje near hart; left holds kapala in meditation mudra; Asana: Meditation

9. Padmasambhava (5′×4′)

(or Guru sakya senge)

Mudra : (*i*) Right hand in Bhumisparsha

(*ii*) Left in meditation, holds patra

Asana : Meditation

Cegs : Two

10. Padmasambhava (5′×4′)

(or Guru Nyima Ozer)

Crown : Five skull crown, ferocious expression

Mudra : Right hand holds khatvanga, left in Skarana

Asana : Lalitasana

11. Padmasambhava (5′×4′)

(or Guru Senge Dradok)

Crown : Five skull crown, Three eyes

Mudra : Right hand holds dorje

and left in karana mudra; both stretched up

Asana: Steps right, standing.

12. Padmasambhava (5′×4′)

(or Guru Dorje Doloe)

Eyes : Three eyes, ferocious expression

Vahana : Tiger

Legs : Two, wears mongolian Zablam

Symbol : Right hand holds dorje, left holds phurba

13. Padmasambhava (5′×4′)

(or Guru Tsokye Dorje)

Crown : Padmasambhava hat

Symbol : (*i*) Right hand holds damaru

(*ii*) Left holds damaru near heart

Asana : Meditation

Asana : Lalitasana

Legs : Two

Eyes : Two

Garments : (*i*) Shawl upper and shantab for lower limbs; wears zablam

Thankas opposit wall of the statues in Namling

14. Padmasambhava (5′×4′)

(Guru Padma Gyalpo)

The statue of Padmasambhava is made as a king of Udiyana. He holds kapal in one hand.

15. Padmasambhava: (5′×4′)

Guru Loden Chokse)

Crown: Lefeat Crown

Mudra & symbol: (i) Right hand's one finger up; left holds patra

Asana : Lalitasana; Wears Zablam

This Photang has five rows for lama seats, has two musical drums; established in 1968. There are some photographs hanging through the ceiling in Namling are: Drigung pa lige.. viz. Dorje chang, Tilopa, Naropa, Marpa, Milaraspa Phagrupa, Gomboba and Skyova Jigsten Gonpo (Fig.17.2).

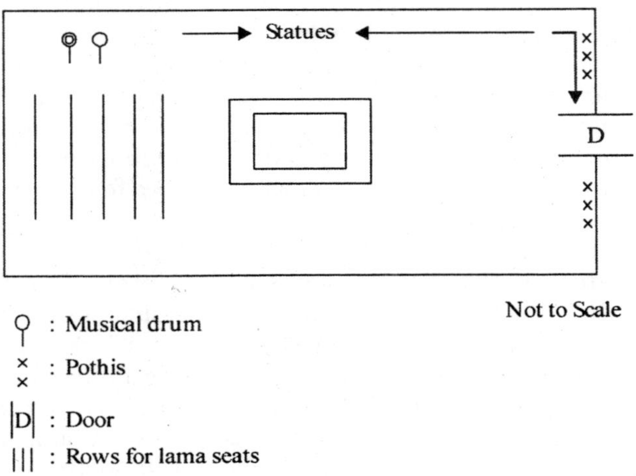

Fig. 17.2 : Photang Urgyan Dorji Choszeng

Notes and References

1. **Skyova Jigstengompo (Phon. Jigten Gompo):** Tib. Jig. rten mgonpo (1143-1217).

He was the disciple of Pagmogrupa (or Phakmotrupa) and founder of Drigungpa order, a suborder of the Kagyudpa. He founded Brigung (Drigung) monastery, 128 km northeast of Lhasa from which the sect took its name. Jigten Gompo was known Drigung rinpoche (Tib. Brigung rinpoche). Cf. Finegan, Jack: Tibet: A Dreamt of Image' Tibet House, 1986:96.

2. **Samvara:** Tib Demochok, Skt equivalent to Cakrasamvara. He belongs to Vajrayana or Tantra of highest yoga which emphasizes on cultivating the clear light. He subdues the Rudra of ego through transmutation of passion, embraces his consort, who represents intelligence energy; together they symbolise the union of the wisdom of nirvana and samsara. Thus during yab-yum form Samvara stands on Mahadeva whereas Shakti as Umadevi who is the symbol of ego. Cf. Batchelor, stephan, 'The Tibet Guide', wisdom Publication. London; 1987: 410-,12

3. **Changchub chorten:** Chorten is known in Hindi as stupa, which literally means an "offering holder." as the chorten is usually construted in Tibet, steps lead up to a square, base above which a few more steps support a bulbous structure which may be surrounded by wheels or umbrellas (thirteen standing for the thirteen heavens), culminating in a crescent moon and sun or other ornamental top piece. The chorten may be a funerary monument (normally only for a prominent person, the disposition of the dead otherwise customarily being by burial exposure to the vultures, etc.), or the chorten may simply contain sacred books etc. which are put inside when the structure is built or inserted afterward through special openings. The changchub chorten correctly spell as byan c'ub mc'od rten and it means chorten of illumination, has a square base with one or more steps round the foot; above this is a round drum, the bumpa or 'pot', above this again are seven or thirtteen 'umbrellas' as said above mounted on a central axis which traverses each of them; and at the top of the whole structure is a metal ring, usually gilded, supporting a crescent and circle which respectively represent the moon and sun. Cf. Waddell, L. Austine: Buddhism and Lamaism of Tibet' Reprint 1974, New Delhi: 262.

4. **Sakyamuni Buddha:** Tib. shakya Tubpa Phon. Eng. Tubpa " The Englightened one" or the Awakened one". Historically known Gotam Buddha. In 6th century B.C. he descended to the world to show the right path to the fortunate beings by taking birth in a royal family in Lumbini. Later, married Yasodhara and gave birth to a son Rahula. Besides, he did not like to involve in the worldly pleasure, inspite felt happiness to show the right path to all beings. consequently he practiced Bodhisattva activities for countless aeons to attain enlightement. Finnally under Bodhi tree at Bodhgaya he attained emlghtenment. Thereafter, he turned the three wheel of Dharma in three different places: Varanasi Grdrakuta and Vaisali. Besides, he went to Tusita loka and preached gods and goddess alongwith his mother. He also turned the wheel of Tantra at Sri Dhamyakuta by menifesting himself into Lord Vajradhara. The essence of his teachings is known Pratiyasamutpada. At the age of eighty he got Mahaparinirvana in Kusinagara.

5. **Buddha (Chamba):** A Bodhisattava and is the future Buddha who will show the way to nirvana. At present Chamba or Maitreya is in Tusita loka in the form of Bodhisattva. While painting on wall or cloth and as a statue form he is known as a Buddha Dharmacakra mudra with his feet resting on a moon disc and a lotus. In painting he may be depicted as a Bodhisattva with a yellow body, wearing the clothing and ornaments of Bodhisattva and holding the stems of two lotus blossoms that bear his emblems: A vase and a Dharma Wheel.

6. **Tsongkhapa Yabsras sum:** Tsongkhapa with his two chief disciples: Gyal tsabje and Khasdupje usually depicted on his right and left.

7. **Dolma (or White Tara):** She embodies the fertile aspects of compassion and her realm is the day. In her ordinary white form she is represented by Astamahabhaya-Tara and Mrtyuvancana Tara. Cf. Bunce. Fredrick W: An Encyclopaedia of Buddhist Deities, Demigods, Godlings, Saints and Demigods, Godlings, Saints and Demons; Vol. I; dK. Printworld Ltd. New Delhi 1994: 542-'43.

8. **Tshe-dpag-med:** The Bodhisattva of longevity who is

invoked for long life, health and happiness. Cf. Bunce, Fredrick W; op. cit: 13.

9. **Namgyalma:** She is called the queen of enlightenment and the mother of all Buddhas, and is a popular goddess of long live or longevity. Cf. Finegan Jack; *op cit:* 136

10. **Padmasambhava:** Pron. Guru Rinpoche' an Indian Tantric invited by king Trisong Detsen in the Eight Century A.D. in Tibet. He brought Buddhist Tantra there and subdued the local deities and demons while constructing the Samyas monastery. He helped Santaraksita in his works on Buddhism, as a result Buddhism was amazingly spread in Tibet. He was thus recognised as the second Buddha. cf. Batchelor, Stephen; *op. cit.:* 420.

11. **Jamyang: Skt. Manjusri.** He is shown in yellow white, red blue and black forms; beautifully handsome young mahabodhi-sattva and bodhisattva or god of wisdom science and agriculture; and is considered by the northern Buddhists as one of the eight Dhyani Bodhisattvas, with his sword he destroys ignogance and darkness. He is frequently shown with Dhyan Bodhisattva Avalokitesvara and Dhyani Bodhisattva Vajrapani. These three together are popularly known. Rig sum gonpo'. Cf. Bunce, Fredrick W; *op. cit.*:33

12. **Cakrasamvarr (Yab-yum):** He belongs to Vajrayana or Tantra of highest Yoga which emphasizes on cultivating the clear light. He subdues the rudra of ego through transmutation of passion. He embraces eith his consortw who represents intelligence and energy; together they symbolise the union of wisdom of nirvana and samsara. Yab-yum form, Samvara stands on Mahadeva whereas Shakti as Umadevi who is the symbol of ego. Cf. Batchelor, Stephen; *Op. cit:* 410-'12.

13. **Vajrapani:** He is the Bodhisattva of energy and power. During peaceful aspect, he is represented as a blue Bodhisattva holding a lotus. Cf. Bunce, Fredric W.; *op. cit.*:397.

14. **Vaishravan a Tib. Namtose.** He is the guardian king of the north and Buddhist god of wealth; vahana: white lion; golden yellow in colour. c.f. Batchelor, Stephen; op. cit: 426.

18

Theghchen Chosling (Tib. ltheg Che Chos Gling) Monastery

In late evening about 8.30 P.M my student Sonam Lhadol rang me, asked do you visit Palam gonpa? I responded affermative and said: "On Sunday mornig about 10 o'clock I'll come Choglamsar bridge, then we'll go to see the monastery."

Next day on 18th May 2008, she received me at Choglamsar bridge. She derived me to Thegchen Chosling gonpa. It is situated about 16 km from Leh and 8km from choglamsar bridge at the left of Indus river. Near the gonpa Sonam Lhadol stopped car and went to a house for key. After some time she came alongwith an old lady, who had key. She opened the main door of the gonpa. It had one room about 10′×12′, some Buddhist statues were placed in a glass almirah, walls were decorated by fresco paintings, which seem to be about 10-15 years old. Sonam Lhadol asked: "Ama le! In which year this gonpa was established, who constructed this?"

"This gonpa was established in 1963 by Palam Kachen Lozang Thapkas (Tib. dpal lam dk'a chen blo bzang thabs mkhas) and Palam Tongopa (Tib. dpal lam grong' ago pa), later named it theg chen chos ling (Tib. ltheg chen chos gling).

× × × ×

The statues in the gonpa were placed along the wall infront of the door (Fig.18.1).

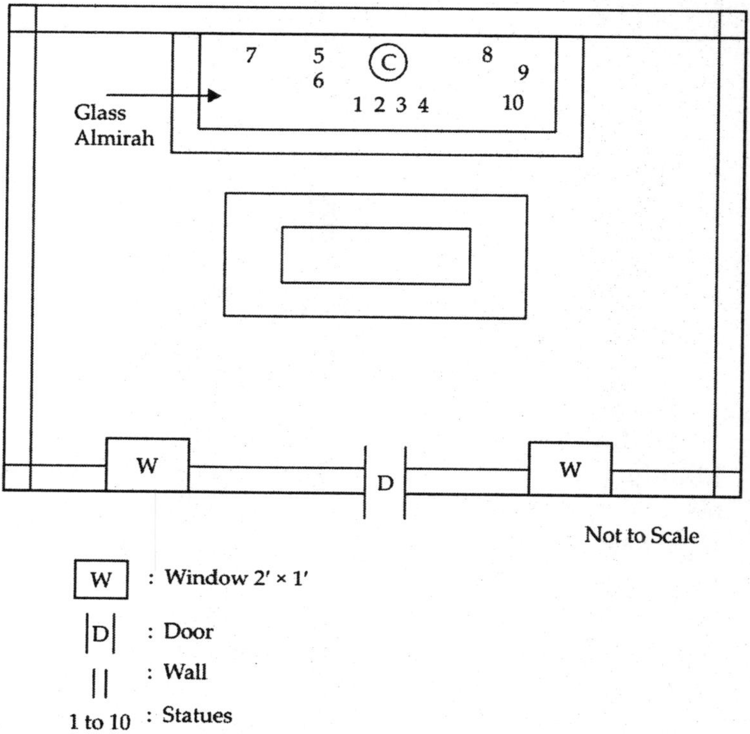

Fig. 18.1. Statues in Thegchen chosling gonpa.

(C) Avalokitesvara[1]

Body	:	White
Group	:	Tantric
Heads	:	Eleven
Arms	:	Eight main arms and at the side 1000 arms.
Symbols	:	(*i*) Right frist hand holds Mala (*ii*) Second holds Cakra (*iii*) Third hand in Varada (*iv*) Right and Left two centre hands in namaskar mudra (*i*) Left first hand holds padma. (*ii*) Second holds capa & sara

(*iii*) Third holds kalasa

Height : 3′

Width : 2′

1. Tsongkhapa

Arms : Two

Mudra : Dharmacakra; right hand holds sword on padma and left holds pothi on padma.

Asana : Meditation

Height : 4″

Position : Ahead of the centre statue

2. Vajrapani (Skt. Candavajrapani)[2]

Arms; Two; holds Vajra in uplifted right hand ; left in Karana mudra

Legs : Two; standing, steps to right

Height : 6″

Width : 4″

3. Avalokitesvara[3]

Group : Tantric

Hands : Four

Mudra : Two centre arms in namaskar Mudra

Symbal : Mala and Padma

Asana : Crossed legs (or meditation)

Height : 8″

4. Manjusri

Group : Bodhisattva

Hands : Two

Symbal : Right hand holds flame sword uplifted, left holds pothi on padma

Asana	:	Crossed legs (or meditation)
Height	:	6″
Width	:	4″

5. Sakyamuni Buddha[4]

Arms	:	Two
Mudra	:	(*i*) Right hand in Bhumisparsha (*ii*) Left in Meditation
Symbol	:	Holds patra in his left hand
Asana	:	Meditation
Height	:	$2\frac{1}{2}'$
Width	:	2′
Position	:	At the right up of the centre statue

6. Green Tara (Skt. Syamatara)[5]

Group	:	Non-Tantric
Ornaments	:	Bodhisattva
Garments	:	Bodhisattva
Head dress	:	Five leafed crown
Mudra	:	(*i*) Right hand in varada mudra (*ii*) Left in Vitarka mudra. (*iii*) Left hand holds utpala at left shoulder.
Asana	:	Lalita
Position	:	Below the Sl. No. 6
Height	:	2½′
Width	:	2″

7. Tsongkhopa[6]

Arms	:	Two
Mudra	:	Dharmachakra
Symbol	:	(*i*) Right hand holds sword on padma at right shoulder.

(*ii*) Left hand holds pothi on padma at left shoulder

Asana : Meditation

Garment : (*i*) Zanggos : Red

(*ii*) Shantab : Red

Head dress : Conical yellow hat

Height : $2\frac{1}{2}'$

Width : 2″

Position : At the right of the centre statue next to Sl. No. 5 & 6.

8. **Avalokitesvara**

Group : Tantric

Arms : Four

Mudra : (*i*) Two centre arms in Namaskar mudra

(*ii*) First right arm holds rosary

(*iii*) First left holds Padma

Asana : Meditation

Height : $2\frac{1}{2}'$

Width : 2′

Position : Left at upper shelf

9. Buddha : Sakyamuni Buddha

Asana : Meditation

Mudra (*i*) Right arm in Bhumispharsha

(*ii*) Left in meditation.

Symbal : Patra in his left arm.

Height : 1'

Width : 6"

10. Vajrapani : Candavajrapani

Arms: Two : (*i*) Holds vajra in uplifted right hand

(*ii*) left is in karana mudra

Legs	:	Two; standing, steps to right
Eyes	:	Three
Ornaments	:	Bodhisattva
Garments	:	Bodhisattva
Expression	:	Firocious
Height	:	2½′
Width	:	2′
Position	:	Below the vajrapani

This gonpa has some good wall paintings of Buddhas and Bhodisattvas (Fig. 18. 2)

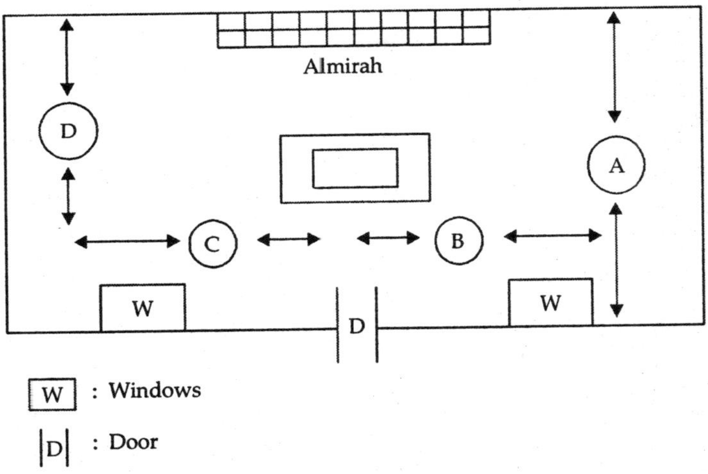

Fig. 18.2. Paintaings in Tegchen chosling gonpa

Paintings on the wall (A) at the left of door

1. Namgyal ma	:	rnam rgyal ma
Group	:	Feminine Bodhisattva in Tantric form
Colour	:	White
Heads	:	Three; yellow white (centre), and black.
Eyes	:	Each face has three eyes

Arms & Mudra :
- (*i*) Origional hands are in near heart, holds a visvavajra
- (*ii*) First right hand holds jambhara
- (*iii*) Second holds arrow
- (*iv*) Third in varada mudra
- (*v*) First left hand in fearless posture or Abhaya mudra
- (*vi*) Second holds a bow
- (*vii*) Third holds kalasa (urn) in meditation mudra.

Asana : Meditation

Experession : Mild anger on each of the faces

Head dress : Five leafed crown

Garments :
- (*i*) Scarf : Green
- (*ii*) Lower limbs : Red

Height of fresco : 3′

Width : 2′

2. Amitayus[7]

Arms : Two

Mudra : Meditation

Symbol : Holds long life patra in lap

Body : Red

Asana : Meditation

Head dress : Five leafed crown

3. White Tara[8]

Arms : Two

Mudra:
- (*i*) Right hand in varada mudra
- (*ii*) Left near heart holds utpala flower

Head dress : Five leafed crown

Ornaments : Bodhisattva viz. Earrings, necklace, Armlets, etc.

Garments : Bodhisattva eg. scarf for upper body green and shawl for lower limbs red

Eyes: Seven ; Two eyes are on her face, one on the forehead , two on her two palms and rest two are on her two feet

Asana : Meditation

Height of the fresco : 3′

Width : 2′

4. Manjusri

Head dress : Five leafed crown

Group : Bodhisattva, non–tantric

Body : Yellow

Asana : Medition

Symbol : (*i*) Right hand holds flame sword

(*ii*) Left holds pothi on padma, rest near heart

Mudra : Left hand in vitarka mudra

Group : Non–Tantric, Bodhisattva

Ornaments : Bodhisattva viz Earrings, Necklace, Armlets, Bracelets wristlest, Anklets, etc,.

Garments : Bodhisativa e.g. (*i*) Scarf – green

(*ii*) Shawl for lower limbs: Blue on red.

Height of the Fresco : 3'

Width : 2'

5. Avalokitesvara : Sadaksari

Body : White

Group	:	Tantric
Arms	:	Four
Mudra	:	Two main arms are in namaskar mudra
Symbol	:	(*i*) first right hand holds mala
		(*ii*) first left holds padma
Asana	:	Meditation
Garments	:	(*i*) Scarf for upper body green
		(*ii*) Shawl for lower limbs blue on red

His Holiness Dalai Lama is the incarnation of Sạdaksari.

6. Vajrapani : Candavajrapani

Arms	:	Two; holds vajra in uplifted right hand; left in karana mudra
Legs	:	Two; standing, steps to right
Ornaments	:	Bodhisattva viz. Earrings necklace, armlets, bracelets, wristlets, anklets etc.
Head dress	:	FIve leafed crown
Body	:	Dark blue
Expression	:	Ferocious
Eyes	:	Three
Garments	:	Lower body covered by lion skin
This fresco height	:	3′
Width	:	2′

Paintings on the wall (B) :

7. Paldan Lhamo[9]

Body	:	Dark Blue
Symbol	:	Danda and Kapala
Vahana	:	Mule with eye in haunch

Special Characteristics	:	Ferocious manifestation. Seated sideways on a mule which has an eye in the haunch and is covered with a demon skin, mule is white, has dice hanging between the forelegs, bridle and trappings of serpents and skulls.
Ornaments	:	Dharmapala viz. Garlands of heads, has serpents in her hair.
Eyes	:	Three
Arms	:	Two; (i) Right arm holds danda raised up. (ii) Left holds kapala near heart
Head dress	:	Skull crown; flaming hair
Fresco height	:	3′
Width	:	2′

8. Cham–Sring[10] (Tib. lcam – sring equivalent to Beg – tse (beg – rtse or Bhegtse).

Face	:	One, fierce, three eyes, hair stands on end ferocious.
Arms	:	Two (i) Right hand holds flame sword lifted (ii) Left hand holds human heart (iii) Left armpet has a bow arrow and a banner
Body	:	Wears breast plates
Legs	:	Two (*i*) Wears Mongolian boots (*ii*) Right foot strands on horse (*iii*) Left on a human form.
Body	:	Red
Face	:	Red

Head dress	:	Five skull crown
Ornaments	:	Wristlets, anklets, necklace, garlands and belts of skulls or freshly severed heads
Fresco height	:	3′
Width	:	2′

Paintings on the wall (C) other side wall along door

9. Neser[11]

Head dress	:	Five skull crown
Vahana	:	white horse
Arms	:	Two
Garment	:	Long coat red inner green
Symbol	:	**Norbos** in patra (*i*) Right hand holds dhavaj at the top sword (*ii*) Left holds jewels in patra
Asana	:	Seated on horse

10. Tara : Khadiravani

Body	:	Yellow/ orange colour
Head dress	:	Five leafed crown
Mudra	:	(*i*) Right hand varada mudra rests on her knee. (*ii*) Left near heart holds flower.
Asana	:	Meditation
Garment	:	(*i*) Scarf for upper body green (*ii*) Shawf for lower limbs blue on red
Ornaments	:	Bodhisattva viz. Earrings, necklace, armlets, braclets, wristlets, anklets etc.
Fresco Height	:	3′
Width	:	2′

Paintings on the wall (D) at the right of door

11. Buddha : Sakyamuni

Arms	:	Two
		(*i*) Right hand Bhumisparsha
		(*ii*) Left holds fruits bowl in meditation mudra
Asana	:	Meditation
Body	:	Yellow colour
Fresco Height	:	3′
Width	:	2′

12. Buddha : Bhaisajyaguru

Arms	:	Two
		(*i*) Right hand varada muder with myrohalain
		(*ii*) Left holds patra in meditation
Asana	:	Meditation
Garments	:	(*i*) Shawl for upper body red
		(*ii*) Lower limbs robe red
Fresco Height	:	3′
Width	:	2′
Body	:	Blue colour

13. Buddha : Abhijnaraja

Arms	:	Two
		(*i*) Right hand in varada mudra
		(*ii*) Left in meditation
Body	:	Red
Symbol	:	Holds patra in his left hand
Asana	:	Meditation
Fresco Height	:	3′
Width	:	2′

14. Buddha : Suvarnabhadravimalaratnaprabhasa

Arms : Two

(*i*) Right hand in vitarka mudra

(*ii*) Left in meditation mudra

Legs : Two

Asana : crossed legs (meditation)

Body : White

Fresco Height : 3′

Width : 2′

15. Buddha : Svaraghosaraja

Arms : Two

(*i*) Right hand in medatation mudra

(*ii*) Left in meditation mudra

Symbol : Patra in his lap

Asana : Meditation

Body : Red

Fresco Height : 3′

Width : 2′

16. Buddha : Dharmakritisagaraghosa

Arms : Two

(*i*) Right hand in vitarka mudra

(*ii*) Left in meditation mudra holds patra in his lap

Asana : Meditation

Body : Yellow

Fresco Height : 3’

Width : 2’

17. Buddha : Svaraghosaraja

Arms : Two

(*i*) Right hand in varada mudra

(*ii*) Left in meditation; holds patra in his lap

Asana	:	Meditation
Fresco Height	:	3′
Width	:	2′
Body	:	Yellow

18. *Buddha: Supari Kirtitanamasri*

Arms : Two

(i) right hand in Abhaya mudra

(ii) Left in meditation mudra, holds patra in his lap.

Asana	:	Meditation
Fresco height	:	3′
width	:	2′
Body	:	Yellow

Besides I saw some photographs and chortens as listed below:

(*i*) His Holoness Dalai Lama (14th Dalai Lama)

(*ii*) Padmasambhava

(*iii*) Jamyang (Manjusri)

(*iv*) Changchub chorten : Behind the Tsongkhapa statue in the shelf of glass almirah.

It took me about one hour to study. The paintings and statues in the monastery. Sonam Lhadol was closely watching my activities in the gonpa, she didn't disturb me, the village old lady was also remained in the monastery till I finished my work. Thereafter, we returned by Maruti car to Sonam Lhadol house. She offered me nice lunch. Her father is working in defence, also a nice and honest person. Sonam Lhadol also had lunch. Later we againg derived to choglamsar bridge. She went Leh by bus, I came to my house by 2 P.M.

Thus it was my short, but interesting journey to Palam village.

Notes and References

1. Avalokitesvara : Tib. spyan ras gzigs, the lord who looks down with compassion is a manifestation of Amitabha, is shown in white colour, has Om mani padme hum as his mantra, is the special protector of Tibet, and is incarnate in king Songtsen Gompo and in Dalai lamas. He is represented in many different forms. The statue in form of Arya Avalokitesvara, has eleven heads and thousand arms. This form with eleven heads is explained by the story that when Avalokitesvara looked down upon the many beings in need of deliverance in the hell of Yama, the god of death, his head broke into ten pieces out of his great compassion these were put together by his spitriual father Amitabha; Thus in the figure there are nine gentle faces arranged in three tiers of three each, above that one wrathful face and at the top, the head of Amitabha, thus making eleven heads in all. With his thousand arms Arya-Avalokitesvara holds numerous attributes with which to communicate unlimited love to suffering beings. *Cf.* Finegan, Jack: 'Tibet: A Dreamt of Image' Tibet House, New Delhi; 1986: 130–31.
2. Vajrapani (skt. Candavajrapani) : Tib. Phyag – na - rdo - rje, Pron. Chhana Dorje, holders of the thunderbolt. He is the Bodhisativa, who is a manifestation of Akshobhya is usually shown as dark blue colour, with a crown of skulls and holding the dorje, and sometimes with a snake (naga) as bearer. *Cf.* Finegan, Jack; *op. cit:* 130.
3. Avalokitesvara : Bodhisattva is a manifestation of Amitabha.
4. Sakyamuni Buddha : He descended to the world in 6th century B.C. to show the right path to the human beings, and may attain freedom from the cycle of existence.
5. Green Tara (skt. Syamatara). Tib. sgrol ma ljang gu. Pron. Drolma Jang–gu or "green savioress" is probably the form of Tara incarnate in wencheng, the chinese wife of king Songtsen Gompo. She is green, sites in the royal posture on the moon disc and lotus flower, her right leg extended, with its foot resting on a small lotus blossom. Cf. Finegan Jack; *op. Cit.* 136.
6. Tsongkhapa : Tib. rje-rin-po-che, tson kha-pa Phon. Eng. Tsongkhapa. He was the founder of Gelukpa tradition of

Mahayana Buddhism in 14th century A.D. considered to be a manifestation of Manjusri. Cf. Batchelor, Stephen: 'The Tibet Guide; Wisdom Publication. London; 1987 422.

7. Amitayus : Tib Ts'e dpag med, Tshe-dpag-med, che-dpag-med, Tshe-dpag-med-lha-dgu, Phon Eng. Tsepame. "Dispenser of long life." The Bodhisativa of longevity who is invoked for long life, health and happiness. Cf. Bunce, Fredrick W: 'An Encyclopaedia of Buddhist Deities, Demigods Godlings, Saints and Demons; Vol. - I; D.K. Printworld Ltd. New Delhil, 1994 : 13.

8. White Tara : Tib. sgrol ma sgrol ma dkar po Phon. Eng. drolma karpo. She embodies the fertile aspects of comassion and her realm is the day. In her "Ordinary" white form she is represented by Astamahabhaya. Tara and Mrtyuvancana Tara. Cf. Bunce, Fredrick W; *op. cit.* 406 - '07.

9. Paldan Lhamo : Tib. dpal ldan lha mo' "The Glorious Goddess" is one of the most importent protectors of the Geluk (or Gelugs) pa order of Buddhism and the guardian of Lhasa: Cf. Batchelor, Stephen : 'The Tiber Guide', Wisdom Publication. London, 1987: 423-24.

10. Cham - Sring : A Dharmapala and a jig-rten-las-das pa ai sung- ma of some importance is Tibet and called a maha - yaksa, lord commender of all ma-mo, head of the gshin-rje God of war and protector of horses. His father is the Dharmapala gnod - sbyin- zangs - kyi - ral-pa - can "The yaksa who has locks of copper' and his mother is Srin-ma-khrag-gi-ral-pa-can "The raksa with looks of blood", lcam-sring as synonymous with Mahakala. Cf. Bunce, fredrick W.; *op. cit:* 290

11. Neser : Ne - ser - Io-bo-chen-po or Phying-dkar ba or aka dga ldan-brog-ri 'ai dge bsnyen, Gangs - btan - pa. A dge - bsnyen and a Dharmapala of some importance.

19

Thuptan Donag Shedup Choskhorling

On 18th April 2008 afternoorn I alongwith Anupam Bharadwaj[1] and Tundup[2] of Central Institute of Buddhist studies, Choglamsar;[3] visited Thuptan Donag Shedup Choskhorling (Tib. Thup bstan mdo sngags bshad sgrub chas 'akhor gling) monastery, at Kharnakling Colony,[4] near the central Institute Buddhist Studies new campus. It belongs to Ningmapa[5] tradition of Mahayana Buddhism has two main temples :

(*i*) (Tshe-dpag med) Dukhang

(*ii*) Padmasambhava temple

Tsepagmed (Tib. Tshe-dpag-med) Dukhang

This Dukhang was built during 1995-'96, later opened for public after *pranpratithana* of Tshe-dpag-med statue in 1998. This temple has only big statue of Tshe-dpag-med[6] statue. Here follows the details (Fig.19.1):

Tshe-dpag-med: statue

Skt. Amitayus

Arms	:	Two
Mudra	:	Both arms in Dhyana mudra
Symbol	:	Holds patra of longevity in his lap.
Asana	:	Dhyana
Throne	:	Padma
Height	:	14′
Width	:	8′

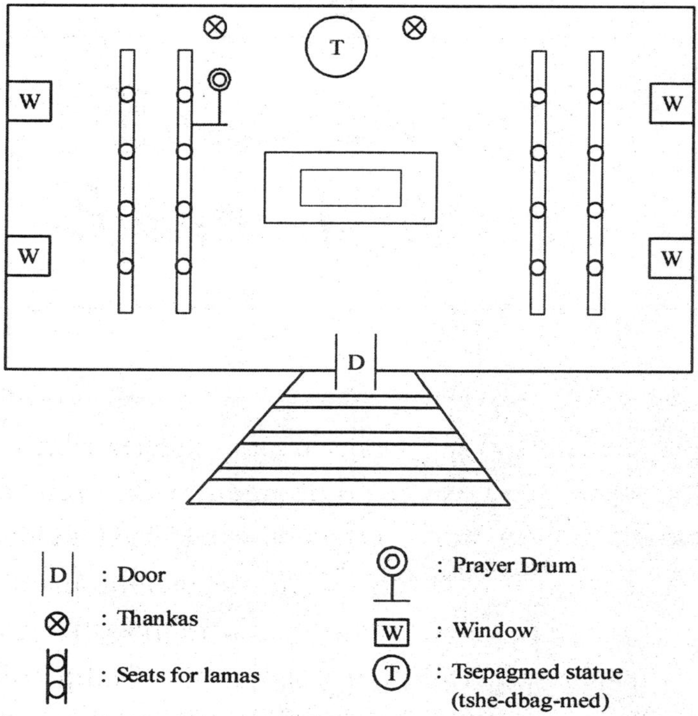

Fig. 19.1. Statues and Thankas in Thuptan Donag Shedup Choskorling Gonpa

Thankas

The Dakhang does have many Thankas, has two big Thankas, which are hanged through, the ceiling :

1. Avalokitesvara[7] :

Eeyes	:	1000
Hands	:	1000
Heads	:	Eleven ; eight main arms.
Body	:	white
Posture	:	Standing
Height	:	10′
Width	:	6′

Position	:	At the right of the Tshe-dpag-med statue
2. Padmasambhava	:	Ningches Sinche tho[8]

The following Buddha and Bodhisattvas are depicted in his mandala.

(*i*) Khenpo Bodhisattva[9]

Arms	:	Two
Symbol	:	Padma
Mudra	:	Dharmacakra
Position	:	Right to the Padmasambhava

(*ii*) Thrisong Detsen[10]: King of Tibet

Arms	:	Two
Mudra	:	(*i*) Right hand in Bhumisparsha (*ii*) Left rests near his knee

(*iii*) Amitaba (tib. 'od-dpag-med)[11]

Body	:	Red colour
Arms	:	Two
Mudra	:	Meditation
Symbol	:	Holds patra in his lap
Asana	:	Meditation
Position	:	Right of the Padmasambhava

(iv) Avalokitesvara[12]

Arms	:	4
Group	:	Tantric
Mudra	:	(*i*) Two centre arms are in Namaskar mudra (*ii*) Right first lifted up with mala (*iii*) Left lifted up with padma.

Body	:	White colour
Asana	:	Meditation

Next to the Padmasambhava thanka tselzee made by butter to offer the concern deities viz. Thing lu, Gyalpo tongpon etc. Besides, has four poles; Tsetul Rinpoche[13] throne, at the right of the statue, one more throne made for the convenience of Rinpoche. It has comparaively low in height, left of the statue. On the right of statue has His Holiness Dalai Lama Throne.

The Dukhang has four rows for lamas on which they sit and offer prayer. Umjat[14] starts prayer by beating drum, ringing bell and using dorje. Outside along the wall surrounding to the building has so small prayer wheels. At the entrance of the monastery also has two big prayer wheels.[15]

× × × × ×

There is one more temple at the left of the Tshe-dpag med Dukhang, which was under construction. Moreover has one big brass statue of Padmasambhava of about 14′×6′ (Fig. 19.2).

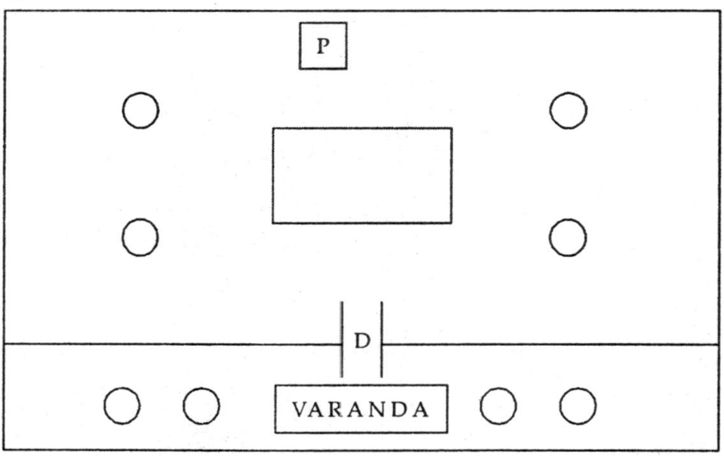

Not to Scale

Fig 19.2. Padmasambha Temple in Thuptan Donag Shedup Choskhoring.

O	:	Pole
P	:	Padmasambhava Statue

Padmasambhava: Statue

Material used : Brass

Arms : Two

(*i*) Right hand rests on his knee.

(*ii*) Left holds Kapala in his lap, in meditation mudra

Symbol : (*i*) Kapan,

Asana : (*ii*) Lalita

Legs : Two, wears mongolian shoe (Tib. Zablam)

This temple has eight poles, four inside, and four outside at the varanda.

Both the temples do not have wall paintings. (Fig. 19.3)

O	:	Rooms for lamas
×	:	Rooms under construction
□	:	Stairs
ΔΔ	:	Lamps

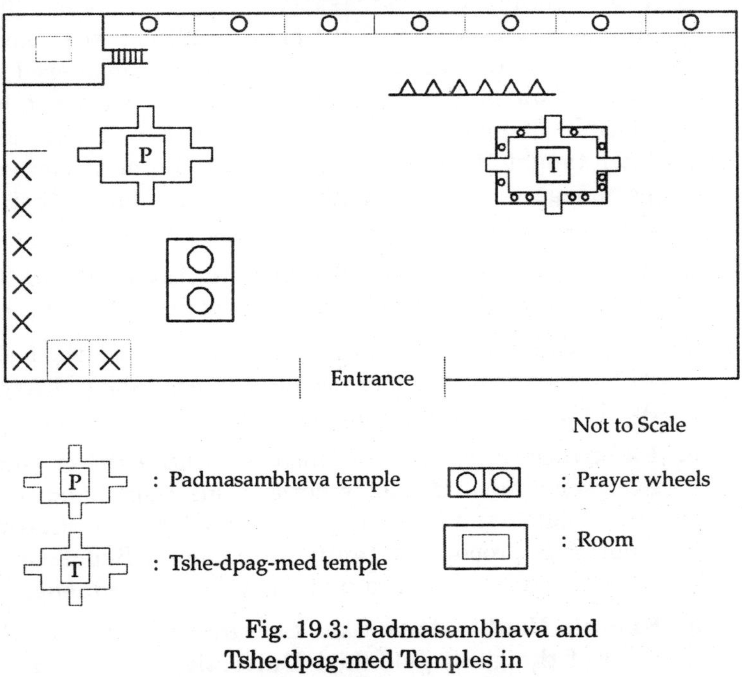

Fig. 19.3: Padmasambhava and Tshe-dpag-med Temples in Thuptan Donag Shedup Choskholing

Notes and References

1. **Anupan Bharadwaj:** He is my collegue at the Central Institute of Buddhist Studies, Leh-Ladakh.
2. **Tundup:** He is my collegue at the Central Institute of Buddhist Studies, Leh-Ladakh.
3. **Central Institute of Buddhist Studies Choglamsar:** It was established in 1959 in view to promote Manyani Buddhist Culture and Religion, and to protect the ancient Old Buddhist Culture and Tradition.
4. **Kharnakling Colony:** It is developed near central Institute of Buddhist Studies Choglamsar. The inhabitants are migrated from Kharnak and nearby areas of Changthang sub-division of Leh district.
5. **Ningmapa tradition:** It is the ancient tradition, the lineage of the order is described as beginning with the Adi Buddha, who is known by various names as Samantabhadra (Tib. kun tu bzang po), Vajradhara (Tib. rdoje chang) and Vajrasattva (rdorje semspa). The lineage enters the level of human tradition with Garab Dorje, and Indian or Tibetan teacher considered an emanation of Vajrasattva. Garab Dorje taught his disciple Sampe Shenyen, who taught Sri Singha, and later taught Padmasambhava. He is the most eminent personage of this tradition. Cf. Finegan, Jack: Tibet: A Dreamt of Image) Tibet House, 1986 : 82.
6. **Tshe-dpag-med:** Skt. Buddha Amitayus. He is the Buddha of longevity, a slightly variant form of Amitabha.
7. **Avalokitesvara:** Tib. spyan ras gjigs the lord who looks with compassion, is a manifestation of Amitabha; as Arya-Avlokitesvara has eleven heads and thousand arms.
8. **Padmasambhava:** Tib. Ningches Sinche tho or Guru Nangsey silnon: He holds dorje in his right hand near heart, left hand holds kapala in his lap in meditation mudra. He propogeted Tantric teachings of Buddhism in Tibet, recognised as the manifestation of amitabha.
9. **Khenpo Bodhisattva:** Skt. Santarakshita, he was the head of the great Buddhist University at Nalanda in

India, was Known for his work 'Tattvasangraha'. Cf. finegan, Jack; 49.

10. **Thrisong Detsen:** Tib. khri srong lde brtsan, was born in 742, the second great religions king of Tibet.
11. **Amitaba:** Tib. 'od-dpag-med. He is the Buddha of infinite light is known as the fourth of the Dhyani Buddha families, the embodiment of compassion.
12. **Avalokitesvara:** He is in this form is known Padmapani as holds the lotus.
13. **Tsetul Rinpoche:** He is the head of Sakti monastery, which is the only big Nyingmapa monastery in Ladakh.
14. **Umjat:** He is the senior lama in the monastery.
15. **Prayer wheel:** It contains Mane mantra scripts in thousands and thousand number i.e. around ten carore.

20

Some Buddhist Monuments in Chushod Village, Leh-Ladakh

On 24th November 2007, Leh had clean weather, Tashi Tharik asked me:

" Guruji, would you like to visit Chushod?"

"If you will show me some Buddhist monuments in the village, it would be my pleasure."

Tashi Tharik had a nice white colour Alto car, responded affarmative. about 2 o'clock afternoon he derived car to Chushod village, stopped near 'Dug Cang Cub Zang' monastery in Chushod Yogma. The monastery area was covered by boundary wall, at the entrance of the monastery Tashi Therik constructed Changohub chorten[2] in a couple of years ago (Fig.20.1).

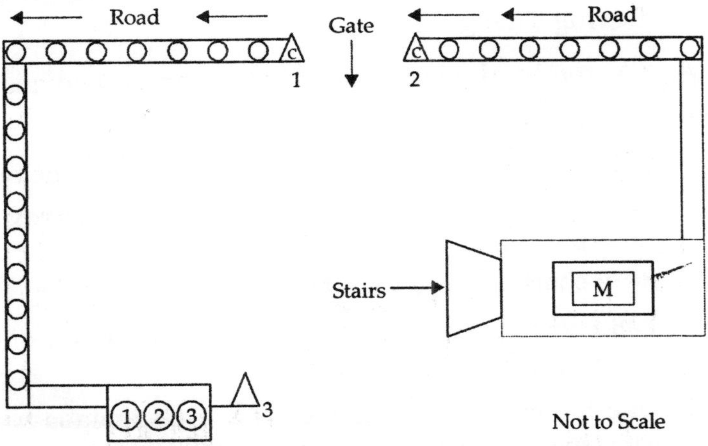

Fig: 20.1. Dug Cang Cub Zong Monastery in Chushod Yogma.

$\triangle_1$: Changchub Chorten, constructed in 2004

$\triangle_3$: Changchub Chorten, repaired by Tasi Tharik

◻◻ : Mane wall (Height 5′ and width 4′)

[M] : Monastery

$\triangle_2$: Changchub Chorten

①	:	Namgyal Chorten	Rigsum gonpo
②	:	Changchub Chorten	
③	:	Namgyal Chorten	

These chortens were constructed in the co-operation of eight following chushod Samma villagers :

1. Phunchok Dorje Tharik
2. Nurbu Ulu
3. Dechen Nagli
4. Lhadol Thakcot
5. Tundup Wangyal Thakcot
6. Syaltsen Spangstot
7. Late Chosgyal Pupu
8. Tsering Thang

$\triangle_1$: At top inside had Avalokitesvara statue and about 14′ high, it costs about Rs. 2 lakh.

$\triangle_3$: This chorten had Padmasambhava statue at the top, covered by glass. Nearby I saw some destroyed chortens viz.

1. 8–10 chortens area were being occupied by villagers.
2. 108 chortens were destroyed along the road, only their ruins could be seen.
3. One big chorten at the memory of Gongmapa was constructed after Kargil war in 1999. He was the son of Tering Norbu who died in Kargil war.

The Dug Cang Cub Zong (Tib. prug byang thub dzong) monastery is a branch of Hemis. It has some Buddha and Budhisattva statues (Fig. 20.2)

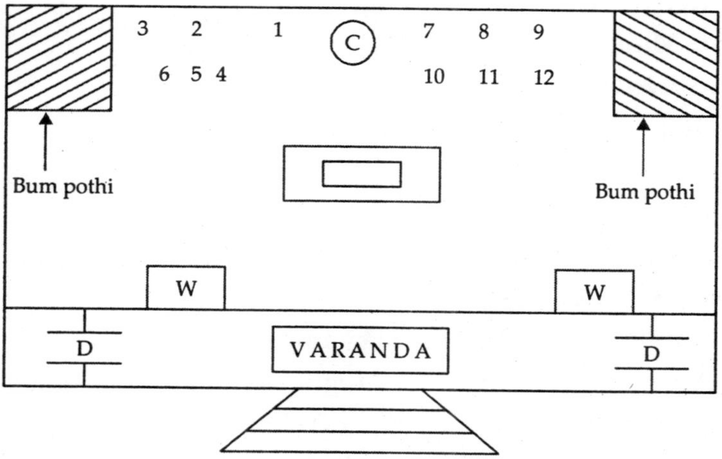

Fig. 20.2. Statues in Dug Cang Cub Zong gonpa in Chushod Yogma

(c) Padmasonleha :

Arms : Two; right hand holds dorje and left hand holds kapala, rests on his lap.

Asama	:	Meditation
Height	:	4½′
Width	:	3′

1. Ton yod jag pa

Position	:	Right to Padmasambhava
Arms	:	Six

2. Sakyamuni Buddha[5]

Arms : Two	:	(*i*) Right hand in Bhumisparsha. (*ii*) Left hand in meditation; holds patra in his lap.
Height	:	3′
Width	:	$2\frac{1}{2}'$
Asama	:	Meditation

3. Kunkhen Padma Karpo[6]

Arms	:	Two
Mudra	:	Dharmacakra
Head dress	:	Red hat

4. Manjusri : Body: yellow /brown[7]

5. Avalokitesvara[8]

Body : White

6. Vajrapani[9]

Body : Blue

4, 5, and 6 Boddhisattvas[10] represented three chortens in yellow, white and Blue.

7. Sakya Thubpa (or Sakyamuni Buddha)

Arms	:	Two; (*i*) Right hand in Bhumisparsha (*ii*) Left hand in meditation; holds patra in his lap.
Asana	:	Meditation
Height	:	2′
Width	:	1½′

8. Padmasambhava

Arms	:	Two; (*i*) Right hand holds dorje (*ii*) Left hand holds kapala
Height	:	1½′
Width	:	1′

9. Buddha

Height	:	6″
Width	:	4″

10. Stag-tsang-raspa[11]

Arms	:	Two; (*i*) Right hand in Bhumisparsha (*ii*) Left hand holds parta
Height	:	3′
Width	:	2½′

11. Atisa[12]

Arms	: Two
Mudra	: Dharmacakra
Height	: 2′
Width	: 1′

12. Kungkhen Padma Duba:

Height	: 1′
Width	: 6″

On the left and right sides of the statues are thirty two bum pothies, or sixteen pothis in each side almirah.

Wall Paintings in Dug Cang Thub Zong

This Dukhang has some lamas and Bodhisattvas mural paintings (Fig. 20.3).

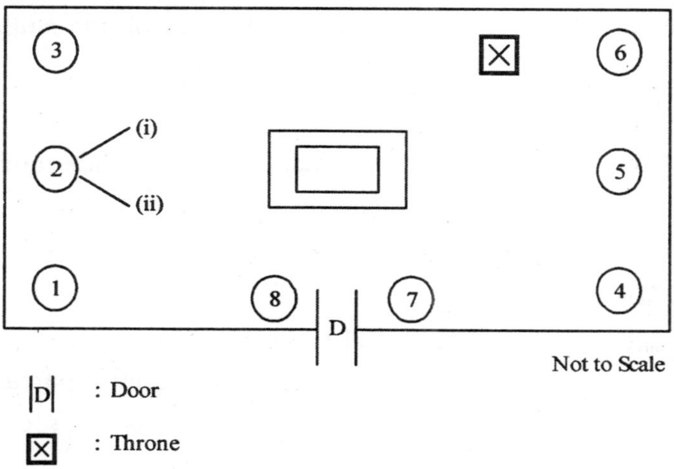

Fig. 20.3: Wall paintings on the walls in Dug Cang Zong Gonpa.

1. Stag-tsang-ras-pa

Arms: Two; (*i*) Right hand in Bhumisparsha

(*ii*) Left hand in meditation; holds patra in his lap.

Body : White

0rnaments : Earrings

Height : 3′

Width : 2′

Asana : Meditation

2. Kunkhen Patkar Sum

Centre figure : Kunkhen Padma Karpo

: Arms - Two

(*i*) Right hand holds doje with lotus;

(*ii*) Left hand holds bell with lotus

Legs : Two

Asama : Dolma stye

2. (*i*) ---------?

Arms : Two; (*i*) Right hand in varada mudra.

(*ii*) Left hand holds patra

2. (*ii*) -------?

Arma : Two; (*i*) Right hand in varada mudra

(*ii*) Left hand holds patra

Tashi tagyat are depicted before the above freseos.

3. Milaraspa[13]

Arms : Two; Right hand raised up near ear; left hand in meditation, holds patra in his lap.

Asana : Lalitasana

Height : 3′

Width : 2′

4. Singdongma

Arms : Two: (*i*) Right hand holds dorje ; left hand holds padma.

Legs : Two; trample one man lying on earth, right leg raised up and trample the man by her left leg.

Height : 5′

Width : 4′

5. Guru rinpoche

Arms : Two; (*i*) Right hand holds vajra near heart :

(*ii*) Left hand holds kapala in his lap in meditation

Asana : Meditation.

Measurements : Height - 4′

Width : 3′

6. Tandin (Hayagariva)[14]

Arms : Two; (*i*) Right hand holds sword

(*ii*) Left hand holds rope

Symbol : Horse headed and wrathful form.

Height : 4′

Width : 3′

7. Four friends : (*i*) Elephant

(*ii*) Monkey

(*iii*) Hare

(*iv*) Parrot

8. Tashi Tagyat[15]

☒ : Dukchen Rinpoche Throne

Atisha statue in this monastery is a powerful statue. In olden days once pujari did not offer prayer, as a result the statue did not like pajari's behaviour and threw his hat. Since then one pujari regualarly offer daily prayer. Besides, the monastery has eight forms of Padmasambhava thankas. Seven of them hanged through ceiling in Namling and one hanged at right side wall of the door.

After finishing research work at Dug Cang Thub Zong gonpa, we derived towards Zabuck village. On the way I saw some repaired and white washed chortens, asking about them

Tashi; Tharik replied: "In 2001, he repaired Mane ka-bum near masque in Tyapa Chushod and in 2005 five chortens at the surrounding, later white washed them. These chortens were in Zabuk village one chorten was being destroyed."

At Zabuk, of Chushod Gungma I saw two big ka-bum mane near the Tong-go-pa house. The old man of this family informed me that 70 years ago maximum families in Zabuk were Shia muslim Baltis, Buddhists were either converted into muslims or adopted Islam, only six families did not adopt Islam. They were:

1. Tong-go-pa (Ist Buddhist house)
2. Kang chen-pa
3. Cang ns-can
4. Kyang ba
5. Ta-ka-pa
6. Za-buk

Now Tong-go-pa family has 23 houses (families).

The Zabuk village has one Sakya gonpa, constructed in 1990 (Fig. 20.4)

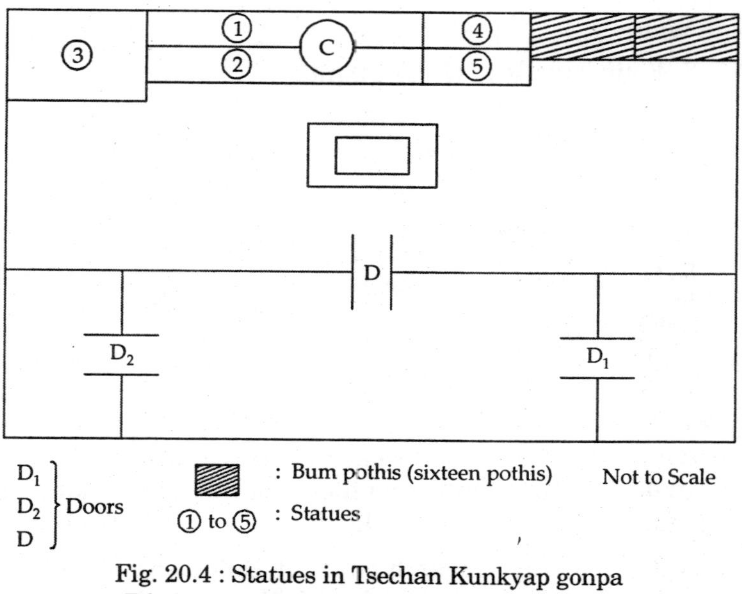

Fig. 20.4 : Statues in Tsechan Kunkyap gonpa (Tib. brtse chen kun khyab chos gling dgonpa)

(c) : Sakyamuni Buddha

Arms : Two; (*i*) Right hand Bhumisparsha
(*ii*) Left hand in meditation; holds patra in his lap.

Height : 5′

Width : 4′

On his right and left are Sariputra and Monglayayan

Height : 3′

Width : 2′

Both are in standing posture.

1. Unidentified

2. Avalokitesvara

Arms : Four

Form : Tantric

Mudra : Two main arms in namaskar mudra;
(*i*) right hand raised up holds rosary
(*ii*) Left hand raised up holds padma flower.

3. Padmasambhava

Arms : Two; (*i*) Right hand holds dorje.
(*ii*) Left hand holds Kapala.

Asana : Meditation

4. Dolma

Arms : Two

Height : One feet (1′)

5. Sakya Pandita[16]

Height : 1′

This gonpa had four pillars and three windows, had flower paintings on wooden almirah below the stutues and on beams (Tib. Kavas).

Notes and References

1. **Tashi Tharik:** He is an old villager of chushod, which is about 12 km from Leh towards Leh-Manali Highway.
2. **Changchub chorten;**
3. **Avalokitesvara:** A Bodhisattva of compassion.
4. **Padmasambhva:** He was a great tantric, brought Budhist tantra in Tibet from India.
5. **Sakyamuni Buddha:** He showed the right path to all living beings to attain freedom from the cycle of existence.
6. **Kunkhen Padma Karpo:** Tib. kun mkhyen. Pad ma dkar po, meaning lotus, He was a famous scholar of Druk-pa during 16th century A.D. His retreat centre was at a palace called the essence of Perfection (Byangchub snying po) in the southern mountains of khar-chu, in the southern part of Tibet and adjoing the eastern corner of Bhutan, from where he was influential in the introduction on of the Druk-pa into Bhutan. He was a poet and the author of works on astrology, medicine, philosophy, and other subjects, and most important of a religions history called the sun which causes the lotus of the teaching to open dealing chiefly with the Druk-pa sect, and of an epitome of the long handed down teachings of the *mahamudra*, the Great Seal, which has always continued to be foundamental in the philosophy and yogic practice of the entire kagyu-pa. Cf. Finegan, Jack: Tibet: A dreamt of Image, Tibet House: 1986: 97.
7. **Manjusri:** Tib jam dbyangs "charming splendor," is the Bodhisattva of wisdom and literature with two lotus blossoms as his attributes or with the sword of knowledge in his right hand and the book of transcendent wisdom (prajnaparamita) in his left. Cf. Finegan, Jack; *op. Cit.* 131.
8. **Avalokitesvara:** He is the manifestation of Amitabha.
9. **Vajrapani:** Tib. Phyag na rdo rje, holder of vajra (thunderbolt), is a mimifestation of Akshobhya.
10. **Bodhisattvas:** They are represented to Manjusri, Avalokitesvara and Vajrapani:

11. **Stag-tsang-raspa:** The name of stag-tsang-raspa derived from the tigernest cave (Tib. stag tshand) in Bhutan where he spent some years in meditation and was said to have attained the vision of all the eighty four Indian Mahasiddhas and was himself recognized as a great 'perfected one'. It was in 1613. after he had already travelled widely in Central and Eastern Tibet and into China stag-tsang ras pa set out for the west. He passed through Zanskar in the time to Jamyang Namgyal who invited him to Ladakh, but he went on to Uddiyana (Swat), then came back in 1616 through Kashmi and Zanskar to Ladakh, where he thereafer spent much time during the reign of Sengge Namgyal and into the reign of Daldan Namgyal. Cf. Finegan, Jack; *op. cit.:* 180.

12. **Atisa:** His origional name was Chandragarbha and his monastic name was Dipankara. He was born in 982, the son of king in Eastern India. In his childhood he had a vision of the goddess Tara, who became his tutelary deity. Later he went to Rajagriha the capital of Magadha and was initiated into the tantric cycle of Hevajra by Rahulaguhyavajra a practitioner of this system at the Black Mountain, later spent three years in Uddiyana, where he participated in tantric ceremonies. At this point he was being established in the tantric methods of the Vajrayana. He then went abroad to study with the teacher Ser Lingpa. After twelve years returned to India and became a famous teacher at the Vikramasila University. Cf. Finegan, Jack; *op. cit.;* 61-62.

13. **Milaraspa (or Milarapa):** He was the disciple of Marpa, was able to endure the coldest weather in only cotton clothing.

14. **Tamdin (Hayagriva):** He is the Dharmapala, and protector of Buddhist doctrine.

15. **Tashi Tagyat:** The Eight Glorious Emblems; white parasol, two fishes, seashell, lotus, standard, vase, wheel and endless note.

16. **Sakya Pandita:** Tib. kun dga 'rgyal (Pron. Kunga Gyentsen). He was the abbot of Sakya.

21

History of Lamayuru Monastery During 1834–40

The manuscript was written by Rangdol Nima when Zorawar Singh invaded Ladakh during 1834-40. His soldiers came via Lamayuru and destroyed Lamayuru monastery badly. Lama Rangdol Nima hid in the nearby place and watched Dogra army activities closely. As Dorgra army marched to Leh he came to the monastery on the request of villagers to re-build the same. In his historical manuscript Lama Rangdol Nima not only described the details about the history of the monastery but explained how he could able to re-founded the monastery. In the following paragaraps I'll endeavour to cover the important historical portion of Lamayuru monastery,

In the middle of 13th century A.D. Zhawa-mer tradition took its hold in Tibetan political administration, likewise Ladakh and Lamayuru in particular was influenced. Rangdol Nima says:

"Lamayuru monastery influenced was by Zhawa-mer tradition during 13th century, in those days this monastery had good political and religions relations with central Tibet. The monastery used to send lamas to Yangspachen monastery in Tibet for higher studies in Buddhist philosophy." At the end of 14th century Lamayuru monastery was first time destroyed by Kashmiri Army. Rangdol Nima writes:

"The Tibtan Army under the command of Galdan Tsewang invaded Ladakh. To defend his kingdom Ladakh king asked help from Kashmir Mugal emire. Kashmir Badshah sent a huge army to Ladakh. On the way between

Kashmir and Leh, they saw Lamayuru monastery. Some Kashmiri soldiers entered into the monastery, took away precious statues, besides 'Chosje chatangpa statue'. They thought to bring the statue to Wangla village, later carry to Kashmir. The statue, by spiritual power became heavy and they could not carry the same to Wangla. Thus they left the statue in the monastery, later marched to Leh. Near Basgo Tibetan army attacked, Kashmir army was fully equipped with arms and amunation, and defeated the Tibetan army. Later agreements took place between Ladakh king and on behalf of Kashmir Badsah. Thereafter Kasmir army started returning to Kashmir. At Lamayuru monastery, the Kashmir army commander once again ordered his soldiers to bring 'Chosje Chatangpa' statue. Soldiers went to the monastery, as they touch the statue, it became so heavy that they could not carry even to a small distance. At last they prayed statue to become lighter and poured water on it. The statue remained heavy, later they left it near to the monastery. Kashmir, army when marched to valley, villagers who lived nearley came to the statue and carry it to the monastery.

In the beginning of 15th century, Hors invaded Ladakh, They marched towards Lamayuru monastery, but Chosje 'Chantangpa' statue through its spiritual power diverted their direction. Subsequently the monastery became famous in Ladakh as well as in the neighbouring countries. The kings and Sultans also decided not to harm it.

Lamayuru monastery as the boundary between Buddhist and Muslim areas. Both communites made an agreement that they would protect the monastery jointly. Thus the monastery was popularly known 'Yung-Dung-Tharpa-Ling' Lama Rangdol Nima says:

"The king of Ladakh issued an order in favour of Lamayuru monastery, under which whoever would come to the monastery for shelter may be pardoned. In case anyone who needs shelter, may reach up to the monastery's boundary or even come up to 'Terchen' or would throw anythings from the distance to the boundary of the monastery was entitled for pardon. As a result the monastery was popularly known Yung-Dung-Tharpa-Ling".

In the middle of 15th century Ladakh was divided in many 'zongs', Lamayuru was the first 'zong' of 'Gyathim' in Shyam. As soon as Lamayuru declared 'zong'. Its political power also increased. Ladakh king Tsewant Namgyal and his minister Tsewang Tondup had given their full support in the propogation of Buddhism in Lower Ladakh. Consequently it became famous not only in Lakakh, but in Kashmir valley. Like Ladakh king official orders often sent to the administrative head of Lamayuru monastery". Rangdol Nima writes :

"Kantham, Duran, Gyuran Duran Baba etc. These were the official orders or related documents of king Ashaling, who used to send them to "Nangstens', Kushoks of Lamayuru monastery and kings of Ladakh.

In the 16th century Ladakh king Tashi Namgyal invited Dhenma Kunga Trakpa to establish Drigung monastery in Ladakh. He founded Phyang monastery under the said tradition and put Lamayuru under its administrative control.

After 16th century to till the end of eighteenth century, time and again invaders attacked Ladakh and plunder the monasteries' property. Rangdol Nima writes:

"Dangi Malik a Kashmiri officer, representative of Kashmir in Ladakh often plundered villagers in Shyam region. Sometimes he looted villagers crops with the help of his 300 men."

In the beginning of 19th century every year British officers visited Central Asia via Ladakh. In Ladakh at every stoppage Begars i-e. Ladakhi labours were ready at their free services with their horses. Lamayuru monastery was exempted from this Rangdol Nima says:

"Ladak his as well as neighbouring countries heads had great respect upon Lamayuru monastery. In the middle of 16th century at many occasions high ranked lamas of the monastery acted as mediator and stopped Ladakh vs Balti wars. The Kusoks of Lamayuru monastery had good relations with Baltis as well as Ladakh kings. They paid their respect to Kushoks and used to send presents on the occasion of Losar and New Year. In response they received gifts from them. In this way Lamayuru monastery was exempted from all kinds of taxes levied either king of Ladakh or Skardu Cho. The monastery was one of the rechest monastery in Ladakh and was the only main Buddhist centre in Lower Ladakh which had about 350 Buddhist monks."

In 1834, Dogra army under the command of wazir Zorawar Singh invaded Ladakh. Tsepal Namgyal the king of Ladakh was badly defeated. Dogra occupied Ladakh. Later Wazir Zorawar Singh invaded Tibet. In 1843 on his request Maharaja Gulab Singh sent a huge army under the command of Harichand to Ladakh. Harichand when reached Lamayuru monastery, saw many precious things, thus looted the monastery. Lama Rangdol Nima remarks:.

"After the Ladakh occupation, Wazir Zorawar Singh invaded Tibet. Ladakhis refused to join his army. He asked Maharaja Gulab Singh to send more troops. Maharaja sent a fresh Dogra army under the command of Devan Harichand. As he reached Lamayuru, saw many precious idols. He ordered his soldiers to bring all important statues and precious things from the monastery. The soldiers did the same, they destroyed monastery, even didn't close doors and windows. In autumn war stopped. Dogra army started returning to Jammu. When the army reached Lamayuru, once again the army commander ordered his soldiers to bring the important statue of Chorje which they left earlier. They again went to the monastery and tried to bring that statue, but unable to do so. Thus, bound to leave it near the monastery. After sometime, Dogra army marched further towards Kargil. Villagers then collected pages of Kagyur pothis, which were scatterved here and there, and placed Chosje statue in the temple. Animals were tied in rooms, they were crying loudly. Lama Rangdol Nima ran away to

Dumkhar. Later on the request of villagers, Lama Rangdol came to Lamayuru, He was informed:

"Dogra soldiers beat Lhopon and lamas so badly that some that of them as a result died the rest of them ran away to high mountains of their respective villages.

Subsequently, with the kind co-operation of villagers Rangdol Nima called all lamas of the monastery and established Buddha Sangha, gradually arranged ritual objects for daily prayers. He remarks:

"We are thankful to Lamayuru villagers, with their co-operation we were able to purchase a bell of without head from the nearby village, later made 'rolmo' from this, and started daily prayer,"

Soon after Lama Rangdol Nima started to rebuilt temples in the monastery. Villagers happly came froward and voluntatily removated the destroyed temples. On this occasion Cama Rangdol Nima informed villagers about his dream:

"While returing to Ladakh from Tibet, saw 'Skyabgon' in his dream. Who was giving me instruction to go to Ladakh carefully, later he presented white shawl and disappeared. Subsequently, on his way to Ladakh, near a mountain top, from where he could see Mount Kailash started reading religious pothis and covered the whole distance easily. Near Lamayuru monastery he spent one night and again saw a dream, that except one idol everything from the monastery were taken away by some enemy soldiers, temples of the monastery were destroyed Phyang lama Tsewang Tashi appeared and informed, the monastery could be removate and still hope to re-establish Bhikshu Sanghu."

Lama Rangdol Nima later conducted villagers meeting and asked then to donate cash and kind for the renovation of temples in the monastery. He repaired temples and printed Kangyur Pothis. He writes:

"Ladakhis have strong faith upon Buddhism, Lamayuru monastery, which was destroyed by Dogra soldiers, renovated by the blessing of '**Tri-Saran-Gaman**' and Eeedan Khando lamas population increased, They strickly follow vinaya rules.Unfortunately by muslim invation from western side of Kashmir, many villagers of Purig were converted to muslim. However, this religion could not spread its roots to the upper regions beyond Lamayuru monastery ."

After the establishment of Bhikshu Sangha. Rangdol Nima faced food shortage. He says:

"Bhikshu Sangha was established, but we were facing food shortage. To solve this problem we had two options: (i) to cultivate monastery land and grow wheat and vegetables (ii) to give monastery land on rent under the agreement to give some portion of food products to monastery annually. Finally we decided to give monastery land on rent to villagers and asked them to get back food products. In this way we were given tax excemption by Ladakh King."

In conclusion Lama Rangdol Nima observed that Lamayuru monastery as an important monastery in the Lower Ladakh, it was built during 11th centrry A.D. and followed Kadampa sect earlier. It had good relations with Tibet as well as with Kashmir till 16th century. When Dhanma Kunga Oragpa established Phyang monastery near Leh on the request of king Tashi Namgyal, Lamayuru monastery was taken under its control. Since then it is functioning under Drigung Ka'gyud tradition. Further details see the following Tibetan manuscript.

Roman Translitesation of Tibetan Manuscript on Lamayuru Monastery (Pl. see text in Appendix-I)

thabs khas thugs jes sha kyi regs su thungs. zhan gyi mi thub dud kyi pung joms pa. Ser gyi lhun po lta bur jed pal sku. Sha kyi gyal po de la chag tshal lo. Zhes chod par jod pe tshig gis ngon sus te loṅ var ja ve don la de yaṅ maṅ yul ṅa ris la dgas cam chogs chi pa daṅ naṅ pe sa tshams su khod pe thub stan yun duṅ gon gyi lo gyus sa cad tsam kod pa la sṅon bod chos dyal gyi duṅ gyud pa dags la phebs dus la dags stod chogs nams su ni yul doṅ ma chags par thaṅ stoṅ daṅ yuṅ stoṅ du yod chiṅ . Cam chogs nams su yul chags pa nams dog pa shes la los zuṅ nas luṅ pa re nas joṅ chuṅ ri jas cig la cig da jag gyod cin sña ve thes yu ru shes pe yuṅ pa di tsho ru kyil nas yo ṅ skad re cig do nyi ma guṅ pa gya gar nas kha che yul du phebs skabs cig la lho chogs dir phebs pas yul di luṅ pa ni tsho ru kyil te yoṅ pas shar chogs kyi ri ser phebs te zigs pas tsho kyil ve us na gad pa bur po shig tse thon te yod pa kun gyis thoṅ va de la chag stan te pha gyi tsho de skams pa daṅ kyil bur po dei sto ṅ du ston pa sha kya thub pe chos do s ṅags zuṅ dol gyi stan pa rin chen ge dun gyi sed daṅ cas pa tshug par gyur so. Shes luṅ stan zas pas shar ri sa chogs de la skam bur shes mi ṅ du thogs de nas do ni ma yuṅ pa zhu thul gyis tsho kyil gad bur tse der pheb naś zhi dag gi lu sog la hu for cin nas chag. der, phebs nas shi dag gi lu sogs la chu tor sjin nas chag gis khar sil kyaṅ ste toi tso jug zhu thul gyis tal nas kha chei yul du phebs soṅ nas dam siṅ ṅis thon pas sa der seṅ ge sgaṅ zhes mi ṅ du thogs chu tor dsad dus kyi tor zhi nas bus chogs la spu ṅ pa gang stoṅs daṅ lan des do yuṅ duṅ ris kyi jaṅs pe myu gu skyes yod pas jes su shi der gon pa chags dus yuṅ duṅ gon zhes miṅ du thogs dug de jes jo na so gya gar nas kha chei yul du phebs pe dus cig la lho cogs nas zans kar jo ṅ s khul phug tu phebs ci ṅ de nas gyud sa chogs der phebs te yuṅ duṅ myu ga skyes pe khaṅ pe tse der phug sa jas dan chags pa thog mar ni na ro pe shags kyis cags pe dan sa yin dug cin jes na ro p'a sku thog nas zons kha che yul nas yuṅ duṅ gondi bar gyis yul sde thams cad la na ṅ pa sa ṅ s gyas pe chos lugs dar dyas su yod tshul ya ṅ de tabu rig gi yiul maṅ po daṅ sbal ti yul sogs la sku nian ga gyi dag da ṅ lha kha hul po ma khi chod ten neng pa sogs stan pe lag jes pa yod skaṅ daṅ je diguṅ pa jig ten pon poi che va jod pai dam las kyaṅ nub chogs na du sha daṅ gyi ling chun chad ng'i og du tshud cissu ṅ s pada ṅ thun dug pa da ṅ des shu ṅ s gon dii chos de dar gyas yod tshul ya ṅ dub thob chen po du ṅ pa sjo ṅ pa shes pa la togs bod na dan phebs pae skyes bu dam pa ga nas stan pa dsin skyo ṅ s sped sum yod pe thos lo da ṅ thul med shib ti gi yig cha yod pa re ni stan pe dar gud kha shas ju n̂ thal ve tshams su chas kyi tho sto n̂ s skabs je su yal bas da ta rags rim tsam gyi thos lo ni n̂ on thog skabs shig ta thi pon tag tar kyabs chip pe pon po shig gis kha chei sa tshams nas ma n̂ yul la tshun thad srid du ju n̂ ste yod skad des n̂ a ris skor sum na tshan yo n̂ s su dags pe lo tse va rin chen za n̂ po dan da n̂ s te kha ches tshams du n̂ shil nas zu n̂ s te soi la tshun chad du chod ten gya da n̂ gyad lha kha n̂ gya da n̂ gyad she n̂ s pa sogs stan pe ja va labs po chei sgo nas jo n̂ s dii skyes doai sod nams kyi nin jed sal bar djad pas deai na n̂ tshan yu n̂ du n̂ gon dii yul gyi chogs zhi us da n̂ n̂ a ma lha kha n̂ n̂ a gyud ste zhi ten da n̂ ten par cas pa dis bur tha yas pa da n̂ chi ru gyud nas su n̂ s pe chod tenma n̂ po zhe n̂ s dug pe de tar thun mo n̂ da n̂ thun mo n̂ ma yon pe dza n̂ pe sgo nas ka dams kyi stan va cin tu dar va zhig ju n̂ va yin tshod la de zhig gon pa der ya n̂ den ju n̂ s bod yul us nas khan po zhig phebas srol tshugs te sde pa zhu n̂ gi ka cag gi yig cha las kya n̂ yu n̂ du n̂ khan por dos khal dug cu zhes phod ci n̂ de tar na n̂ yod pa da n̂ chis su gon di de gu n̂ pas dag dzin dzad pa nas za n̂ s rim gyis di nas dos khal sum cu skor du yod skabs bod gyal tshab tsho mo li n̂ pe sku thog la lo chag pa ma n̂ khan gyis lam yig ka sog ni n̂ pa ka shag tu phul nas Aag mad khan de ni sku tshe jes so n̂ nas de n̂ chin chad lam yig ka shog chag tags res na n̂ va da n̂ mi na n̂ va nis su dug cid de tar lo tsa va rin chen za n̂ gi chag jes chod ten sa bun re da n̂ us kyi lha kha da ta n̂ skyon med du zhugs yod ci n̂ de tar ka dam kyi chos lugs dar zhi n̂ gyas ra n̂ zhin can da n̂ de jes bar skabs shig la ma yul spu ra n̂ s gu ge sum la bod chos gyal gyi du n̂ gyud gyal po gon sum zhugs pe du n̂ gyud sras shig la dags la phebs te thog mar sle ru dan sa chags nas chu reai dro n̂ tsho tshugs de nas she chu shod can la yur va don nas yul tsugs shi n̂ shan chogs dog yul nams la mag da n̂ pa sogs kis mag da n̂ pa sogs kyis n̂ a ba n̂ s che gyas va da n̂ jes su la dags stod sham thems cad du gyal va ni mi nen gyi stan pa dar zhi n̂ gyas par gyur va ni to nas gar zhi yul tshun tshud la dags gyal poi n̂ a zhabs su togs pa da n̂ nub na kha chei yul tsho kha shas su rig gyud nas la dags thug chabs cig pa dañ nub jañ na du sha dañ gyi liñ nas shi khar gyud la dags su togs shin dam pe chos dar gyas yod va sogs sñ ar gyi thos lo dañ da tañ de nams su lha khañ chod ten dag la kos pe sku zugs sogs yod va de nams su slab pa thams cas kyi mig lam du gyur dug de dar gyal bañ s chos srid thabs shes gan gi sgo nas zhiñ nas dar zhiñ gyas par gyur nañ. la dags joñ s di pon bañ s nams la dar gud mañ po juñ yoñ skad dañ yañ chos zhin skoñ pe gyal po sku sod nams dañ lan va rim shin zuñ sde dam chos kyañ je cher gyas pe dar ni jes su sa skya pa ni ma dug pa di guñ pa sogs dub tha mañ poi chos sed da dai bar du yod cid gon dia bar skabs shig nas gyal rabs kha shas kyi riñ la chos lugs zha mar yod pe skad cha dañ da gyun jan yañ s pa can du go lugs yud pe thos lo dañ di gi chas kyi srol ka gyud pe sgom zha sul med ñ id soñ mañ pos khom sum zhi skañ s yod pa dag gis kyañ thon cho je ja dañ pa zhes pe la mi sku yan cin can ka nan pa zhig da di bar du nañ ten gyi tso bor zhugs yoñ sku nan di la tse cig tu mos pa nams la sol va gañ tab thun tu dub pa dañ gon dii char togs pa gañ la mi srun pe ja va jas pa nams la tags dañ tshan ma ñ on sum du juñ va sogs thams cañ gyis liñ dug yods kyi lins mo la bod na ga dan tshe bañ zhes pe mag puñ la dags la sleb skbas kha chul nas kha chei mag puñ che bar thon pas gon dii ka nams sdu sog jed kabs nañ ten rin po che wan la zhes pe yul du sbar var dan zhus pas wam le lun sgo nas phar la sus kyañ ma theg par yu ra di gar tshur dan zhu gos juñ ve skad dañ de tar ñ es can yin pe dag kuañ wan li luñ s goai zhiñ kyil tu nañ ten gyi zhugs thi zhes pe cigas pa dug chi zhig na mag kha chul du log skabs kha cheai mag pon gyi den kha chul du khyer bar yu ruai lañ s gor mig thoñ tu gyur nas kha che nams kyis lag tsid du chu mañ po zhig thor nas zhag soñ va dañ. rañ rai mig cig gis tshur dan zhus pa yin zer ve liñ jod dug ciñ de tar buai tags tshan mañ po dug pe ten kyañ par can dañ stañ jin pe dus sde sogs dar gyas yod ñ añ gyal srid kyi joñ s skabs shig tu sbal tis non pa sogs ja ziñ tshams su dar gud juñ bañ rañ shis la dub pas bar skabs gon pa di dag djin jed sa chun ba zhig tu gyur skabs shig la la dags gyal po zhig gis snyur li gun sar thañ la yul jug sar la dagas stod sham thams cad kyi bañ s sdus ti he mis roñ thil gyi la du nas chu roñ du dañ ve thabs dzad nas ri dam nas yur ra ba zos shiñ la go nas ched tsam dus pa la deai sa doñ nas tsans pe zugs sewam gyi tshad tsan zhig chos thul tu thon juñ bas las mi nam kyis tog stse gyabs te sat pas deai kyen gyis gyal po jam yans nam gyal zhu va zhig snun dze dag pos thebs nas gyal shin du che bas sman cad rim do sogs gañ gi sgo nañ ma pan pas gañ s te yiai di guñ gon pa da gyañ dags nas chos jes dan ma zhes dub pa thob be nal jor pa chen po sa lam la nas pe sod nam kyad du pahgs pe la ma zhig zhugs pa de dan den zhus te rim do zad pas gyal po'i yun dzang dal du vag sa te nas chos jes dan ma gyal ve bu lar khur nas ngon tis chos dzong shes pa chos zhi su phul nas der gon pa tab de dang tags yung dung gon di chos sring dan sar phal va dang lhag don du gon pa di chi nang sa tsham su yong pe kabs yin par ten thar pa ling da yang nga sol nas/gyal pe nga zhabs su togs pe chi pa dang pa tod sham kun gyis kur gos pa dang pon.

bañ s gañ la nes par gyur ve nag can srog la bab pa sogs kyañ gon pa diai zhabs jus la oñ s pa nams yul go yul jug gi dar ngar po cheai nañ tsun chad du lep pa thams cad gon pe srol tañ der ma tsad la dags sham chogs kyi joñ s jog kha shas la gyal thims kyi de du cho thims kyi luñ gyug pa sogs kha dag she mo zhig chos gyal chen poai tshe vañ nam gyal dañ chos lon chen po che vañ don dub bar gyi sku thog tu dul ciñ de zhin du gon pa thar liñ du ña sol te kha chai gyal po ca Aa gañ ga shes pe ka tham dañ du ran na ta va gyal po nams kyi ka shog kha chea yi ge dañ nañ ten gyi shugs thi kha chul nas phul pe shi shi me loñ la bar tsai gi ge kos pe dan chos shep mor yod par ten kha chul gyi pha na dañ s gyi ma lig shes pa khor yog nis gya sum gya dañ cas lo ño sum bar du yoñ skabs la dags stoñ sham nams kyi lam thams cad la thog com sogs sdañ stsub yod kyañ yul dir ta bul su lag sogs ciañ mi bab ciñ thog com sogs stañ stsub jed pa phar shag nas tha na yul du me di skad tsam cañ mi chog par kha che nams kyis kyañ tsi jog gos pa sogs yod pa dañ de tar chiñ ñ chos lugs thams cad kyi mos tud sde stan gyi nas yin pas des nas la dags daṅ sbal ti. sogs thab tsod chen por jaṅ tse gon pa des nis kyi tshams na legs dum gyi phyin dig pa daṅ yas mas kyi chad thoai yaṅ jed pa sogs chod jog pa jas te gon pa di nas la dags gyal lon nams la lo sar gyi tses chag daṅ sbal ti gyal po skar donai jo la lo chagpa pho na zhig dzaṅ va ma nas la dags gyal lon nams la lo sar ggi tses chang daṅ sbal ti gyal po skar donai jola lo chagpa pho na zig dzaṅ va ma togs chos srid la thal rigs du tsam med pe raṅ tsan pa yin ci ja va lugs nis gaṅ gi sgo nas logs lam phun sum chogs shin ge dun gyi sde sa saṅ sṅon thog maṅ skabs sum gya zhi gya nas mi nyuṅ bar dom che tsam tshogs shiṅ ten ched sogs. kyaṅ phags zaṅ la dos che va looṅ s jcod ni nam thos kyi bu la dan nus pa tsam raṅ khos la bag na ma yin pa daṅ ma dig pe sgo gaṅ yaṅ meṅ ciṅ chi naṅ gi shyabs nas do va la miai chod steṅ du tshags te lo maṅ lon pa daṅ la dags chos gyal rin phebs kyi jug cos dyal chen po pal nam gyal gyi sku thog tu la dags gyal srid jam mu ra ji ṅ a oog tu chud soṅ de nas lo ṅ o gu tsam na jam muai ka lon das nas ji jo ra var zir va daṅ bod thugs skabs la lags pas bod la dun stan pas jam mu nas ho lan ha ri can zir va shig gi tsos ma ga pun ne degs te dkha thul nas la dags daṅ tsiai bar du mag puṅ gis ṅ a bas te dus la dags yul ste joṅ khag thams cad sham stod lo jun ma lus par lag soṅ gon pa diaṅ zhu ga lam yin shis yul mi nams ni ri la dos pas jar thog cig gi riṅ la mag dul nas yul. daṅ gon la daṅ thams cad saṅ sum den ched cha la sogs pa nams joms nas sdoṅ s pa ma tshad naṅ gi sgo kar khuṅ dyod jug tsam ma lus par soṅ va de nas sten tsams su gyal khag yas mas chin dig steṅ jam muai mag nams log zin pa daṅ mi nams ri nas yul du bab ste na tus la daṅ tiai ten dis bur thams cad kyi naṅ na di guṅ nabs duṅ ste no padme gyan gyi da sku sman dam las dab pa thu khan pa nig ni sus kyaṅ las ma thug par dug de daṅ cha las nams kyi naṅ na gor sbub cha cig lus dug de nis ma t ogs zhan khyer dod pa nams la ni kyer nas mi dug ciṅ mi gos pa nams ni shig nas dod pa nig cig kyaṅ ma lus shiṅ gyal ve ka gyur rin pe che daṅ duṅ du phub ma gyañva zhin du lug nas te dañnam du khañnañgi phubs nams su ti bi cag sogs ta nams dañjug khor du biu bañbu sogs kag nas gon khañgi dab skar nañji ruñtas te bon bus ñar da sgog pa sogs de tar tan pi gegs chags ci mi legs pa thams cad dug ciñtsogs pe slo pon gyis tsos da pa kha shis kyañdeg duñtson sogs kyis tons dug de jes ge du gyi sde thams cad kyañ rañ rañ soai yul sogs su dos pa ta bus thor nas tsogs gyu riñskabs cig la thog mar dug ste zhig dzoms nas dzai med dam zhig bum pa jas dzai chod koñteñre ned pe chod cha jas yul sruñkha che zhig gi lag na yod pe dil bu skye bud cig nos te rol mo jas te das po zhi ga gi jañsteg gyis dug de ta bu nyam thag su thug gi nañla yod skabs su nos la miñkon chog rañdol nyima sñon du mag ziñskabs jañ chogs to khar gyi bhu la dos te ja kyed cig tu scil bu zhig tsigs te sga sed yoid par de ra yu ruai yul mi thun moñbod mi nyis leb te la dang di khang stoñdu chur pas mi yin gyi dim dul tshag tshig reañ thos dug zhig soai do khur zhig jed khan poñtshe ños nams kyi ma zhin kun tsad la zhag ste gos cha ri gañcogs skub gyu yin zer juñños kyi sam pa la khoñmi skya nams de tsam gyi lo yod na ña doai sam pa zhig dañyañsñon du ños rañ bod nas nas skor pe tsul su yoñs skabs goñs ri zhin mi lam tu di guñskuabs gon nam nyis gyun mis chad du jal va dañ mar yul la thon pe zhag de de bar soñ zhig suñs sam snyim nam nyis kyi kha tag da kar poai sba dar ri nañyod pa ra jal di nas chin ma jal pe ngos kyi sam tsul da jag chom kun sogs la kyi jigs pa thams cad las thar va yin da snyam nas oñas te tse bo thog chen gyi se ra luñdu do ve dabs lam zhig na gñas ti siai u tse jal ran pa dañpha yul du leb bezang ñan ci jeñyoñgi nam dog khur nas jam pal tshan jod don gyin yods pas tsañs pe yul sa tse nas non zhes pa dañ gñaskyi bu tse jal bas ge ve las re sdub na lam do yjoñ nam sam de ta buai tas zañre ña yod sdun soñsnyam nas yu ru la yon ve khar lañs deai nub mo mi lam du nañgyi cas sku thams cad ma zhig par ta lam me yod par thoñthams cad zhig zer va yin dum sham pa deñsgañsñon gyi bu tse vañta tis da ve da pa zhig gis kyaṅ ste nyen raṅ mi dug zer dug nyid sad pa daṅ tsan ma zaṅ nyam ste do ve lo thag chod chi lo jar smad la yu ru la sleb nas chogs gaṅ de re la sod snyopas slod mo re skul ba daṅ raṅ laṅ than bu re gaṅ yoṅ bod cad nas zhig so la go tsug pas lo nyis kyi ri ṅ la sman dam las dub pe sku nams legs par dub de nas lo nyis kyi riṅ la gyal ve ka kyur rin po ches tsos suṅ rab nams dub de jes lo kha shas riṅ la chod che rig daṅ gon po dang ka dyad nyis ke tor log gar tsams sdgas pe chas thams cad dub de nas yaṅ stod sham yoṅs dsogs la sloṅ mo na va zod la thug gi bar du yaṅ nad yaṅ du skul va jas thabs ci dag gi sgo nas chod pa nyams chag nams kyaṅ sos te sci thog nyer las re skal te thog mar nya stoṅ la so sjong daṅ kyad roṅ nam gaṅ la so sor thar pe do don pa daṅ nas cu nyis choga tsugs de dar la va reai ṅ o re la thses sum daṅ nyer sum la do je phag moai kyil chog tshes gyat la sman lai do chog ches cu la pad liṅ dag poai sgo nas ches cuai chod pa tshos cub zee la goṅs pa yaṅ zab las dyal va zhi khoai kyil chog tsogs la mi thug chug cu gu la ka gyad de dus diṅ jaṅ po'i tshogs chod nyer lags la la ma chod pa nyir gu la de gon gyi skaṅ solk dyas yang chos nga nyir dug sogs la sjin dag re skur nas sdol kar ma la zhim cas dan zhin yaṅ tsoga par sṅa chiai dam tom pag ste chos skyed smon lam daṅ cas pa daṅ dus gyun du zhi sum nad suṅs pe gyid chags sum pa daṅ chu tor gya tsa chag med cas dub gyud di pe lugs kyi chogs don nams zai koṅs su tsaṅ thans daṅ gyor chags kyi gon pa chos de zhin dag dzin jed pe ge dun gyi ste tsugs thabs su raṅ khos la pag pe stan pe zhags deg tsam zhig dub naṅ chos nor daṅ kyaid ṅa thaṅ stobs daṅ dan pa nams kyi thoṅ yul du ni jes pe tsed mo tsam gyi va las med pas niṅ je ai yul du zigs las che naṅ dag raṅ ni ja va zhan paṅs pe ri thed pe lugs la gyur pas gyu cas lag thog tu ciaṅ med pa zhig daṅ dad dan gyi sjin dag nams ni de dus tha mag gis shigs pe sogs kyi thabs sdug naṅ de tsan dub pa te ni la ma kon chog kyi jin thu daṅ yi dam tho sruṅ mi thil thugs jeṅ on sum du jum te gang gos la thogs pa med pa ta buai daṅ nas ka tsogs med par lhun gyis dub pe zhig pa teṅ nas jed na ya tsan gyi nas su gyur dug la dañ gi chi nañ par sum tsa ve tse scod sogs ni sus kyañ sog thub khan ma juñ sa thog du ni maha ra dzi nul sdal sogs ma togs ge dun tso ve thum gyen la phan pe des pa ma shis ñ ub chogas kha che nas gyud su rig gi se thams cad phyi pa la loai chos lugs rim zhin dyas te gon pa di dañ ny skod du leb yod pa dañ nab jañ sbal tiai yul thams cad chi pas kyab ste gon pa diai stan pe sjin tag gi sa tsams la thug yod nañ da tai bar du ni yul dañ gon pa chos dañ sdes kyab ste de nad gyen la loai chos ma dyas pa yin dug kyañ da ni tso ve thun kyen shan pas tsogs ve zhal dañ s gyañ s ñ ar du las di nañ da ta chogs zhes tha dag stoms te phogs thob rigs nyes dyai skor zigs tsam zhugs yod pe da chin dus sed tsugs thabs su gyun ja zhing gos gal dug kyañ de ni stan don lar dyar dzas pe goñ sa pon bo zhig la rag ga las pi de tai snyan sdon mi reañ zhu spos pa su yañ med pe snyims las kyi dañ nas stan pa je lod kyur va las zhan mi dug gan cag nams kyis ge sjor du migs nas cuñ zat re sdabs kyañ da dus sdar lam du yod pe dyal bi ka gyur rin po che suñ sdos jed pe gyu zhig ni thabs gañ gi sgo nas kyañ ma dig par yod lo re zhin s ñ ar thims tar dag don zhig sdub gyus na stan pa tañ sems can gyi don du gyur ñ es shiñ dag zhin del thogs nams kyi tso rabs kun la phan pe mi lus la snyiñ po len pe skal can du gyur va ni ton mi za ve sto va shin tu chen ñ a nas skabs kyi dus di la thabs de va zhig zhi nas ma juñ pe tsul ni tsa pe tsi spod la du nas shig nyer la zhag na ni mi ded pon du gyur zhiñ dag po yog tu gyur te mal du lus pe re va mi dug sa zhiñ re zhag na ni ma ha ra dza tiai ñ a zhabs su togs pe sa zhiñ na yod pa la ñ ul tha babs payin chin teañ ma deb sogs kyis lus yod ciñ gon pa di dañ po tsugs pe gyu dus sun gyi gyal va sras cas nams kyi jin labs te ñ as can stan pe sgo tan tu chi nañ so tses srun pi nyer por dub pa zhig yin des dug pe di nes dag ta bu snyom chuñ gyin pe rañ shes can nam kyis kyañ lhag sam nam par dag pe smon dug ni dzam liñ ñ as can di na nam den zhi pe stan pa dzin skyoñ dzad pe goñ ma nams la gon de scan dyañ gi jigs pa nas skyoñ nas da duñ ge dun tsogs pe tso va zhis pa s ñ ar srol zhin dyas pi thog slab sum dzin pe dus ste dar zhi n̂ dyas te gyal va zas tsa n̂ sras kyi stan rin po che chi na n̂ gis tsams dins dzin spel sum thub pa da n̂ gyal pe ka gyur rin po chea n̂ di don log sum kyun mi chad du nub cin stan pa yar phel yo n̂ vis this yar za dan jar tsoai da n̂ dub par shog cig pe smon lam gyi n̂ a n̂ nas zhas po zhes rab ja n̂ a ji n̂ na n̂ tsan n̂ a chen loai chu stod za ve na n̂ jis heb kah mir nas la dgas la phebs dus la dags stod nas sku dag thams cad dan su ru phebs skabs ru shod pon ga ga tse gi n̂ tis da n̂ zhil dis par ten da ta ga n̂ s can zhi n̂ khams de je dan nyis pe yul bus lo chag gi this dzad sgo la phebs skabs jen skyems snyan gyi dud ri thod tom bu ve ga n̂ dan gyi dseg de na thugs na n̂ deg pe stgo nas zhus pa yin pe---- tshol jonas thol med pa shu zhes yu n̂ du n̂ ---- la gyus s n̂ on du ji tar ju n̂ ba da n̂ da tar ji tar yot tsul s n̂ on rabs kyi na bar gyud pe thos lo da n̂ yul chogs ga no lha kha n̂ tsugs lag kha n̂ re zhe n̂ s pe kar chags re da n̂ ma n̂ yul chos gyal rim phebs gyi gyal rebs deb thor sogs ga nas lu n̂ rig cad sum gyis te yun du n̂ la zur ko chog ra n̂ dol nyi mas zur shag ta shis nyima kyil pa nas dis pa sar m n̂ ga lam.

22

Tibetan Inscriptions on the Walls Inside the Temples of Alchi Choskhor during 11th and 16th Century A.D.

In 1981 after attending National conference on Buddhism in Himalaya at central Institute of Buddhist Studies, Choglamsar; Leh–Ladakh, I got chance to visit Alchi choskhor alongwith scholars. That time I saw some Tibetan inscriptions on the inside walls of temples alongwith frosco paintings. Thereafter in 1982 I once again visited and endeavoured to write some portion of these incriptions with the help of my lama student. Later I was informed that Yusuf Gergan had collected these incriptions. To see his book on Ladakh hiostory written in Tibetan language I saw some of my collected inscriptions had similiarity. Later I saw David L. Snellgrove and Tadeusz Skorupski book on Ladakh 'The Cultural Heritage of Ladakh' in two volumes, in the second volume I saw my collected Tibetan inscriptions were almost the same. Therefore, I left further research work on isncriptions.

I am here presenting the Roman transliteration of the Tibetan classical language text as collected by Tadeusz Skorupski with mild corrections.

These inscriptions were ineligible, therefore there may be possibility of some mistakes. However, in the interest of research scholars, particularly about the Buddhist history of Ladakh these inscriptions are impörtent.

As we know Ladakh first dynasty starts with Nyi–ma–mgon, who migrated from central Tibet in 9th century A.D.

But through the collected Tibetan inscriptions we have come to know that Ladakh had some princely states before 9th century A.D. When Nyi–ma–mgon migrated, he married with the royal lady of Bro–clan and established his kingdom in Upper Ladakh. Gradually his relations were established with other governors and principalities of Ladakh. He was a religious king, therefore, without any harm got his influence over the heads of principalities. As a result Lotsatva Rinchen bzang po established Nyar–ma monastery near Leh, later with his initiation Alchi and Sumda monasteries were construted.

Summary of the Tibetan inscriptions

Inscription No.1: Salute to Buddha, Dharma and Sangha. By the blessings Alchi temple is constructed. Now people may offer prayer and get puniya. The frescos and wooden art are strange. To see these people may get peace and will be attracted towards religious works; build gonpa, stupa and statues. Thus they may not take birth in the Bhava Cakra[1] and attain Buddhahood.

Inscription No. 2: Salute to Buddha by body, speech and mind. All sentient beings by ignorance take birth in Bhava cakra, skal–ldan–shes–rab[2] who built the Dukhang of Alchi Choskhor says: (i) Bodhisattva[3] vehicle perceives the two aspects of truth[4], pursues the advantage of others. (ii) The Pratyekabiddha[5] perceives the concept of realization pursues own advantages. (iii) The Sravaka vehicle[6] percieves the concept of devoid selfhood, pursues own advantages. (iv) The vehicle of laymen has faith in dharma, pursues the ten vertues[7] and observes the sixteen precepts[8].

Inscripition No. 3: By Buddha blessings skal–ldan–shes–rab got victory over four opposing evils and became the scholar of Sutra and Tantra from Nyarma. We praise his works which he did for the welfare of living beings.

Inscription No. 4: Buddha teachings are useful to all sentient beings. I salute to Buddha with my body, speech and mind. In this world all living beings take birth by ignorance, therefore are suffering some or the other way. Budhisattva like precious tree, selflessly always ready to remove their sufferings and show them the path of enlightenment. By his industrious work living beings started to involve themselves in religious activities, may they get puniya.

Inscription No. 5: The frescos of mandalas representing Aksobhya[9], the thousand Buddhas, Maitreya[10], prajnaparamite[11] etc. May we attain the attributes of Manjusri[12].

Inscription Noi. 6: By the blessings of Manjusri, through four stages of lift one may attain enlightenment after practicing religion correctly. To remove bodily impurity Lama Tshul–khrims 'od has set up Manjusri image to remove vocal impurities, set up Avalokitesvara[13] image and for the removal of mental impurities, set up Maitreya image.

Inscription No 7: Salute to Buddha, Dharma and Sangha[14]. At the north of Jambudvipa many practitioners possess the knowledge of Enlightement. Here by the patronage of Tshul – Khrim 'od , Sumtsak temple at Alchi in Lower Ladakh is built.

A mamber of 'Bro clan arrived Ladakh via Guge – Purang. Later resided at Nyarma and became governor of Phobrang – dbang-lnga. This family after some times established relation with Sumda teacher Byan-chu, who married with the girl of 'Bro clan, had three sons. The eldest was ldan 'od did religious works at Sumda. His nephew was the great teacher was appointed lama with the three wisdoms, planted the victory banner of Dharma.

Inscription No. 8: After the establishment of Alchi choskor, Tshul – khrim 'od popularly known as 'Garland of Butter lamp'.

Inscription No. 9: Lama of 'Gar" Tshul –khrim gyung – drung has written the inscription about Alchi choskhor.

Inscription No. 10: Tashi Namgyal[15], the king of Ladakh is the manifestation of Avalokitesvara, has defeated enimies of Mon–kha[16], Hor[17] etc. extended his kingdom from Rudok to spiti, Suru to Dras, Nubra and Zangskar under his control.

Inscription No. 11: By the initiation of Rin – chen bzangpo[18] the path of the two truth adopted by lamas and by doing religious works protect living beings and Buddha darma.

Inscription No. 12: For the good health of blo – bzang – shes – rab, custodian of Alchi choskhor, devotees arranged sufficient medicines,fragrant water and curative pills.

Explanation of the Inscriptions

Alchi choskor was contructed by the initiation of Lotsava Rinchen bzang po who founded Nyarma monastery, 10 km from Thiksey near Leh towards Leh Manali highway. Skal–ldan–shes–rab then in the middle of elventh century A.D. founded Dukhang and other temples in the Alchi choskhor campus. He got education on Sutra and Tantra from Nyarma under the guidance of Lotsava Rinchen bzang po, later became good scholar of Buddhist tantra and decorated temples in Alchi with the tantric Buddhist deity mandalas. Popular among these are Varocana, Akshobhya, Prajnaparamita and one thousand Buddhas. The inscription No. 10 reveals that during king Tashi Namgyal, temples which were partially damged, repaired with the help of artists, migrated from Kashmir due to muslim invaders. Their interest was to fulfil the gap, intead order. We can see Persian influnence.

The inscriptions inform us the early history of Ladakh when Tibetan empire collapse in the middle of 9th century Nyi–ma–mgon migrated to Ladakh, he married 'Bro – caln lady and established first Ladakh dynasty. We also come to know 'Bro clan families migrated earlier to 9th century from Guge and Purang sides and established states in Ladakh. As 'Bro descendent, lived during 10th –11th century at Nyarma acted as governor. During 16th century king Tashi Namgyal patromised Drigung pa tradition. He considered Alchi choskor as a Drigung pa monastery. Later he sent some artists to repair damaged temples (*Appendex: 2*).

Notes & References:

1. **Bhava Cakra:** Tib srid pa'i khor lo Eng–Pron. Wheel of life. Yama the god of death, cluthches the whole wheel. In the smallest circle at the centre a bog, a snake and a cook symbolize the three cardinal sins of ignorance anger and lust, and are biting are other's tails to show that these evils are inseparably connected. In the narrow circle arounded the innermost circle the light half at the viewer's left shows figures ascending to higher levels of existence, the dark half at the right shows figures descending to lower levels. The six main segments of the wheel depict the six worlds of existence, the dark half at the right shows figures descending to lower levels. The six main segments of the wheel depict the six worlds of existence. In the upper half are the relatively happier realms of the gods (in the centre) the asuras or demigods (at the right), and human beings (at the left). In the lower half are the more wretched realms of the animals (at the left), the pretas or hungry ghosts (at the right) and those tortured in hells (at the centre). In the outer rim of the wheel twelve scenes depict the chain of cause and effect, a blind woman (ignorance) a potter (deeds forming karma), a monkey (restless consciousness), two men in a boat (mind and body), a house with six windows (the six senses), a pair of lovers (contact), and arrow piercing the eye of a man (feeling), a drinker served by a woman (thirst and craving), a man gathering fruit (grasping of and clinging to desired object), a maithuna sonce of "pairing" (a new process of becoming), a women living birth (rebirth in a new existence), and a man a carrying a corpse on his back (death). But all of the forms of existence shown in the entire wheel , even that of the gods at the top, are transient and that is why the whole wheel is held in his claws by the god of death. Cf. Finegan, Jack: 'Tibet: A Dreamt of image', Tibet House, New Delhi & Wiley Eastern Ltd., 1986: 152 –'53.

2. **Skal -ldan -shes - rab:** He studied Buddhist Sutra and Tantra in Nyarma, which was built by Lotsava Rinchen bzangpa in 10th century A.D. skal–ldan–shes–rab, later went to Alchi and built Alchi choskhor in the mid of 11th century.

3. Bodhisattva does not take nirvana, always ready to help living beings who are suffering from one or the other reasons.

4. **Two truths:** They are:

   (*i*) Conventional truth Tib. kun rdzom mden pa dang Skt. samvartisatayam.

   (*ii*) Ultimate truth Tib. don dam bden p'o skt. Parmarthsatyam.

5. **Pratyekabuddha:** Tib. rang sangs rgyas kyi theg pa dang; solitary realizer's vehicle.

6. **Sravaka vehicle:** Tib. ryan thos kyi theg pa dang; Hearer's vehicle.

7. **Ten vertues:** Opposit of ten non – virtues (killing, stealing, sexual misconduct lying, slander, Harsh speech, gossip, covetousness, Malicious thoughts and wrong views).

8. **Sixteen precepts:** In my opinion it would be as follows:

   (*i*) Forbearance with the knowledge of Dharma as the truth of sufferings.

   (*ii*) Knowledge of Dharm as the truth of sufferings.

   (*iii*) Subsequent forbearance with the knowledge of sufferings.

   (*iv*) Subsequent knowledge of suffrings.

   (*v*) Forbearance with the knowledge of Dharma as the truth of source of suffering.

   (*vi*) Knowledge of Dharma as the truth of the source of sufferings.

   (*vii*) Forbearance of knowing subsequent realization of source of suffering.

   (*viii*) Subsequent knowledge of the source of sufferings.

   (*ix*) Forbearance with the knowledge of Dharma as the truth of cessation of sufferings.

   (*x*) Knowledge of Dharma as the truth of cessation of sufferings.

   (*xi*) Forbearnce of knowing subsequent realization of cessation of sufferings.

(*xii*) Subsequent knowledge of cessation of sufferings.

(*xiii*) Knowledge of Dharma as the truth of the path.

(*xiv*) Knowleadge of the path.

(*xv*) Forbearance of knowing subsequent realization of path and

(*xvi*) Subsequent realization of knowledge of path.

9. **Aksobhya:** Tib. mi bskyod – pa; Immovable one. He is one of the five enlightened Buddhas.

10. **Maitreya:** He is one of the eight Bodhisatvas, the others are: Gaganaganjah (space treasure), Samantabhadrah (ever auspicius), Vajrapani (Holder of vajra), Manjusri (Lord of wisdom), Sarvanivaranaviskambhi (Eliminator of Obscurations), ksitigarbhah (Essence of earth) and Khagarbha (Essence of sky).

11. **Prajnaparamita:** She is the goddess of perfect wisdom.

12. **Manjusri:** Lord of wisdom, one of the eight Bodhisativa.

13. **Avalokitesvara:** He is the Bodhisattva of compassion.

14. Buddha, Dharma and Sangha are the three jewels of Buddha Dharma.

15. **Tashi Namgyal:** King of Ladakh during 16th century A.D. He fought against an invading force of Hor (Mongols) and killed many. He erected a castle on the summit of the rNam rgyal rte mo. The main peak overlooking Leh, and just below it built a mGon khang or temple of the protective deities (mgon po). At the feet of the images of these guardian divinities he laid the corpses of the slain Mongols; so by the building of this temple he obtained power to command the services of the demon who turns back hostile armies. With respect to the Buddhist orders, Tashi Namgyal sent gifts to the monasteries in Tibet of Drigung, Sakya, Ganden, Lhasa and Samye, but among the several orders evidently had preference for the Drigung pa. In particular he invited chos rje ldan–ma and then, in association with him, built Phyang (Tib. Phyi dbang) monastery, 16 km northwest of Leh along the Leh–Srinagar highway. Lamayuru monastery, which was originally kadam pa order, was taken under Phyang. Cf. Finegan, Jack; *op.cit*; 174–'75.

16. **Mon - kha:** It seems me that when Tashi Namgyal invaded Spiti, he might faced army from Manali side, probably called Monali army, which would quickly pronounced Mon–kha.

17. **Hor:** In Ladakh Hor means Mongol during Tashi Namgyal regime, Mongols invaded Ladakh from Nubra side. He faced Mongols bravely and killed many.

18. **Rin–chen–bzangpo:** After interruption in the middle of the ninth century due to the persecution of Buddhism by king Langdarma (839 – 842), translation of Sanskrit Buddhist texts was resumed and new Tibetan Buddhist writings were produced as well. Of the translators of this time one of the most illustrious was Rin chen bzang po (953–1055), under whose leadership a whole school of scholars and translators arose to render from Sanskrit into Tibetan not only Sutras and Tantras but also many of the numerous and extensive commentaries attached to these works. It is estimated that by the thirteenth century nearly one thousand Indian scholars and five handred Tibetan translators had worked togather in this large translation works. Cf. Finegan, Jack; *op – cit.*: 13–14.

Roman Transliteration of Tibetan Text on Alchi

Text No. 1

Om tashis par gyur cig /
kon chog lama yid dam lha ces la /
kun ne tang pe kus par chag tshal nas /
rang zhan nges shes kyid chir sal deb tsams /
ling gyi ling chog lhoi dzam bu ling /
ri tho sa tsang pu gyal pod kyi yul /
sa chogs cig achi gon nas su /
dad gus mos pe rin chen tsug lag zhengs /
shing tang rimo zo nams mi × × × × tas /
zhan vang gyud pe × × × × ka × × × × tus kyi
nying ma × × × × tse × × tang longs cod
sod nam / (2) × × × × /
sog du gyis kyi go lo god /
thab tsod thugs long shin tu mang /
sa bon ci tab legs pa nyung /
char chu tus su phebs pa ka /
ton thog das bu thob par ka /
kyen tang lhags pa shin tu mang /
kha dag yin na thog tu. ong /
khan man yin na long du ong
lags la ba na su yang gu /
thel tang ngo tsha su la ang med /
tug gis zhu na su yang tshong /
tug srin mang na jan mo tar /
phug na yod pe jan mo sku /
to na yod pe khor× × × tos /

lo dos tod × × × su la ang med /
de di dus × × nying ma la / (3)
ge va ced pa shin tu ka /
de tar ka var gyur na yang /
ton ka zan gong jin pa pas /
yar ka kul ma mi ga am /
dang la sha chang cin pa pas /
tog × × kho lag mi ga am /
te zhin tus kyi nying ma la /
cin pa chung tu tang na yang /
sod nam chen po yod par ka /
cin pa chung yang tang var ca /
mi dam thob nas cang chub ma dub na /
ngan song sum tu dub pe nas skab met /
tsha dang tug ngal shin tu zod thang chad /
tis skom nyis kyis dus kyang shin tu dub /
sha zhud nyis kyis (4) skad kyang tar zhin tar /
cig kyis cig sod gyug cing dos pa las /
cang chub dub pe dal khom ga la yod
ti mug gyur pas gar do mi shes na /
thar pe lam la dzeg pa ga la shes /
da ta di ru thar lam ma tsal na /
chi dus deb pa din la tshon pa dzug /
cid kyi mi lam bzhin du na tshog thul /
tha med khor var shin tu yum ring khyam /
khor ve dug ngal pag med rab tu nong /
chi mi gyag che ti ru ma song na /
chi me shul thag ring po ci yis dot /

chi me gos lham ti ru ma song na I
thul thag ring poi gos lham su yis jod I
chi me gyags che song tu yod pa la I
mi song dug sogs jet pa shin tu thul I
nas sogs long cod gyuma yin pa la I
chag shing zhen pa te bas shin tu thul I
sog chot nying je met pe zhen pa yang I
sog la bab kar gyot pa cher skyet I
the tsom met pe kye bu ci te tam I
dal khom mi lus thob pa shing tu ka I
dad tson shes rab dan pa te vas ka I
ma nor ton tang the pa te vas ka I
ti ru nges shes kyed pa te vas ka /
ka zhi ti × × × × tu yod pa la /
gyi na tod pa shin tu thul tshab che /
dod nas ma kyes nam tag sems nyid tang /
nam kha tha med ta bur kun khyab /
khyab kyang do dug las kyis khor var khyam /
khor va thon man de dug du ma nyung /
ngan song sum gyi dug ngal zod thag chad /
dos kyang mi phan ting zhin dod du × × × /
mas kyang mi phan shintu × × × × mi thad /
tsol yang mi phan × × × pa reg tu yong /
zegs kyang mi phan × × × kyin × × × × nyung /
gon skyabs ced pa cig kyang thong va med /
sod sog zer va chog nam kun nas lang /
nyun pas did pas thar lam thong pa med /
× × × cing ngang pas kad kyang ngar zhi dar /

tha med khor ve dug ngal ya ri × × × × × /
Khor va tha med di la yid chug nas /
mos gus dad pa loi ting nas kyed /
ma tags gyu ma de la ci chir chag /
di ru dug long med pa yod pa thong /
dus sag yid × × ge va ci mu ca /
ma nor don dang thad na ci zo /
gyi las dos × × × × pa dang /
da ta drang kyen zom pa dang /
la me din gyi don me yis /
ya × × ma nod don dang thad /
dug ngalma pang cang chub chen poi lam
dod yon ma pang gang nang dogs su char /
nang dag ma pang ye nas chos kyi ku /
khor va ma pangs nya dan das pe ngang /
du ze ma pangs ngo vo nyid kyi ben /
dos kyang mi gos ded khen cig kyang med /
dases pa mi gos das sam jod las das /
tsol yang mi gos thams cad nyen du do /
zegs kyang mi gos cang chub de chen nas /
tsal med lhum dub × × × dag chen po yi tsa ci zhin × × × × × /
dan to rang tengs sems nyid nyug me dad /
× × × × med lhum dub cang chub chen po sku /
dus sum gyur med mi da lam du longs /
thar thug das bu sku sum ye shes nga /
gom pa nya ngan thob gyur the tsom med /
tshegs chu don tshe mi bad su yis mod /
jig ten la thong yen nas gon pa dod /
tobs su gyur na gang du nad kyang de /
gyal poi pho tang la sogs gar nod kyang /
te nyid ton na mi dal lhum gyis dub /

× × × × kal pa ---- shes rab --- nyal ba dang /
× × × × kal pa × × × pe do sal /
de shes skyed chir sal debs don ma tsems /
rin cen tsug la lha khang zhings pa tang /
sal debs don ma tsams pe /
ge va dag gis gang thob tes /dag tang thayas
sem can kun /comdan ter segs mi thusgs pa yi /
ge va chen zhos ca ve /
zhing chog tsang mar skyed par shog /
chod sog nyen kur ced par shog /
dam chos tshul zhin nyen par shog /
nyan chad bur du nyes par shog /
tshul zhin togs pa skyed par shog /
× × × × shog /
com tan ter shegs nyi thungs pe /
skil tshad thang sung gi tshad /
thugs kyi tsad tang yon tan tshad /
yon tan thin las dzad pe tshad /
sku tshe yi tshad tang dul ci tshad /
de tag tshad nams thams cad kun /
dag gis nyam par × × par shog /
dzad pe thin las re res kyang /
khams sum sems can tha yas kum /
ngan song gar ma gyis kag nas /
tho ri nas su tan par shog /
tho ri nas pe sems can kum /
thar pe lam la gor par shog /
nyur tu cang chub thols par shog /
ta shis par gyur cig /

zhus legs par gyur cig /
mon lam that × × × gyur cig /
ci cas tsogs su do var gyur cig /
ngang va rang sar dol par gyur cig /
lam la var chad med par gyur cig /
sal debs don ma nges shes skyed pe chos /
nges shes skyes pas tshogs nyis rab ty dzogs /
tshogs nyis dzogs pas dib pa nyis dang dal
de pa nyis dang dal vas /
dzogs sangs gyes /
ge long kal dan shes rab dag gis tsam /
tsam pe las nam tha ru kyol var ca /
tho ru lus na rang gyod mi yang× × × ×
tsam pe las nam tha ru skyol var ka /
ge ni thog ma var tang tha × × × ge
thog med dus nas khor var yun rings khyams /
ta ni khor va di la ce gyas debs /
lus sem dal kar ga × × × reng de do /
long ni tab pas kun nas rab tu long /
tab pa med na chos la jug mi gyur /
chos la mi jug sem can nyon re mong /
mi du la ten la khor va dol /
kal ni chos la kal te rig pa labs /
zhon pe tus su rig pa ma lab na /
gas pe tus su lab pas thar mi kyol /
gun gi me tog var va lhag pas khyer /
dan ni kal par dan te shes rab dan /
kal pas rang zhan re tod skong var ced /
shes rab kyis ni × × × nam zed par tol /

sid sum nam las yang tag dol var gyur /
shes ni nang sid khor das gyu mar shes /
gyu mi vang zhin yin las zhen pa log /
zhen med tos × × × chos kyi sku /
sku sum cer med no vo nyid gyi sku /
rab ni tog pa rab ste nyis me tog /
nyis dzin rang re sa tos da × × × nas × × /
ma tsal nyun po ri va tang gis zhib /
tus sum der shegs ngas ma chin × × /
tag ni tag med nyis × × × × /
tag dzin nyis dal × × × × /
× × × dal med lhum dub chen poi ngang
khor va ma pangs rang dag chen poi log /
gyis ni ge va × × × × ced /
zhan tag ge ve × × × × /
rang ton dub pa mi ge shug la dub /
rang zhan nye × × × × the tsom med /
tsam ni sal debs don ma × × × × tsams /
× × × × /× × × × / rang zhan nges shes kyed pa
ton pe chos /
tsig gi deb ma leg shing ngon / × × × ×
dog na kye vo khas nam zod la zod /
ma nor ton tang dig gyur na
chag tang dang pe yid dor la /
ge tsogs zhang dze ci mi jod /
sod nam nyam par thob par shad /
sal debs don ma zhes ca va /
shag kyi ge long kal dan shes rab kyis dab /
jog so /.

Text No. 2

sku sum tag nyis sngs gyas kon chog tang /
lung tang togs pe dag nyid tam chos tang /
nyan tang cang chub sem pe ge dun la /
lus ngag yid sum tang vas chag tsal te /
dul ca dul ced dul thabs nam sum tang /
dum dum thegs kyi tan chog shad par ca /
ma rig gyu la × × tog gyen gis kyed /
thas bu thar med khor ve nas su kyes /
do va ris tug thul ve nang par shar /
dug ngal sum tan gyad tang cu cig gis /
dung shing zod kyi dug ngal nyams su mong /
te dog dul chir ston pa nam sum jung /
chos skui ston pa cin gyi lab kyi chad /
long skui ton pa rang ge ngo vas chad /
tul skui ston pa tsog tang yig ger deb /
dul ci ton chir khor lo nam sum kor /
chos kyi go mo gyad ti zhi stong sum /
rig can sum la theg pa sum du nang /
nyan thos rang gyal cang sems theg pa sum /
rang tes thong ve den pe tshig sum /
den nyis yir med cang sems thegs pa togs /
pha rol thin tug du × × × × dag gyi
ton por zhan gyi ton du cod /
bu tang chu × × × × go tang ka lag tong /
zang zing long cod × × × × ×
zung va rang zhin med pa rang gyal theg pas tog /
ten del cu × × × × × × /
mi tan nang gi ngos po tan la beb /

rang ton tso che zhan ton cha shas cod /
nyan thos × × × × zag dag med tog /
den pa zhi la yeshes cu tug gis /
nges shes kyet nas nyam su len × × × /
kha na ma tho sum ngas dag gi ton du chod /
vang pe yang tha mi lhai theg pa yis /
las pa nam min chos la yid ches shing /
ge va cu chod mi chos cu tug sung /
zhan ya tus cas ge khyad vas /
log ton skor va chod ten tsig las la sog /
ge ve tsa va sa tab do tab ced /
tshan tags zhi tang danpe yon × × /
yul la tshan sol lob pon sum da va /
nas la tshan sol lob pon Alchi pa
tus la tshan sol lop pon dom ton te
ton la tshan sol kal dan shes rab bo /
kal dar dan pa mi lus tsang ma thob /
jor va dan ma zas nor tong phul che /
shes rab dan pa zab moi tog pa /
rab ga sog sa cu tab cig cig dot /
don la tshan du sol ve lob pon gi /
khor ve tshan nyid gyu ma ta bur tog /
zar nor long chod nying po med shes pa /
stong me nying po la × × × ve chir /
gom ra long don lha × × × × zhengs su sol /
de la ten na zes nor longs cad tang /
× × × × × × × × × /
zhon nu rig pa lebs na gas na gyod pa med /
× × × × la ja nas de va chi ma dabs /

dub pa pa den tsheg tha chog /
zhan yang Alci yul tang de la nas pe mi /
dei nas lug chung zad shad par ca /
phu sum ri yis skor vas ku thog chos kun nyung /
da sum chab kyis cad pa da long ta ra met /
sa la ci tab × × × pas rin chen du nat chung /
gya × × ngam thot med pas so nam thot par la /
de na nas pe pe tsan nyid ni /
tsun chen ge zhung dam pe chos sung vas /
shes nyin yon tan tham cad ve nas /
ya rabs dung seng ngo tso /
thil dan dan pas /
nga zhung chi thag thams cas ve nas /
shar pa dap tsal kher kham dang dan pa /
gyog shor she mong tham cad ve nas /
de la so × × × × yon tan tha yas chog /
yon dag jor pa car gis gyu cas shing /
lha zo rig pa can gis kyen cas te /
lha khang tsug lag chen zheng pe /
ge va di med sod nam kun che o ?
shag kyi ge long dags dan aod kyis deb
nong pa chis na khas nam zod pa zhes /
mang po dag la bu kye ci zhin tu /
khas nam ge legs zang zes zod par rig /
tan sun tan sum dul × × × × ai thig pa sum /
dam dam thigs kyi cang ser dzogs zhes ca.

Text No. 3

kal pa du mar tsogs sag las /
dan par ka ve dal jor thob /

shes nyen phu yu jung pa yis /
rab chog mug mi don la kal /
dan pa phun tshot khen pa yi /
dal jor don yod don nyis chir /
chog nam me lus thug su chud /
zab mo don tog las tho dan /
shes ça ma lus tag pe chir
do va nam kyi tso va teb /
nam dag nying zhus yong kheng pa /
dol ve thab ni na tsog shes /
rab chog dam pe chos la skal /
nyis med zab moi tog pa dan /
nod dan nams kyi dul thab shes /
di chir na kun pa rab /
ca thabs di la lags thab sum /
log zhin lags tang lug zhin lag /
dum bu dum bur lag pao /
tang po nyid kyis tsan zhi tan /
nyis pas cii yon tan stan /
× × × × × × × × × × × × ×
× × × × × × × × × × × × ×
× × × × × × × × × × × × ×
sum pas dzad pe yon tan stan /
zi pas khyad par yon tan stan /
shes rab dam vas legs pa ma shes kyang /
aol tam gyis pas khas nam dzad par zhes /
om ta shis par gyur cig /
nyi thun chog kyi dud zhi las gyal var gyur cig /
di ta chos nam kun kyi dag po ni /

kye med kha da jod med kun la khyab /
gyur med na tshog ton la chag tsal nas tan /
pe nam zhag dzad la chag tsal tod /
ci tar zho tog mar zhin tu /
rig dug nas su lhun kyis dub /
chos nam mi las tshul tsam tu /
kyong dzad cang chub sem pe rigs /
ge ve shes kal dan shes rab khong /
zho nu rab tu jung nas ka thub nyam su langs /
do gyud nyis la thar lam tsel ve rig kyi bu /
da ma jang pe las tho can la chag tshal tod /
thos sam lob nyir dzad pe dus da tu /
mar yul nyar ma choskyi pho dang du /
khan po la sog khas pa nam kyi thug zin nas /
khas pa mi tog dang tsi ta bu cud kyis khengs /
kho nyid bung va ta bus thug kyi cud nam jibs /
shes rab jag kyi de nod bung tsi ta bui /
dam chos du mi ro nyong khong la chag tshal tod /
ge ve shes nyen kal dan shes rab khong /
chag gya chen poi ton tog do don chog cur shar /
nying poi don la tshon med tshig gyi do dog dal /
ma cos × × × × ton la kal dan pho mo tod la tod /
las can mos pa kha cig khyed la × × × × cas nas /
pag sam /
shing chen ta bur yon tan tham cad gyal /
bum pa zang po ta bur kun gyi re dod kong /
rin chen ter gyi jung nas kho la chag tshal tod /
kun gyi ge ve shes nyen kal dan shes rab khong /
dam nang nad kyis zin pa zung zin dud pa dol /
cin labs tsos ma da vab thul pe kho dog gyur /

do don thun gyis dub la chag tshal tod /
ton tshe sod nam sags pas ta ta jor pa dan /
thug la ser na med pas cin pa thog med tong /
cas pa din du zo vas zhu la din lan sags /
do va kyab chir ka vas dzong dang zam
pa dzad mig med ge va gom ra yang tang yan tu dzad /
sod nam sam mi kyab pe gyal yum dang kyi sel /
yab zhui dzad tshal nyag chir tsug lag khang chen di /
dad pas gyu cas jor vas khyen vas nas /
jor va du sa Al ci yul dir zheng /
cam sem dam pe pu gyal dod /
rig pe jung nas nga ris tod /
yon tan kun dan Alci nas /
rig gyur dan pa doi de /
khyen pa nyis dan × × × pon gyis /
khas gyog nyis dan ta zo la /
chag med dod yon nga phul nas /
lha khang khyad phag di zhing pas /
yon dag chod nas khor cas nams /
sod nam ye shes tshog dzog te /
ku sum ye shes nga dan pe /
tham cad khyen nyid thob par shog /
pod pa gom chen jung nas shes rab kyi /
zhung tang man ngag la ten cas nas /
od zer sal ve tshig gi theng va di /
lo la shar tshad tsam zhig deb pa la /
khas pa mod pe rang zhin te /
khas su re nam ci chir mod /
tshig la tag nas kyon jod na /
kun khyen la ya kyon chag pas khas /
dzog so /

Text No. 4

com dan das mi thung pa la na med pa /
yang dag par dzog pe camg chub tu don /
par dzog pe sang gyas shid nam pa tham /
cad khyen pe ye shes nyes par gyur pe
cang chub kyi shing rin po che na dun las dub pa /
pad du pag tshad dum yod pa /
tei dong poi pang du pag tshad gya yod /
dom su gyag dag ched kyi khors la /
dei yal ga nam ni pag tshad dun tong dun stong yod /
tei khot yug tu ni pag tshad zhi thi yod de /
cang chub kyi shing dei yal ga tang lo ma tang yal ga thiu dag/
lung gyis kun du skyod pa na /
te dag la nyan pa tang yid du od pa
tang chag par gyur pe da kar cung va ni /
lhai sel nyan yan lag dum tang dan pa
dag rol moi lob pon khas pa sil va dag
las kyang jung par mi gyur ro cang chub kyi shing te las /
pha rol tu chin pa than cad kyi da dang ngon par shes pa tang /
dang po tang /
tob tang /
cang chub kyi yar lag tang /
lam gyi yan tham cad kyi da kad lhi
yang la shin tu das pa
nyin zhing yid du ong va dag jung te /
sem can gang dag gis da kad thos par gyur
va de dag than cad kyang dod chag dad
dal va sem pa jes su dan pa zhes ca ve ting nas zin thob bo /
zhan yang ngas gyas kyi zhin te na /
ngan song sum dag med te sem can nyal dad /

dud doi kye nas tang /

shin jei jig ten ni /

ter kyes pe sem can te tag tham cad ni /

ge va cui lam tang dan pe she tag go /

zhan yang ngas gyas kyi zhing te na /

sem can nam la jei am dan gyi ce dag tu ce va med te /

tei mi nam la kol ve shos × × × yur len pe /

sam pa yang me do /

te cii chir zhe na sem can nam la dag tang dag gyir zhin pa med pa med pe chir ro /

sang gyas kyi zhin dei sa zhi tham cad thang thil ṭar nyar va /

kan tsha lin di ka tar rig na de zhing /

ser gyi ka kha tog tar tug la /

lhai nor bu rin po che cas shing /

pad ma ser gyi dog can dab ma ce va thag tong dang tan pa dag gis leg par gyon pa /

me tog man da ra va tang man da ra va chen po dag don par tam va /

× × × × × dum tang /

tsher ma tang /

gyo mog tang /

seg ma med pa /

dam dog tang da pa tang mi zang va dor sel med pa do tang ri med pa te sa zhi de la khang pa zhag × × × ×× × ×ram zhes ced la /

deg re sar zhes med to /

zhan yad sang gyas kyi zhing dei mi nam la /

kha dog ngan pa tang di mi zhim pa dag tham cad kyi thams cad du med to /

te cin chir zhen deai sems can nam ni nyon mong pa dug sum chung chir ro /

zhen yang sang gyas kyi zhing te na sem can nam la /

sad pa tang tshing va tang /

go dar zhung pa dag thams cad kyi tham cad du med do /

sang gyas kyi zhid de na mu tegs tham cat kyi tham cad tu met do /

sang gyas kyi zhing te na shid jon pa nam tag tu me tog tang das bu chag pe sha tag go /

zhan yang sang gyas kyi zhing de na mi nem kyi gos ni pag sam gyi shing las cung ve gos /

kha dag gos kyi ca va cet /

gos te dag kyang dog sal zhin di zhim po tang tan la /

kha dog mi nyam pa sha tag te /

per na lhai me tog nam kyi di sung na

tsgag ci da va di zhin du /

de dag gi gos kyi di yang de dag da la /

pag sams kyi shing de la dug pana de dag gi di ci da va zhin du /

de tang gis yong su lod cod da yong di de dang da va nyid tu gyur bas /

gos te tag gi di tang kha tog la nyam par gyar va med la /

te tag gi gos na mas shin tun mang zhin phal che ve chir /

te tag yang tang yang tu je zhin tang zhin gon par cet to per na sum cu tsa sum ve lha nam yit la ci sam pe kha zas ga jung va te zhin tu /

jig ten gi kham tei mi te tag kyang kha zas ci lha bu dag tod pa de ta bui kha zas tag /

tam tu rin po chei not dag nas jung do /

mi te tag gi kha zas te tag ni kha dog tang di am ro lhai kha zas tag /

ma dag las mi thuo /

mi te tag sang pa tang ci va tang chi lam tang nabs dag med /

dod pa na cod pe lha nam zhin no khang tu mi dag dug pe nas /

rin po che na dun las dub pe khang pa tsog pe nang na rin po che na dun las cas pe thi dag gi tang tu /

shing bal par tshang can gyi tan leg par teng pa tam pa tag jung va gyur zhing khang pa tseg pa de tag tu khang × × × × pe yong su cad va khnag las /

mi nam chui ca va ced pe jing nam pa na tsog yan lag gyad tang dan pe chus gang pa jung te dzeng au te dag gyang ser gi ce ma × × × ×× × × ×× × × ×lhai shid nya ngan tshang kyis kor pe sha tag go /

de dag gi mi nam tam pe chos kyi ga las ga var ced cig nas so /

mi de dag gi dung du yan lag gyad dang tan pe chus kang pe jing dag jung zing /

gal te jes su dang bar /

dod na yang jes su dang par gyur la /

mi mang par dod na yang mi nang bar gyur ao /

sang gyas kyi zhing de na ha cang yang mi do ha cang yang mi dang ve lung /

tag dang te jam va tang de va tang × × × × dag dang do /

di zhim pa tang yid tu ong ve lung tag dang te /

lung te dag gis mi de tag tang lha de tag gi los kyi ca va kam /

kham ced to /

gal te la la zhig dag la lhung tang vad gyur ro /

gal te zham tag mi dot na /

te tag mi × × × × pi lung gyis phog par mi gyur zhin gang tang gang gyi tsho /

tod pa te tab di te tag la lung dang var gyur so /

sang gyas kyi zhing de na ta ta × × × × sang gyas kyi zhing ten /

bud med tag la yong pe kyon tag med na /

sang gyas gyi ti na bud med ni dag mi sung /

zug mi gas pa × × × × × dis pa met × × × × jed × × × ×

dod pe long cod tag × × × ×shes pa cas pa mi zo va tho va tang ci nyis su mer va tang /

dag tog tang zhi chog kyis vo ceng pa tag yin te /

sha sii bu sang gyas kyi zhing te na /

bud med la bud med kyi kyon te tag met te /

te ni sang gyas kyi zhing tei don gyi mon lam gyi khyad par gyis gyur pa yin no /

de dag gi but med ni yon tan tham cad tang tan pa yin te /

bud med rin mo che ri miai bud med kyi yon tan tag las shin tu tas shing /

lha mo'i yon tan tang tan × × × × × × × × /

sang gyas kyi zhing te na bud med rin mo chei × × × × × × × × san ggyas kyi zhid de na bud med kyi tan gang yin pa de tag ni /

de tag gyi yon tan gi gal na /

bud med rin mo chei yon tan dag ni gya'i char yang nyi var mi do /

tong gi cha tang /

gyai tong cha tang /

ce va gi cha tang /

ce va gya tong gi cha tang /

ce va gya tong gi cha tang /

ce va thag thig gyi tong gi cha tang /

dang tang × × × tang pa tang /

pes tang /

gyur yang mi zod to /

sang gyas kyi zhing na /

kyes pa tang bud med tag × × × × tu × × × pa cad pe chir /

dus jar med × × × × × × × × tas pa tsam khyis kyes pa dei dod chag rab tu zhi var gyur te /

shin tu yang yid jung zhing pang nas /

mi dug pa la dod chag tang dad ve ting de dzin thob vo kyes pa des bud med la tas pa tsam gyis dum par gyur te nuis kai dod chag zhi var gyur nas ma la na nas pe khyeu am bu mo lus tang sem kyis kyang di da ve de va per na /

sum cu tsa sum pe lha nam /

rin po chei × × × × zhal med khang na ga zhing chog tu × × × × ced na /

× × × × × × × × va zhin no de na me la na nas pa de dag nyin zhag dun gi var du de va nyong nas tsa var gyur zhing /

budi med dum me lus tang sem kyis kyang /

sam tan nyis pa la nyom par zhung pe ge long tham cad kyi tham cad tu de gyur pa zhin no /

bud med bu tsa va na yang / mi zang va dang × × × × × × mi × × × × dag med de /

sang gyas mi khyung pa dei sang gyas kyi zhing na

gang gi tshe kyes pa dang bud me × × × khyeu am bu mo dag can thong × × × × × × × × dog par gyur te de ni sang gyas dei don gi mon lam gyi khyad par gyis gyur pa yin no de na sang gyas chos kyi gyal po las gyal po zhan med do. /

Text . No.5

× × × × × × phel tar va nyam × × × × rang × × × × zad por gan gyur cig /

ngas mas mi da zung × × × × ngan /

sem can don la gong pe la med kon chog sum /

yid kyis tul cig tsham pe nas × × × × × × × lus dang cas te sheg su × × × × /

kon chog sum la chag tshal lo /

kon chog sum la kyab su chi /

× × × × × × kul nya dan mi da sol va × × × × × × × ge ve tsa va × × × × /

× × × × × sems /

dam pa dag gis kyed par gyi mon pe sems dang rab tan zhing /

jug pa pha rol chin dug cod /

× × × × × × × ×× × × × /

do va phan chir sang gyas dub par shog /

chog cui sang gyas dang gyal × × × la sog pa dum sum gyi × × × × × ×thob pa med pa × × × × tha ma dal thug × × du /

× × × × med pa nam pa dan × × × × /

mi ge va cu dang /

kha na ma tho va sum dang ci va zhi tang /

log pa gyad tang /

× × × × chos la kur va tab pa tang /

zhan × × × × sog ngag kyi tam chig tang /

× × × × jang chub sem pe dom pa tang gal va tang /

× × × × tho × × × × tang gal ve ga chag ci ches × × × × /

sang gyas × × × × par gyid × × × × × × tag

gis kyil khor gyi lha tshog tang /

mi thung × × kod × × × /

kal pa zang poi sang gyas tong tang jam pa tang /

tso gyad la sog pe ten zhing pa tang yum shes rab kyi pha rol tu chin ma zheng pa tang × × × × sog pe dus cas tang du ma jas × × × × ge ve tsa va ci gyi gyis pa la tan nas tag × × × ×yas pe sem can tham cad kyi tsa na med kyi ja × × × × thob × × × × gyur cig /

× /

× × × × × × × × × × × × × × ×me tog pat ma la /

kat cig te la dzus nas kye var sog /

jus kyes kad × × × × × × × × la ni /

jam pal ta bu top tang kha tog zi jid shes rab than sum tshog pa tang /

lha tang lui gyal po × × × × ×long cot phum sum chog × × × × tsang pa ta n'ai × × × × jang /

kun pa yi × × × × × × × × com dan de sheg mi thung la /

chag tshal chod × × × × × × × nyen kur jed par shog kam /

Text. No 6

Om ta shi par gyur cig /

× × × × rab rang zhin jam gon la dud de /

tan × × × × × × × tshod zhin pa di var ja na tshot tang po cis pe tus kyi tshe /

nga gyal tsa tang tu ve las las med /

yon tan tag gyang lab pas mi lab te /

chu la ri mo dis pa ci zhin no zas tang long cad × × × pe du shes med

snyon va tag gi shes pa dag tang tshu /

na tshod nyis pa dar la bab ve tshe /

so nam na zhis zas tang long cot bags /

gyu tsal yig tses phong tsal las sog jang /

thos tang sam ve ses rab la vat la .

rig pe nas nga dag la khas par lab /

yon tan med la zhan dag kur mi jed /

cho ris med la zhan dag mi kur zhing /

yon tan can gyi thabs dun na dod /

yon tan can tang sa dag rgyal po nyis /
rgyal po rang gi ngas ris dag gis kur /
yon tan can la kun kyis tod cing kur /
de chir yon tan dag la rab tu vat /
nor ni jig ten mi gyan /
nor gyis lo phang kyed pe gyu /
zas tang long cot la ten nas /
kon chog la ma chot cas pa /
chi mi lam na den ve kyen /
nor gyis jei thug kyang zin /
de zhin phur mi za yang srong /
nyam po og tu nor gyis chut /
de chir zas tang long cot bags /
× × × × × pe kye bu ni /
de ni jig ten lo zat yin /
per na shi ve ro zhin no /
na tshot sum pa dar yol tshe /
nying je dug cing phong pa so /
jang chub sem pe cot pa yin /
dad pas lha tang kon chog chot /
jig ten chi me gyags che yin /
gus pas la ma × × × × ten /
sem nyid ton pe me long yin /
tang po la ma tam pa la /
tos pa met pe nyen kur gyis /
la ma tam pa nyes jas la /
de jes gong pa ngon par ja /
× × × jung shes rab kyis /
yang tang yang gom par ja /
sem nyid sal ve don tog na /

cod lam nam zhi chos kyi ku na tshod ve pa gas shing gud pe che /
zhon pe lang tsho zang tang za mas zad /
go la sha met kha la so yang met /
mig gis mi thong na va da mi thos /
do yang mi nus gus nas gog cing do /
mig pa mi sal dam pa nyam par gyur /
nyam len mi nus tha mal dag tang tshung /
de chir zhon ve che la chos la bot /
mi lus rin can thob nas tam chos ma cat na /
rin can ling nas × × × cas pa tang /
gya tshoi ling du gom tin shi va zhin /
te chir zhon ve dus su chos la bot /
yon tan can la tham cat mon pe zhi /
dag med lam tu long na thar pe lam /
ge ve las la tson na tho ris thob /
long va dag la nying jas cin pa tang /
tshul zhin tam chos cad na jang chub thob /
thim don tam la nas pa kun kyi dog /
'od sal gyad la kyes na tshe dir das bu thob /
yon dag ge long tshul thim 'od /
long cod nying po med pa la /
tong ve nying po bung ve chir /
ku sung thug kyi dung ten zheng /
lus kyis dib pa cang pa tang /
tul ku thob par ca ve chir /
kui ten tu jam pal zheng /
ngang gi dib pa can va tang /
long ku thob par ca ve chir /

sung ten can ras zigs tang zhang /
yid kyis dib pa cang va tang /
chos ku thob par ca ve chir /
thug kyi ten tu jams pa zhang /
dag pa tha yas gyal ve ka /
dan pa phun tshog × × × × sal jas /
od sal jung jug gyud la kyes /
dag tan od ches te la gyi /
shag kya ge long dag tan od kyis deb pa lag /
nong pa chis na zod par sol /
dag cag ge ve las nam de dag gis /
khan po lob pon dus sum khyen × × × /
tha yas ma lus sems can tham cad × × /
shar chog ngon gi zhin du kye var shog dzogs so. /

Text No. 7

Om ta shis par gyur cig /
ter met cos dal nam khe ngo ao nyit /
mig met thug je chen poi lho tin phob /
chi met dut tsii char pas do ve /
ge ve lo tog kyet pe ngas gyas chot /
nam × × × ying thar pe jo vo las /
dub ve phag lam gyat kyis nyi ma kar /
ton pe × × × gi ot zer chog cur khyab /
do ve ma rig sel ve tam chos chot /
cang chub sem kyi dong po nying jes kyet /
yon tan yal ga lo das me tog gis /
do ve dung sel lha mii go phang /
chag lam das cas ten pe ge dun chot /
× × × dog gon jigs su rung var ni /

ti mug gis tong thar × × × lam tor vas /
thog met dus na yun ring khyam pa la /
mig cet that lam ton pe la ma chot /
ling gi ling chog lhoi dam bui ling /
ren chen ca dung ji × × gyis khyab /
pag tshat tung tong ta gya shing ti cibs /
gyal vas cang × × chot nyes × × × dan /
ti met dud tsi jung nas gyal poi khab /
yon tan dan par ḍag pe nas chen mang /
dzam ling cang chog kha va can gyi jong /
ri tho sa tsang pu gyal bot kyiyul /
cang chub sems tan dub thob namskyi gang /
khas tsun tu mi jung nas ng'a ris tot /
mar yul mat kyi la dvags Alci dir /
tsu lag khang chen rin chen tseg pa di /
zhing pe yon dag lob pon tshul thim ot dung
rus che × × ya rab doi de /
gung don kyil na nyi za nyis po dzes /
dog moi sa la do chog nyis po che /
tong pe don tog lob nyir ja mi tsal /
rus pa do × × ge tsang chat mi chal /
se per × × yul ge du dang kyi /
× × × doi khyar bar tag zang di /
co kyes zhang dung sa ja × × nu jor /
chii da dul nang gi bu bang kyon /
jei × × zin × × × chi bor kur /
lha × × kor la sog la × × ×/× × × skab ri tsam na /
tsho las bo zing gang las × × ×
× × × kyi nyad mar stad /

pho dang bang lai lon po cas /
× × tsei bar × × × × × × × × /
kan zhi phu das bar ling cat /
sum di lob pon cang chub × × × × × /
cam mo khim thab jas nas sras sum × × /
sras kyi che shos × × × dan ot /
og min de dan nas × × × × sum bar /
mig met thug dza do ve don la con /
khas tsum nyis dan cin lab nus pa che /
de lha nam thong sras kyi ngos dub phul /
jor pa che zhin zas nor tong pa × × × /
tug phog kun kyi nyen chog mi go /
kui gya ma tum × × × khang zhens /
dei on po lab pon chen po ni /
tan don mi × × × gyi pal /
man la nying tse la ma mi bor kur /
shes rab sum gyis × × × nang do tog cad /
dul ja mang po thar pe lam la kong do ve
gon po shag kya seng ge'ai /
tan × × × nub kar chos kyi gyal tshan tsug /
khas pa chen po de not sum la cang /
khyud te zhii mang dag rin po × × × /
tsheg cad /
gyad la lag thab dug /
tang po kyus su lag pa tang /
de na × × × yig lag pa tang /
tang por nyis par tshig bar dun /
thed la lag pe thab yin no /

de nas thur tu tshan tshan lag /

× × × tshil yig de zhin × × × /

chig cat gyat la × × × gyur /

jod ja cir tod sum tang ni × × × × × met gyis tod /

cu ru shes na khas pa yin /

× × × × tshig gyad ma tod pa cu /

tshig cad nyi shur gyur × × × × shag kyi ge long gar gyis kod.

Text No. 8

tsag lag khang di zhing pe sod nam kyis /

dag tang nam kha mi sem can nam /

nyur tu dzog pe jang chub thob na ni /

× × × × ×× × × × × × × × × × × × × × ×

bo ban lob pon tshul thim × × × × ×

× × × × × × × tsug lag khang zheng

pe tshul mi ton chos mar mei theng va zhes ja va /

ton pa shag kyi ge long ngos dub shes

rab gyi dis pa las jung sod nam ci ches pa /

Text No . 9

Tei dong can gar gyis rab tu kod /

sha kyi ge long gar lo tsha tshul thim yung dung.

Text No . 10

Omi sva ti set ha /

khen pe kha la /

thug je'i nyi ma shar /

lo dos 'ot zer chog cur rab ga nas /

do ve ma rig mun pa sel dzat pe /

tin la ma nam la chag tshal lo /

zab zhi tos dal 'ot sal du ma cas /

tag chad tshan mar rang dol bu mi lam /

phan de cung nas ye shes con pe zot /
yum chen pha rol chin la gus chag tsha lo /
zhon nu nyid las tan las rab tu cung lab
pa sum la mig das ta bur ces /
dur mig dzin pe che tu var dag pe /
chog las nam gyal zhab gus tshal /
kye lag shes ce kha la rab kyil khor gyas /
do dag chos kyi od zer × × × × /
ka zang tu ci tshog nam min dzat ve
shes rab chos zang zhab la gus pas dud /
ling gi chog gyur lhoi dzam bu ling khu khab cor nam sa nyis kyi bar /
Thong ngam dzes pe ku khar tho la tsan /
Thos pas zil non Alu di gum dir /
nam cag thog bab sing gei tsal tang /
thung pha rol da te jom × × pur tsal gya /
dang de nyen go kyong zhing din can pha vas lhag mi vang gong ma ta shis nam gyal la lus dag yit sum gus phas chag tshal lo /
bot yul sot nam tos las leg /
thung pe can ras zig vang cul ve gyal po khyet /
kun gyi tsug tu khur vas kyit pe nyi ma shar /
ta shis nam gyal tag tu gyal gyur cig /
Ae ma ho /
mon kha hor sog va da nam tul /
ru tog be ti man cat /
su ru hem pab kyen cat /
nang gong nub ra zang kar tshin da ris nga yog /
cas tung pa kun kang tse cas chos kor gyut pe lug la /

shes rab sod nam tag gi bu gon cog kyab zhig sod ca va la ge ve kul ma ce pe dog la /

Alci chos don dub lo do de don dub kyab cun nyis /

ta shis kyab don dub ta shis don dub pal cor tsun pa nam kyi tsug la ga khang di la zhab tog phul /

pul kul la tag mo od cam kyi dung × × yu tshal ca tud pa lag cor ris × × yu cung cig × × thong cig ge long sod nam pal car 'ai thing tang ma thig si tung vas rag bum cig /

tung pa lo zang de legs kyi nat de la nas khal gyat chang nga /

yu ru na de pas tshal zo dun kag /

tshal li cos dul thsal gya ram cung /

mul ve co co je mas kag /

pheng kya rag /

pho gar na tsk cos ras /

cag nang cig kye rag /

dan na pa cag cig cung /

bon mo che don dub pal /

kon cog kyab gang nam la zhab tog cas /

chos kar ras mug ton par ton cas /

don× × × × × sod nam ta shis × × yul pa sa ni /

nam gye si ka ru pon nam tsim rab cas /

geo leg so /

ta shis par gyur cig /

Om su va ti va dzu ye sva ha /

Om sva ti si dm vo mo na cung nam kyi lob zang da va zhang /

pon nam shes pe zhab tog leg phul /

ta shis par gyur cig /

mon nam sha chan g kyis

tshim par cas nas zhing /

he he he.

Text No. 11:

la ma ka gyud sang gyas kal zang tang tshung zam ling con /

chos je do gon yab sras nyam med tse va chan po yis /

rin chen nor bu vang gi gyal pos do nam tsim pa dzad /
la ma tsung med do ve tet pon nam la kyab su chi /
kon chog di med cung va dab kon 'u tu va tar /
gyal va kha tar chos cing tga pa lhun dub dus ma cas /
lo dos tha yas khyen tse nus tang don nyis tan pa yo /
rin po chei cung khung ku sum cer med sang gyas nam la tod /
ka tang tan cos la sog tad gi chos nam vang chen sa zhi da /
kon zad zhi va chag dal gya tso tang tsung den nyis lam /
yon tan phun tshog tog pe chos ni pag sam shing tang tshung /
tam pe don ban dam chos ten chen don ma nam la tod /
dinlan sob chir × × pe ge dun nam la rab tod na /
gi ne das bus ben dur mi log sem tap chen po nam /
dag zhan thar chin tan pe × × × × × /
tung khad tshog kyi phag pe ge dum namla tod.

Text No . 12

Alci gon gyi ku nyer lo zang shes tab ku tsho zang va × × × sung dis ten shing tas va shag kha ve cis cor va yid to dir yang de var chis tshad bul tsa de kha tsug lag khang gi skor kor kyab gon rin po cher nyan bul zhus par gyas pa la thi thag cig tang tid pal tong thag cig tha ma nga gya gyas ting dus sum gyi kor tshad tang kha kong do va tang tang gyi lo zus tang tun pa cas chog pheb cung vas gong jag zhu / ten chag tung cin ten du tsi kye dun sad chab ril bu tang ha kha tag tang cas shes la man khang phul.

Co mo cam pa chos zin pun nyis kyis kor tshad de zhus nas jes su ma ni gya tsa sum zhin dub pas dis kyang ve tan pa dar zhing gyas par gyur cig tis de kab su tshu ang dul a jo pal dzon dul ri cung.

Appendex — 1

Tibetan Manuscript on Lamayuru Monastery during 1834-40

Tibetan Text in classical language

Thabs mkhas thubs rjes sha' khyi' rigs su'khrungs gzhan gyi mi thub 'dut kyi dbungs 'joms pa /

gser gyi lhun po lta bur brjed p'i sku sha' ky'i gyal po de la phyag 'thal lo /

zhes mchod par brjod p'i tshig gis sngon bsus te glong bar bya b'i ton la te yang mang yul mnga' ris la dvags sham phyogs phyi pa dang nang p'i sa mthams su khod p'i thub bstan byung drung dgongyi lo rgyus sa bcad tsam bkong pa la sngon bod chos gyal gyi' gtung brgyd pa dvags la phebs dus la dvags stod phyogs rnams su ni yul grong ma chags par thang stong dang yung stong tu yod cheng /

sham phyogs rnams su yul chags pa rnams 'brog pa zhes kla klos bzung nas lung pa re nas sjong chung ri byas gcig la gcig dgra jag 'gyod cing bsnga b'i tshe byu ru'es p'i lung pa 'di mtsho ru 'khyil nas yong skad re shig dgro nyi ma gung pa gya gar nas kha che'i yul du phebs skabs shig la lho phyogs 'dir phebs pas yul 'di'i lung pa ni mtso ru 'khyil te yong pas shar pyogs kyi ri'i rtser phebs te gzigs pas mtso 'khyil b'i ngus na gad pa 'bur po zig rtse 'thon te yodg pa kun gyis mthong ba de la phyag bstan te pha gyi mtsho de skams pa dang dkyil 'bur po de'i stong du ston pa sha' kya thub p'i chos mngo sngags zung 'brol gyi bstan pa rin chen ge 'dun gyi sde dang bcas pa tshugs par 'gyur so /zhes lung stan mdzad pas shar ri'i sa phyogs de la skam' bur sheis meng du thogs de nas dgro nyi ma yung pa rzhu prul gyis mthso dkyil gad 'bur rtse der phebs nas gzhi bdag gi klu sogs la chu gtor sbyin nas phyag gis 'khar gsil brkyang ste mto'i mtsho mjug rzhu 'phrul gyis bkral nas kha che'i yul du phebs song nas 'dam sing gnyis thon pas sa den senge sgang zhes ming du thobs chu gtor mdzad dus kyi gtor bzhi nas dbus phyogs la spungs pa gang stongs dang rlang 'dres bdo gyung drung ris kyi ljangs p'i myu gu skyes yod pas rjes su sh'i der dgon pa chags dus byung drung dgon zhes ming du thogs 'dug de rjes jo na' rso gya gar nas kha che'i yul du phebs p'i dus gcig la lho pyogs nas zangs kar rjongs khul phug tu phebs shing de nas brgyung sa phyogs 'dir phebs te gyul drung byu ga skyes p'i gang p'i rtse dir phug sa byas gdan chags pas thog mar ni na ro p'i zhabs kyis ba cags p'i gdan sa yin 'dug cing rjes na ro p'i sku thob nas bzungs kha che'i yul du nas gyung drung dgon di'i bar gyis yul sde thams cad la nang pa sangs gyas p'i chos yugs dar gyas su-yong tshul yang de lta bu rig gi yul mang po dang spal ti yul sogs la sku nyan ga gyi brag dang lha kha nyul po ma gi mchod rten rnying pa song bstan p'i lag rjes phyong skang dang rje 'bri gung 'jig rten mgon po'i che ba mrjong b'i gngam las kyang nub phyogs na 'aphru sha dang 'gyi ling tshun chad ng'i 'og tu tshung cis gsungs pa dang mthun 'dug pa dang des mtshungs dgon 'di'i chos sde dar gyas yong tshul yang grub thob chen po grung pa sjang pa 'as pa la ngogs bod na gdan phebs p'e skyes bu ngam pa 'ga' nas bstan pa 'dzin skyongs spel gsum yod p'i thos lo dang 'khrul med zhib ti gi yig che yong pa re ni bstan p'i dar rgung kha shas byang thal b'i mthams su thas kya 'phro stongs skabs dbye su yal bas da lta rags rim tsam gyi thos lo ni sngon thog skabs shig tu phri dpon btag rdar skyabs chis p'i dpon po nig gis kha che'i sa mthams nas mang yul la tshun chang srid tu bzung ste yong skad des mnga' ris skor gsum na mtchan yongs su grgas p'a lo ts'a ba rin chen bzang pa gdan drangs te kha ches mtsams mdung bzhilnas bzungs te so'i la tshun chantu mthod rten rgya dang brgyad lha khang brgya dang brgyad bzhings pa sogs bstan pi bya ba rlabs spo che'i sgo nas ljong 'di'i skyes gro'i bsod nams kyi nyin byed gsal bra mdzad pas de'i nang tshan gyu'ng drung dgon 'di'i yul gyi phyogs bzhi dbus dang lnga ma lha khang lnga rgyung ste bzhi'i rten dang brten par bcas pa bris bur mtha' yas pa dang phyi ru rgyud nas gsungs p'i mthot rtin mang po bzhengs 'dug p'i de ltar thun mong dang thum mong ma yin p'i mdzad pi sgo nas ka' gtams kyi bstan ba shin tu dar ba zhig byang ba yin tshod la de bzhig dgon pa der yang den bzungs bod yul dbus nas mkhaan po zhig phebs srol tshugs te sde pa gzhung gi bka' shag gi jig tshang yas kyang gyung drung mkhan por do skhal drug cu zhes phod cing de ltar gnang phong pa dang phyis su dgon 'di bri gung pas bdag 'dzin mdzad pa nas bzungs rim gyis bri nas dos khal sum cu nyi skor tu yong skabs bong gyal tshab mtso mo gling p'i sku thob la lo phyag pa bta mad khan gyis lam yig bka' shog nying pa bka' shag tu phul nas ag mad kan de ni sku tshe brjes song nas deng phyin chad lam yig bka' shog phyag rtags ris gnang ba dang mi gnang ba gnyis su 'dug cid de ltar lo tsa' ba rin chen bzang gi phyag rjes mthod rten sa 'bum re dang dbus kyi lta khang da lta'ng skyon med du bzhugs yod cing de ltar bka' gdam kyi chos lugs dar zhing gyas rang bzhin can dang de rjes bar skabs shig la ma yul spu rang gu ge gsum la bod chos gyal gyi gdung brgyud rgyal po mgon gsum bzhugs p'i gdung brgyud sras gcig la lvags la phebs te thog mar sle ru gdan sa chags nas chu ri'i grong tsho tsugs de nas she chu shod bcas la yur ba bdon nas yul btsugs shing sham phyogs 'grog yul rnams la damg drang pa sogs kyis mnga' 'bngs che gyas nga dang rjes su la dvags stod sham thams cad tu gyal ba nyi m'i gnyen gyi bstan pa dar zhing gyas par gyur ba ni lto nas gar zh'i yul tshun tshad la dvags rgyal po'i mnga' zhabs su gtogs pa dang nub na kha che'i yul mtsho kha shas su rig brgyud nas la dvags thub thabs cig pa dang nub byang na 'bru sha dang 'gyi ling nas shi khar brgyud la dvags su gtogs shing dam p'i chos dar gyas yod pa sogs sngar gyi thos lo dang da lta'ng de rnams su lha khang mchod rten brag la brkos p'i sku gzugs sogs yod pa de rnams su syib pa thams cad kyi mig lom tu gyur 'tug de ltar gyal 'bangs chos srid thabs shes gang gi sgo nas dar zhing gyas par gyur na'ng / la dvags ljongs 'di dpon 'bangs rnams la dar rgud mang poo byang yong skad dang /

yang chos bzhin skyong b'i gyal po sku bsod nams dang ldan pa rim bzhin byang ste dam chos kyang je cher gyas p'i rtar ni rjes su sa skya pa nyi ma 'brug pa 'bri gung pa sogs grub mtha' mang po'i chos sde da lta'i bar tu yod cing dgon ' di'ng bar skabs shig nas gyas rabs kha shas kyi ring la chos lugs zha dmar par yod p'i sked tha dang gra rgyun byang yangs pa can tu 'go lugs yod p'i thos lo dang 'di gi chas kyi srol bk'a brgyud p'i sgom zhva sul med nying song mang pos khom gsum b'i brangs yod pa bdag gis kyang mthong cho rje bya btang pa zhes p'i bla m'i sku nyan byin can bka gnygan pa zhig da lta'i bar du zhang rtan gyi gtso bor bzhugs yong sku rnyan 'ti la rtse gcig tu mos pa rnams la gsol ba gang btab lhun tu 'grub pa dang dgon 'di'i char gtogs pa gang mi bsrun p'i bya ba byas pa rnams la rtags dang mtshan ma mngon sum tu byung ba song thams cang kyis gling 'tug yongs kyi glings mo la bod na dga' ltan tshe dbang zhes p'i dmag dpung la dvags la slab skabs kha chu la nas kha che'i dmag dpung che bar thon pas dgon 'di'i ka ca rnams bsdu gsog byed skabs nang rten rin po che lvam la zhes p'i yul du sbar bar gdan zhus pas lvam li k'aung sgo nas phar la sus kyang ma theg par yu ra 'da gar tsur gdan zhu dgos byung b'i skang dang de etar des can yin p'i rtags kyang lvam li klungs mgo'i zhing dgyil tu nang rten gyi gzhug khri zhes p'i bltsigs pa 'dug / phyi zhig na dmag kha chul du log skabs kha che'i dmag dpon gyi rten kha chul du khyer bar yu ru'i klungs mgor mig mthong tu gyur nas kha che rnams kyis lag bstid tu chu mang po zhig 'thor nas bzhag song ba dar /rang r'i mig cig gis tshur gdar zhus pa yin zer b'i gling brjod 'dug cing de ltar bu'i rtags mtsan mang po 'dug p'i rten khyang par can dang bstan 'jin p'i 'dus sde sogs dar gyas yong na'ng gyal srid kyi ljongs skhabs shig tu sbal tis gnon pa sogs bya zing mthams su dar rgud byung b'ang sang gshes la grub pal bar skabs dgon pa 'di bdag 'dzin byeng sa chung ba zhig tu gyur skabs shig la la dvags gyal po zhig gis smyur li dgun sar thang la yul 'jug sar la dvags stod sham thams cad kyi 'bangs bstus ti nyi mis rong mthil gyi la 'bru nas chu rong du drang b'i thabs mdzad nas ri 'gram nas yur ba bzos shing la go nas phyed rtam brus pa la de'i sa dong nas btsangs p'i gzugs silvam gyi tshad tsam zhig chos 'phrud tu thom byung bas las mi rnams kyis tog stse bgyabs te bsang pas de'i rkyen gyis gyal po'jam dbyangs rnam gyal zhu ba zhig bsnyan ‘adze drag pos thebs nas ’o bgyal shin tu che bas sman dbyad rim gro sogs gang gi sgo na’ng ma phan pas gngas te yi’i ’bri gang dgon pa sgra gya gtags nas chos rjes mdan ma zhes grub pa thob ’a’i rnal byor pa chen po sa lam la gnas p’i sod nam khyad du ‘phags p’i bla ma zhig bzhugs pa de gdan ’dan zhus te rim gro mdzad pas gyal po’i smyun mdzad bral du dvag sa de nas chos rjes mdan ma gyal po’i dbu blar khur nas sngon bkris chos sdzong zhes pa chos gzhi su phul nas der dgon pa bdab de dang sbrangs gyulng drung dgon ‘di chos srid gdan sar phul ba dang/lyag don du dgon pa ’di phyi nang sa mtshams su yod p’i skabs yin par rton thar pa gling du yang ’ang gsol nas/gyal p’i mnga’ zhags su gtogs p’i phyi pa dang nang pa stod sham kun gyis bkur dgos pa dang dpon ’bangs gang la nyis par gyur b’i nag can srog la bah pa sogs kyang dgon pa ’di’i zhabs ’jus la ’ongs pa rnams yul mgo yus ’jug gi dar dar po che’i nang tshum chad du sleb pa thams cad dgon p’i srol dang der ma tshod la dvags sham phyogs kyi ljongs yog kha shas la gyal khims kyi stong du cho khrims kyi lung rgyag pa sogs kha dvag bshe mong zhig chos gyal chen po tsewang rnam rgyal dang chos blon chen po che dbang don grub bar gyi sku thog tu ’dul cing de bzhin du dgon pa thar gling tu ‘dul cing de bzhin du dgon pa thar gling du mang’ gsol de kha che’i gyal po sha a gang go ’is p’i bka’ tham dang rtu ran ta ba gyal po rnams kyi bka’ shog kha che’ yi ge dang nang rten gyi bzhugs khri kha chul nas phul p’i shi shi me long la bar rtse’i yi ge brkos p’i rtan chos zheb mor yod pha rten kha chul gyi pha nya ’gra-gyi ma lig zhes pa ’khor yog nyis bragya bsum brgya dang bcas lo nog gsum bar tu yong skabs la dvags stong sham rnams kyi lam thams cad la ’phrog bcom sogs sdang strub yod kyang yul ’dir rta bul su lag sogs ci’ng mi bab cing ’phrog bcom sogs stang stsub byed pa phar bzhag nas tha na yul du me mang’i skad tsam pyung mi chog par kha che rnams kyis kyang stsi ’jog dgos pa sogs yod pa dang de ltar phyinang chos lugs thams cad kyi mos btud bste stang gyi gnas yin pas des nas la dvags dang sbal ti sogs ’thab brtsod chen por byang tse dgon pa dis gnyis kyi mtshma na legs ’dun gyi phyin ’grig pa dang yas mas kyi mtang tho’i yang byed pa sogs chod ’jog pa byas te dgon pa ‘di nas la dvags gyal blon rnams la lo gsar gyi gyal blon rnams la lo gsar gyi tshes phyag dang sbal ti brgyal po skar mto'i jo la lo phyag pa pho nya zhig brdzang ba ma gtogs chos srid la khral rigs kru tsham med p'i rang btsan pa yin ci bya ba lugs gnyis gang gi sgo nas logs lam phun gsum chogs shing dge 'dum gyi ste sa sang sngon thog mang skabs gsum bgya bzhi bgya nas mi nyung bar dom che tsam tsogs shing rten mchen sogs khyang 'phags bzang la dos che ba longs spyod ni rnam thos kyi bu la 'gran nus pa tsam rang mkhos la dpag ma yin pa dang ma 'grig p'i sgo gang yang med cing phyi nang gi skyabs gnas 'gro ba lta mi'i mchod steng du tshugs te lo mang lon pa dang la dvags chos gyal rin phebs kyi 'jug chos gyal chen po dpal rnam gyal gyi sku thog tu la dvags gyal srid 'jam mu ra ji mang 'ga tu chud song de nas lo na dgu tsam no 'jam mu'i bka 'blon 'gras nas bje jo ra lvar zir ba dang bod; khrugs skabs la dvags pas bod la mdum bstan pas 'jam mu nas rngo lvan nya ri can zer ba zhig gi gtsos dmag dpon re dang dpung re shrags te kha chul nas la dvags grang tsi 'i bar tu dmag dpung gis gang bas de dus la dvags yul ste ljong khag thams cang sham stod lto byang ma lus par brlag song dgon pa 'di'ng gzhug lan yin gshis yul mi rnams ni ri la bros pas dbyar thog gcig gi ring la dmag grul nas yul dang dgon bla 'brang thams cad gsang gsum rten mched cha la sogs pa rnams' joms nas sdongs pa ma tshad nang gi sgo skar khung' byod' jug tsam ma lus par song ba de nas sten mtshams su gyal khag yas mas phuin 'grig steng 'jam mu'i dmag rnams log zin pa dang mi rnams ri nas yul du bab ste lta dus bla 'brang 'di'i rten bris bur thams cad kyi nang ni 'abri gung zhabs drung bste no prm'i gyan gyi 'dra sku sman 'dam las grab pa khru gang pa zhig no sus kyang las ma thng par' dug de dnag cha las rnams kyi nang na rgor sbu cha gcig lus 'dug de gnyis ma gtogs gzhin kyer 'dod pa rnams la ni shig nas 'dod pa zhi ga gig kyang malus shing gyal b'i kja' gyur rin po che dang tung du phung ma bgyang ba bzhin tu blag nas de dang mnyam du khang nang giphugs rnams su ti pi cag sogs rta rnams dang njug 'khor tu dri'u dang bong bu sogs bkag nas dgon khang gi bdab skar nang 'yi rung ltas te bong bus dngar sgra sgog pa sogs.

de ltar bstan p'i bgegas chags ci mi legs pa thams cad 'dug

cing tshogs p'i slo dbon gyis grtsos gra pa kha shas kyang brdeg brdung mtshon sogs kyis bkrongs 'adug de rjes dge 'eun gyi sde thams cad kyang rang rang so'i yul sogs su bros pa lta bus thor nas tshogs rgyu ring skabs shig la thog mar drug sde zhig 'dzoms nas rdz'i med dam zhig bum pa byas rz'i mchong kong t ing re nyed p'i mchod cha byas yul srung kha che zhig gi lag na yod p'i dril bu skye 'bung gcig nyos te rol byas te 'das po zhig gi byang steg bgyis 'dug de lta bu nyam thag su thug gi dang la yod skabs su ngos bla ming dkon mchog rang grol nyim sngon du dmag zing skabs byang phyogs rdo mkhar gyi phu la bros te rja khyed cig tu spyil bu zhig brtigs te sa bsad yod par der yu ru'i yul mi thun mong 'bod mi gnyis sleb ste bla 'brang 'di khang stong tu phyur pas mi yin gyi grim 'grul tshag tshig 're'ng thos' dug zhig gso'i do khur zhig byid mkhan yong tshe ngos rnams kyi ma zhing kun tshad la bzhag ste dgos cha ri gang lcogs sgub rgyu yin zer byung ngos kyi bsam pa la khong mi skya rnams de tsam gyi blo yod na nga 'gro'i bsam pa zhig dang yang sngon du ngos rang bod nas gnas skor p'i tshul su yongs skabs gongs re bzhin rmi lam du 'bri gung skyabs mgon rnam gnyis rgyum mis chad du mjal ba dang mar yul la thon p'i zhag da bde bar song zhig grungs sam snyisn rnam gnyis kyi kha tag dkar po'i sba dar re gnang yod pa ra mjal de nas phyin ma mjal b'i ngos kyi bsam tshul da dgra jag chom rkun sogs la gyi 'jigs pa tham cad las thar ba yin 'dra snyam nas 'ongs de rtse bo thog chen gyi ser lung du 'gro b'i dbas lam zhig na gngas di si'i dbu rtse njal ran pa dang pha yul du sleb p'i bzang ngan ci --r yong gi rnam rdog khur nas 'jam dpal mtshan brjod don gyin yongs pas tshangs p'i yul stse nas gnon zhes pa dang gngas kyi dbu rtse mjal bas dge b'i las re sgrub na lam gro yong ngam bsam de lta bu'i ltas bzang re 'nga yod sgrub song snyam nas yu su la yong b'i khas lbangs d'i nub mo rmi lam du nang nang gyi gcos sku thams cad ma zhig par bkra lam me pod par mthong thams cad zhing zer ba yin 'dum snyam pa dang syang sngon gyi dbu tshe dbang bkris 'dra b'i gra pa zhig gis kyang ste gnyen rang mi 'tug zer 'dug gnyid sad pa dang mtsham ma bzang mnyam ste 'gro b'i blo thag thod phyi lo dbyar smad la yu ru la sleb nas phyogs gang bde re la bsod snyoms slong mo re bskul ba dang rang la'ng phran bu re gang yong bod bcad nas zhig gso la mgo tshugs pas lo gnyis kyi ring la sman dam las grub p'i sku rnams legs par grub de nas lo gnyis kyi ring la gyal b'i bk'a 'gyur rin po ches gtsos gsung rab rnams rnams grub de rjes lo kha shag ring la mchod che rigs dang mgon po dang bka' bgyad gnyis ka' gtor bzlog gar 'tshams sbags p'i chas thams cad grub de nas ynag stod sham yongs rezogs la slong mo rna ba zang la thug gi bar tu yang nas yang tu bskul ba byas thabs ci drag gi sgo nas mchod pa nyams chag rnams kyangs gsos te spyi thog gnyir las re bskal te thog mar nya stong la gso sbyong dang khyad rang gnam gang la so so thar p'i mdo 'on pa dang gnas bca gnyis chog btsugs de ltar jla ba re'i ngo re la tshes dang nyir gsum la rdo rje phag mo'i dkyil chog tshos la sman bla'i mdo chog ches la pad gling drag po'i sgo nas ches bcu'i mchod dpa tses la dgongs pa yang zab las gyal ba zhi gro'i dkyil chog btsogs la mi 'khrug chog bcu dgu la bka 'byad bde 'dus 'bring po'i byang mchod nyer lags la bla ma mchod pa nyis dgu la bde mgon gyi bskang gsol gyas yang tshos nyir drug sogs la sbyin bdag re bskur nas sgrol dkar ma la bzhim bcas dang gzhan yang tshogs par snga phyi'i' dam khom dpag ste chos skyed smon lam dang bcas pa dang dus rgyun tu bzhi gsam nas gsungs p'i rgyad chags gsum pa dang chu gtor bgya rtsa chag med bcas sgrub brgyud 'di p'i lugs kyi chogs 'don rnams zla'i khongs su tshang thabs dnag pa chags 'kyi dgon pa chos 'de bzhin bdag 'dzhin byed p'i dge 'dun gyi sde tshugs thabs su rang mkhos la dpag p'i bstan p'i zhahs 'deg tsam zhig grub na'ng chos nor dang kyang mang' Thang stobgs dang ltan pa rnams kyi mthong yul du na byes p'i rted mo tsam gyi bgyi ba las mad pas snying rje'i yul du gzigs las che na'ng bdag rang zhi byaba gzhin spangs p'i ri khred p'i lugs la gyur pas rggu cas lag thog tu ci'ng med pa zhig dang dad ltan bra gyi sbyin bdag rnams ni de dus tha dmag gis bshigs p'i — sogs kyi thabs sdug zha'ng 'di tsam grub pa de ni bla ma dkon mthog kyi byin mthu dang yi dam

mkhro srung m'i 'phris thugs rje mngon sam du byung ste

gang dgos la thogs pa med pa lta bce'i dang nas dka' 'tshegs med par lhum gyis grub p'i gzhig pa gteng nas byed na ya mtsan gyi gnas su gyur 'dug bla 'brang gi phui nang par gsum rtsa ba' rtse spyod sogs ni sus kyang gsob thub mkhan ma byung sa thog tu ni mha'r dzi dngul na sbral sogs ma gngogs dge 'dun'tsho ba' mthan rkyen la pham p'i des pa ma shes nub phyogs kha che nas brgyud su rig gi se thams cas phyi pa kla klo'i chos lugs rin bzing te dgon pa 'di dang nyi skor tu slab yod pa dang nub byab sbal ti'i yul thams cad 'phyi pas khyab ste tgon pa 'di'i bstan p'i sbyin btag gi sa mtshams la thug yod na'ng da lta'i bar du ni gyung drung dgon pa 'di'i chos dang sdas khyab ste de nas gyen la kal klo'i chos ma gyas pa yin 'dug kyang da ni 'tsho b'i mthun rkyen zhanpas tshogs p'i zhal grangs kyang sngar du las bri na'ng da lta phyogs gzhes tha tag stoms te phogs 'thob rigs nyes bgya 'skor gzigs tsam bzhugs yod p'i da phyin 'dus tshugs thabs su rgyum ja zhig dgos gal 'dug kyang de ni bstan don lar gyar gzigs p'i gong sa dpon po zhig la rag las p'i de lta'i snyam sgron zhume re'ng zhu spabs pa su gang yang med p'i snyams las kyi ngang nas bstan pa je lod'gyur ba las gzham mi 'dug phran cag rnams kyis dge sbyor du dmigs nas cung zad re sgrubs kyang da dus sngar lam du yod p'i gyal be bka' gyur rin po che gsung sgros byed p'i rgyu zhig ni thaba gang gi ------ nas kyang ma 'grig par yod lo re bzhin sngar khrims ltar dag 'don zhig sgrub brgus na bstan pa dang sems can gyi don tu 'gyur nges shing btag gzham 'brel thogs rnams kyi tshe rabs kun la phan p'i mi lus la snying po len p'i skal can du' gyur ba ni gton mi za b'i sphro ba shin tu chen'ng gnas skabs kyi dus 'si la thabs bde ba zhig gzhi nas ma byung b'i tshul ni rtse b'i rtsi sprod la 'bru nas shig gnyer la gzhag na ni mi dred dpon du' gyur zhing btag po yog tu' gyur te mal tu lus p'i re ba mi 'dug sa zhin re gzhig na ni ma ta' ra' dza' di'i mang' zhabs su gtogs p'i sa zhing gang na yod pa la stul khra 'babs pa yin phyin de'ng ma bdeb sogs kyis lus yod cing dgon pa di dang po tshugs p'i rgyu dus gsum gyi brgyal ba sras bcas rnams kyi byin brlabs te gngas can bstan p'i sgo gtan tu phyi nang so tshas srung b'i gnyer por grub pa zhig yin nges 'dug p'i 'ti nas btag lta bu snyoms thung gyin p'i sang gshes can rnam kyis kyang lhang bsam rnampar dag p'i smon 'dug ni 'dzam gling gngas can 'di na rnam 'dren bzhi p'i pa 'dzin skyong mdzad p'i gong ma rnams --- dgon , de spyan gyang gi gzigs pa nas skyong nas da dung dge' dun tshogs p'i 'tho ba bzhes pa sngar srol bzhin gyas p'i thog bslab gsum ' dzin p'i' dus ste dar zhin gyaste brgyal ba zas gtsang sras kyi bstan pa rin po che phyi nang gi sa mtshams dins dzin skyong spel gsum thub pa dang ngyal b'i bka' 'gyur rin po che'ng bri' don klog gsum rgyum mi chad tu zhub cing bstan pa yar 'phel yong b'is phris yar zla dang dbyar mtsho'i dpltar 'grub par shog cig p'i smon lam gyi dang nas gnas p'o zhes rab byung ying kyi nang tshan nga chen lo'i chu stod zla b'i nang bjis heb kashmir nas la dvags la phebs dus la dags sdod nas skyu dvag thams cad gdan bsu ru phebs skabs su shod dpon ga ga tshe ring bkris dang zhal 'dris par brten da lta gangs can zhin khams rdo rje gdan gnyisp'i yul dbus lo phyag gi 'phris mdzad sgo la phebs skabs byen skyems snyan gyi bdud ------ ri khrod ldom bu b'i gang dran gyi tsheg 'de -- thugs nang dag p'i sgo nas zhus pa yin p'i ---- tshol dbying khrol med pa zhu gyung drang ---- la rgyas sngon du ji ltar byung ba tang ta ——— ji ltar yod tshul sngon rgan rabs kyi rna bar brgyad p'i thos lo dnag yul phyogs 'ga' na lha khang gtsugs lag khang re bzengs p'i dkar thags re dang mang yul chos gyas rin phebs kyi gyal rabs deb thor sogs 'ga' nas lung rig dpyat gsum gyis te gyu drung bla zur dko mchog rang grol nyi mas zur shag bkra shis nyim 'khyil pa nas bris pa sar mngga lam.

Appendex : 2

Tibetan Inscriptions on Alchi

1 - Tibetan Text in classical language

Om kra shis par gyurd cig /

dkon mchog bla ma yid dam lhar bcas la /

kun nas dang pas gus par phyag btsal nas /

rang gzhan nges shes skyed phyir gsal debs rtsams /

gling gyi gling mchog lho 'ai dzam bu gling /

ri mtho sa tsang spu rgyal bod kyi yul /

sa phyogs gcig al lchi dgon gnas su /

dad gus mos pas rin chen rtsug lag bzhengs /

shing dang ri mo bzo rnams myi x bltas /

gzhan dbang gyud pas × × dk'a /

× × × dus kyi snyigs ma ---- tshe dang longs spyod bsod nams × /

sog du gnyis kyi go lo god /

thab rtsod khrugs long shin tu mang /

sa bon ci btab legs pa nyung /

char chu dus su phebs pa dk'a ston thog bras bu thob par bk'a /

rkyen dang lhags pa shin tu mang /

kha drag yin na phrog tu 'aong /

khan man yin na slong du 'aong /

rlags la bab na su yang sgu /

khrel dang ngo tsha su la 'ang myed /

tug gis zhug na su yang mtshong /

sdug srin mangs na byan mo bster /

phugs na yod p'a byan mo sku /

mdo na yod p'ai khor × spros /

blo × × bstod × × su la'ang myed /

de dr'ai dus × snyigs ma la /
dge ba byed pa shin tu dk'a
de ltar dk'a bar gyurd na yang /
stond ka zan gong byin pa pas /
dbyar ka skul ma mi dg'a 'am /
drangs la sha chang byin pa pas /
ltogs × × kho log mi dg'a 'am /
de bzhin dus kyi snyigs ma la /
sbyin pa chung ngu btang na yang /
bsod nams chen po yod par dk'a /
shyin pa chung yang btang bar bya /
myi gdam thob nas byang chub ma sgrubs na /
ngan song gsum du sgrub p'ai gnas skabs myed /
tsha grang sdug bsngal shin tu bzod thag chad /
kres stom gnyis kyis dus kyang shin tu dub /
sha bzhud gnyis kyis bskad kyang ngar zhing dar /
gcig gyis gcig gsod rgyud cing bros pa las /
byang chub sgrub p'ai dal khom g'a la yod /
sti mug gyurd pas gro mi shes na /
thard p'ai lam la dzeg pa g'a la shes da lta di ru mthar lam ma btsal na /
bhyis dus debs pa sbrin la mtshon p'a dzugs /
dpyid kyi nyi lam bzhin du sna tshogs khrul /
mth'a myed khor bar shin tu yun rings khyams /
khor b'ai sdug bsngal dbag 'myed rab tu myong /
phyi m'ai rgyags phye di ru ma bsrong na /
phyi m'ai shul thag ring po ci yis gsod /
phyi m'ai gos lam di ru ma srong na /
shul thag ring po'ai gos lham su yis shyor /

phyi m'ai rgyags phye bsrong du yod pa la /
mi bsrong bsdug bsogs byed pa shin tu khrul /
gnas sogs long spyod sgyu ma yin pa la /
chags shing zhend pa de bas shin tu khrul /
srog gcod snying rje med p'ai zhend pa yang /
srog la bab kar gyod pa chen bskyed /
the tsom med p'ai skyed bu ci ste dam /
dal khom mi lus thob pa shin tu dk'a /
dad rtson shes rab ldam pa de bas dk'a /
ma nor don dang phrad pa de bas dk'a /
di ru nges shes skyed pa de bas dk'a /
dk'a bzhi di × × tu yod pa la
gyi na sdod pa shin tu khrul tshabs che /
gdod nas ma skyes rnam dag sems nyid ngang /
nam kha mtha med lta bur kun la khyab /
khyab kyang gro drug las kyis khor bar khyam /
khor ba mthon sman bde sdug du ma myong /
ngan song gsum gyi sdug bsngal bzod thag chad /
bros kyang mi phan sting bzhin dod du × × × × /
smras kyang mi phan shin tu × × × × mi phrad /
btsol yang mi phan × × × pa rag tu yong /
dzegs kyang myi phan × × × kyin × × × nyung /
gon bskyabs byed pa gcig kyang mthong ba med /
bsod sogs zer ba phyogs nams kun nas langs /
mun pas sgribs pas mthar lam mthong pa med /
× × × cing sngangs pas skad kyang ngar zhing dar /
mth'a med khor b 'ai sdug bsngal ya ri × × × /
khor ba mth'a myed di la yid phyang nas /
mos gus dad pa blo 'ai rting nas bskyed /

ma rtags sgyu ma di la ci phyir chogs /
di ru dug long med pas yod pa mthong /
dus sag yid × × × dge ba ci nus bya /
ma nor don dang phrad na ci bzo × × × × /
× × × × gyi las bros × × pa dang /
da lta drang rkyen dzom pa dang /
bla m'ai drin gyi gron me yis /ya × × ma nor don
dang phrad /
dub lnga ma spangs byang chub chen po'i lam /
dod yon ma spangs gang snang grogs su char /
snang grags ma spangs ye nas chos kyi sku /
khor ba ma spangs mya
dan das p' ai ngang /
du dzi ma spangs ngo
bo nyid kyi dben /
bros kyang mi dgos ded khan gcig kyang med /
smras pa mi dgos smra bsam brjod las das /
btsol yang myi dgos thams cad gnyen du gro /
dzegs kyang mi dyos bgang chub bde chen gnas /
brtsal med lhun grub × × dag chen po'ai sa ci bzhin
× × × × /
dran rtog rang dengs sems nyid myug m'ai ngang /
× × × med lhun grub byang chub chen po'ai sku /
dus gsun gyur myed mi d'a lam du slongs /
mthar thug bras bu sku gsum ye shes lnga /
goms pa mya ngan thob gyur the tsom med /
tshegs chu don tshe mi bad su yis mod /
jig rten × × la mthong dben gnas dgon par bsdod /
stobs su gyurd na gang du bsdad kyang bde /
rgyal po'ai pho brang la sogs gar bsdod kyang /
de nyid don na mi bral lhun gyis grub /× × × × skal
pa shes rab gnyal ba dang /
× × × skal pa × × × p'ai gro bsal /

nges shes skyed phyir gsal debs sgron ma rtsams /
rin cen rtsug lag lha khang bzhengs pa dang /
gsal debs sgron ma rtsams p'ai /
dge ba bdag gis gang thob des /
bdag dang mtha yas sems can kun /
bcom ldan bder gshegs mi khugs pe /
dge ba chen zhes bya b'ai /
zhing mchog rtsang mar skyed par shog /
mchod sogs bsnyen bkur byed par shog /
dam chos tshul bzhin nyand par shog /
mnyan chad lbur du nyes par shog /
tshul bzhin rtogs pa bskyed par shog /
× × × × shog /
bcom ldan bder gshegs nyi khrungs p'ai /
ska'ai -------- tshad dang gsung gi tshad /
thugs kyi tshed dang yon tan tshad /
yon tan phyin las mdzad p'ai tshad /
bsku tshe'ai tshad dang zhing gi tshad /
khor gyi tshad dang dul by'ai tshad /
de dag tshad rnams thams cad kun bdag gis gnyam
par × × × par shog /
mdzad p'ai phrin las re res kyang /
khams gsum sems can mth' a yas kun /
ngan song gar ma gyis bkag nas /
mtho ris gnas su dan par shog /
mtho ris gnas p'ai sems can kun /
thar p'ai lam la gor par shog /
myur du byang chub thob par shog /
bkra shis par gyur cig /

bzhur legs par gyur cig
smon lam tha × × × gyur cig /
ci byas tshogs su 'agro bar gyur cig /
snang ba rang sar grol par gyur cig /
lam la bar chad myed par gyur cig /
gsal debs sgron ma nges shes bskyed p'ai chos /
nges shes skeyes pas tshogs gnyis rab tu brdzogs /
tshogs gnyis brdzogs pas sgrib pa gnyis dang bral /
sgrib pa gnyis dang bral bas rdzogs sangs rgyas /
dge slong skal ldan shes rab bdag gis rtsams /
rtsams p'ai las rnams mtha ru skyol bar bya /
phro ru lugs na rang
gyod nyi yang × × /
rtrans P'ai las snams
mtha ru skybo bar ska
dge ni thog ma bar dang mtha × × dge /
thog med dus nas khor bar yun rings khyams /
da ni khor ba di la bye brgyas debs /
lus sems bral kar dga × × reng nge gro /
slong ni dad pas kun nas rab tu bslong /
dad pa med na chos la jug mi gyur /
chos la mi jug sems can myon re mongs /
mi' ai gru la sten la khor ba bsgrol /
skal ni chos la bskal te rig pa bslabs /
gzhon p'a i dus su rig pa ma bslab na /
rgas p'ai dus su bslab pas thar mi skyol /
rgun gi me tog bar ba lhags pas khyer /
ldan ni skal par ldan te shes rab ldan /
skal pas rang gzhan re dod bskong bar byed /
shes rab kyis ni × × × rnams zad par brtol /
srid gum rnams las yang dag grol bar gyur /
shes ni snang srid khor das sgyu mar shes /
sgyu m'ai rang bzhin yin las zhen pa log /

zhen med spros × × × × chos kyi bsku /
sku grum dbyer med ngo bo nyid kyi bsku /
rab ni rtogs pa rab ste gnyis med rtogs /
gnyis dzin rang re sa spros bro × × × nas × × /
ma rtsal lhun p'ao ra ba ngang gis zhib /
dus gsum bder gshegs gnas ma phyin × × /
bdag ni bdag med gniys × × × × × /
bdag dzin gnyis bral × × × ×× × × × /
× × × bral med lhun grub chen po'ai ngang /
khor ba ma spangs rang dag chen po'ai blog
gyis ni dge ba × × × × byed /
gzhan dag dge b'ai × × × × × /
rang don grub pa mi dge shugs la grub /
rang gzhan gnyes × × × × the tson med /
brtsams ni gsal debs sgron ma × × × brtsams /
× × × × × × × × × × × × × × × × × × /
× × × × × × × × × × × × × × × × × × /
rang gzhan nges shes bskyed pa ston p'ai chos /
tshig gi sdebs ma legs shing ngond × × × grigs na /
skye bo mkha rnamms bzod la mdzod /
ma nor don dang grig gyur na /
chags dang bsdang b'ai yid dor la /
dge tshogs bzang zhes cis mi brjod /
bsod nams gnyam par thob par bshad /
gsal debs sgron ma zhes bya ba /
shag kyi dge slong skal ldan
shes rab kyis sdebs brjogs so / /

2. Tibetan Text in classical language

sku gsum bdag nyid snangs rgyas dkon mchog dang /

lung dang togs p'ai bdag nyid dam chos dang /
nyan rang byang chub sems dp 'ai dge dun la /
lus ngag yid gsum dang bas phyag tshal te /
gdul bya dul byed dul thabs rnams gsum dang /
dum dum khregs kyi stan chos bshad par bya /
ma rig rgyu la × rtog kyen gis skyed /
bras bu thar med khor b'ai gnas su skyes /
gros ba ris drug khrul b'ai snang bar shar /
sdug bsngal gsum dang rgyad dang bcu gcig gis /
gdungs shign bzod rk'ai sdug bsngal nyams su myong /
de dag dul phyir stond pa rnam gsum byung /
chos sku' ai stond pas byin gyirlabs kyis chad /
longs sku'ar pas rang gi ngo pos chad /
spral sku'ai sdon pas tshig dang yig ger sdebs /
gdul by 'ai don phyir khor lo rnam gsum skor /
chos kyi sgo mo rgyad khri bzhi stong sum /
rigs can gsum la theg pa gsum du snang /
nyan thos dang rgyal byang sems theg pa gsum /
rang tes thong b'ai bden pai tshig gsum smra /
bden gnyis dbyer med byong sems thegs pa rtogs /
pha rol phyin drug bsdu × × × × bdag
gyi don bor gzhan gyi don du spyod /
bu dang chu × × × × go drang rka lag stong /
zang zing longs spyod × × × × × /
bzung ba rang bzhin med pa rang rgyal theg pas rtogs /
rten brel bcu × × × × × × /
mi dang nang gyi dngos po stan la bebs /
rang don rtso che gzhan don cha shas spyod /
nyan thos × × × × zag bdag med rtogs /
bden pa bzhi la ye shes bcu drug gis /
nges shes bskyed nas nyams su len × × /
kha na ma tho gsum sngags bdag gi don du spyod /

bdang po 'ai yang tha mi lh'ai theg pa yis /
las pa rnam smin chos la yid ches shing /
dge ba bcu spyod mi chos bcu drug srung /
gzhan ya dus byas dge khyud bas /
glog don skor ba mchod rten rtsig las la sogs /
dge b'ai rtsa ba sa btab rdo btab byed /
mtshan btags bzhi dang ldan p'ai yon × × /
yul la mtshan gsol slob dpon gsum md'a bas /
gnas la mtshan gsol slob dpon Alcipa dus la mtshan gsol slob dpon bron ston te /
don la mtshan gsol skal ldan shes rab bo /
skal dar ldan pas mi lus rtsang ma thob /
byord pa ldan ma zas nor stong phul che /
shes rab ldan pas zab mo'ai × × × rtogs pas /
rab dga sogs sa bcu stabs cig cig grod /
don la mtshan du gsol b'ai slob dpon gi /
khor b'ai mtshan nyid sgyu ma lta bur rtogs /
zas nor longs spyod snying po med shes pas /
stong m'ai snying po bla × × × × × b'ai phyir /
sgom ra klog don lha × × bzhengs su gsol /
de la sten nas zas nor longs spyod brtang /
× × × × /
gzhon nu rig pa slabs na rgas nas gyod pa med /
× × × × la bya nas de bas phyi ma dbas /
shrub pa pa bden tsheg mtha mchog /
gzhan yang a lci
yul dang de la gnas p'ai mi /
de 'ai gnas lugs chung zad bshad
par bya /
phu gsum ri yis bskar bas rku phrog

chom rkun nyung /

md'a gsum chab kyis bcad pas sgra slong ta ra med /

sa la ci btab × × pas rin cen bru nad chung /

gya × × ngam grog med pas so nam grod par sla /

de na gnas p'ai mi'ai mtshan nyid ni /

btsun chen dge zhungs dam p'ai chos bsrung bas /

bshes gnyen yon tan thams cad byung b'ai chos bsrung bas /

bshes gnyen yon tan thams cad byung b'ai nas ya rabs gung seng ngo tsha / khral ltan !tan pas / nga

gzhung phyi thag thams cad byung b'ai gnas /

shar pa dpa rtsal khyer kham dang ldan pa /

gyogs shor she mong thams cad byang b'ai gnas /

de la so × × × × yon tan mth'a yas mchog /

yon bdag byor pa car gis rgyu byas shing /

lha bzo rig pa can gis rkyen byas te /

lha khang tsug lag khang chen bzhengs p'ai /

dge ba dri med bsod

nams kun mchi 'ao /

shag ky'ai dge slong grags ldan 'aod kyis sdebs nongs pa mchi na mkhas rnams bzod pa bzhes /

mang po dag la bu skyes ci bzhin du /

mkhas rnams dge legs bzang zhes brjod par rigs /

stan gsum stan gsum dul × × 'ai

theg pa gsum /

dum dum khrigs kyi byang ser rdzongs zhes bya /

3. Tibetan Text in classical language

skal pa du mar tshogs bsags las /

ldan par dk'a b'ai dal byor thob /

shes gnyen phu yu byung ba yis /

rab mchog mug m'ai don la skal

ldan pa phun tshogs khyan pa yis /
dal byor don yod don rnyes phyir /
chos rnams ma lus thugs su chud /
zab mo don rtogs las phro ldan /
shes bya ma lus brtags p'ai phyir /
gro ba rnams kyi rtso ba bsteb /
rnam dag nyig zhus yongs khengs pas /
grol b'ai thabs ni sna tshogs shes /
rab chog dam p'ai chos la bskal /
nyis myed zab mo'ai rtogs pa ldan /
snod ldan rnams kyi dul thabs shes /
de'ai phyird na kun pas rab /
bya thabs di la rlag thabs gsum /
logs bzhir rlag dang lugs bzhin rlag /
dum bu dum bur brlag p'ao /
dang po nyid kyis mtshan bzhi stan /
gnyis pas spy'ai yon tan bstan /
× × × × / × × × /× × × /
gsum pas md zed p'ai yon tan bstan /
bzhi pas khyad par yon tan bstan /
shes rab dma bas legs pa ma shes khyang /
'aol
tsam bgyis pas mkhas rnams bzod par bzhes /
'aom kra shis par gyur cig /
myi mthun phyogs kyi bdud bzhi las rgyal bar gyur cig /
di lta chos rnams kund kyi bdag po ni /
skye myed mkha dra bjod med kun la khyab /
gyur med sna tshogs ston la phyag btsal nas /

bstand p'ai rnam bzhag mdzad la phyag tshal bstod /
ci ltar zho skrogs mar bzhin du /
rigs drug gnas su lhun kyis grub /
chos rnams mi las tshul tsam du /
bskyong mdzad byang chub sems dp'ai rigs /
dge b'ai bshes skal ldan shes rab khong /
gzho nu rab tu byung nas dk'a thub
nyams su blangs /
mdo rgyud gnyis la thar lam btsal p'ai rigs kyi bu /
snga ma sbyangs p'ai las phro can la phyag tshal bstod /
mthos bsam slob gnyer mdzad p'ai dus dag tu /
mar yul
nyar ma chos kyi pho brang du /
khan po la sogs mkhas pa rnams kyi thugs zin nas /
mkhas pa mi tog sbrang rtsi lta bu 'a bcud kyis khengs /
kho nyid bung ba lta bus thugs kyi bcud rnams jibs /
shes rab ljags kyis sde snod sbrang rtsi bu'ai /
dam chos du me /
ro myong khong la phyag mtshal stod /
dge b'ai bshes gnyen skal ldan shes rab khong /
phyag gya chen po'ai don rtogs gro don phyogs bcur
shar /
snying po'ai don la mtshon med tshig gyi sgro dogs bral /
ma bcos × × × × don la skal ldan pho mo sprod la bstod /
las can mos pa kha cig khyed la × × bcas nas /
dpag bsam shing chen lta bur yon tan thams cad sgyal /
bum pa bzang po lta bur kun gyi re dod skong /
rin chen ster gyi byung gnas kho la phyag tshal bstod /
kun gyi dge b'ai bshes gnyen skal ld an shes rab khong /
gdam nang

gnad kyis zin pas bzung dzin mdud pa grol /
byin rlabs mtshos ma dra bas khrul p'ai kho dog sgyur /
gro don lhun gyis grub la phyag tshal bstod /
sngon tshe bsod nams bsags pas da lta byord pa ldan /
thugs la ser sna med pas sbyin pa phyogs myed stong /
byas pa drin du bzo bas zhu la drin lan bsabs /
gro ba skyab phyir dka bas rdzong
dang zam pa mdzad /
dmyigs med dge ba sgom ra yang dang yang du mdzad /
bsod nams bsam mi khyab p'ai rgyal yum grangs kyis bsil /
yab zhu'ai mdzad tshal snyag phyir
rtsug lag khang chen di /
dad pas rgyu byas byord pas kyen byas nas /
sbyor ba du mas al lci yul dir bzhengs /
byams sems ldan p'ai spu rgyal bod /
rig p'ai byung gnas mnga ris stod /
yon tan kun ldan al lci gnas /
rigs rgyud ldan pa bro'ai sde /
khyen pa gnyis
ldan × × × dpon gyis /
mkhas gyogs gnyis ldan lha bzo la /
chags myed dod yon lnga phul nas /
lha khang khyad phags di bzhengs pas /
yon bdag mchod gnas khor bcas rnams /
bsod nams ye shes tshogs rdzogs te /
sku gsum ye shes lnga ldan p'ai /
thams cad khyen nyid thob par shog /
bod pa sgom chen byung gnas shes rab kyis /

gzhung dang man ngag la sten bcas nas /
'aod zer gsal b'ai tshig gi phreng ba di /
blo la shar tshad tsam zhig sdebs pa la /
mkhas pa mod p'ai rang bzhin te /
khas su re rnams ci phyir smod /
tshig la rtags nas skyon brjod na /
kun khyen la ya skyon chags pas /
mkas pa khrel × × bzod pa bzhes /
byang ser 'aod zer gsal b'ai tshig gi phreng ba /
byung gnas shes rab kyis sdebs pa /
rdzogs ho /

4. *Tibetan Text in classical language and Orthography*

bcom ldan das mi khrugs pa bla na med pa yang dag par rdzogs p'ai byang chub tu mngon par rdzogs par sangs rgyas shing rnam pa thams

cad khyend p'ai ye shes rnyes par gyur p'ai byang chub kyi shing rin po che sna bdun las grub pa /

dpang du dpag tshad dum yod pa /
di'ai sdong po'ai dpang du dpang tshad
brgya yod /
sboms su dgyang grags phyed kyis khor la /
de'ai yal ga rnams ni dpag tshad bdun stong bdun stong yod /
de'ai khor yug tu ni dpag tshad bzhi khri
yod de /
byang chub kyi shing de'ai yal ga dang lo ma dang yal ga phre'au dag /
rlung gyis kun tu bskyod pa na /
de dag la snyan pa dang yid du 'aong ba dang /
chags par
gyur b'ai sgra skad byung ba ni /

lh'ai bsil snyan yan lag bum dang ldan pa dag rol mo'ai slob dpon mkha pas bsil ba dag las kyang byung bar mi gyur ro

byang chub kyi shing de las /
pha rol tu phyind pa thams cad kyi sgra dang /
mngon bar shes pa dang /
dbang po dang /
stobs dang /
byang chub kyi yan lag dang /
lam gyi yan thams cad kyi sgra
skad lh'ai dbyangs las shin tu das pa /
gnyen zhing yid du 'aong ba dag byung ste /
sems can gang dag gyis sgra skad thos par gyurd pa /
de dag thams cad kyang dod chags
dang bral ba semd pa rjes su dran
pa zhes bya b'ai ting gnas dzin thob bo /
gzhan yang sangs rgyas kyi zhing de na /
ngan song gsum dag med de /
sems can dmyal ba dang /
dud gro'ai skye gnas dang /
gshin rje 'ai jig rten ni /
der skyes p'ai sems can de dag thams cad ni /
dge ba bcu'ai lam dang ldan p'ai sha stag go /
gzhan yang sangs rgyas kyi zhing de na /
sems can rnams la rje'ao 'am bran gyi bye brag tu dbye ba myed de /
de'ai mi rnams la bkol b'ai shos × × yur lend p'ai
bsam pa yang med do / de ci'ai phyir zhe na sems can
rnam la bdag dang gyir bzhinpa med pa p'ai phyir ro /

sangs rgyas kyi zhing de'ai sa gzhi thams cad thang thil ltar gnyam ba /

kan tsa lin di ka ltar reg na ble zhing /
ser gyi ka kha dog ltar dug la /
lh'ai nor bu rin po ches spras shing /
pad ma ser gyi mdog can dab ma bye ba phrag stong dang ldan pa dag gis legs par brgyan pa /
me tog man d'a ra ba dang /
man d'a ra ba chen po dag mngon par bkram ba /
× × × dum dang /
tsher ma dang /
gyo mog dang /
seg ma med pa /
ngam grod dang /
gad pa dang /
mi bang ba dor bsil med pa /
rdo dang ri med pa ste /
sa gzhi de la rkang pa bzhag × × ×
nems zhes myed la /
bteg na sar zhes med do
gzhan yang sangs rgyas kyi zhing de'ai mi rnams la /
kha dog ngan pa dang dri mi zhim pa dag thams cad kyi thams cad du med do /
de ci'ai phyir zhe na /
de'ai sems can rnams ni nyon mongs pa dug gsum chung b'ai phyir ro /
gzhan yang sangs rgyas kyi zhing de na /
sems can rnams la /
bsad pa dang ching ba dang /
go rar zlugs pa dag thams cad kyi thams cad du med do /
sangs rgyas kyi zhing de na /
mu stegs thams cad kyi thams cad du med do /
sangs rgyas kyi zhing de na shing
ljon pa rnams rtag tu me tog dang bras bu chang p'ai sha stag go /

gzhan yang sangs rgyas kyi zhing de na /
mi rnams skyi gos ni dpag bsam gyi
shing las byung b'ai gos kha dog lngas gos kyi gya ba byede /
gos de dag kyang mdog gsal zhing dri zhim po dang ldan la /
kha dog mi nyams pa sha stag ste /
dper na lh'ai me tog rnams kyi dri gsung sna tshogs ci dra ba de bzhin du /
de dag gi gos kyi dri yang de dang dra la /
dpag dsams kyi shing de la dug pa na de dag gi dri ci dra ba de bzhin du /
de dag gis yongs su longs spyod da
yang dri de dang dra ba nyid du gyur bas /
gos de dag gi dri dang kha dog la nyams par gyur ba myed la /
de dag gi gos rnams shin tu man zhing phal chel b'ai phyir /
de dag yang dang yang du rje /
zhin dang zhing yon par byed do da
dper na gsum bcu rtsa grum b'ai lha snams yid la ci
sams p'ai kha zas dag byang ba de bzhin du /
jig rten gi khams de'ai mi de dag kyang /
kha zas ci lta bu dag dog pa de lta bu'ai kha zas dag /
mdun tu rin po che 'ai snod dag nas byung ngo /
mi de dag gi kha zas de dag ni /
kha dog dang dri 'am ro lh'ai kha zas dag las mi mthu'ao /
mi de dag gshang pa dang lci ba dang mchil ma dang snabs dag med /
dod pa na spyod p'ai lha rnams bzhin no /
gang du mi dag dug p'ai gnas /
rin po che sna mdun las grub p'ai

khang pa rtsegs p'ai nang na / ri po che sna bdun las byas p'ai khri dag gi steng du /

shing bal par tshangs can gyi stan legs

par bting pa bkram pa

dag byung ba gyur zhing khang pa

rtsegs pa de dag tu khang × × × × × p'ai

yong su spyad pa gang las /

mi nams chu'ai bya ba byed p'ai bdzing rnam pa sna tshags yan lag brgyad dang ldan p'ai chus gang pa byung te brdzang 'au de dag gyang ser gi bye ma × × × × /

lh a'i shing mya ngan tshang gyis skyor sha stag go /

de dag gi mi rnams dam p'ai chos kyi dg'a las dg'a bar byed cig gnas so /

mi de dag gi drung du yan lag brgyad dang ltan p'ai chus gang p'ai brjing dag byung zhing /

gal te brjes su brang bar /

dod na yang rjes su brang par gyur la /

mi snang par dod na yang mi snang bar gyur 'ao /

sangs rgyas kyi zhing de na ha cang yang

me dro ha cang yang mi grang b'ai rlung /

dag ldang ste jam ba dang bde ba dang × × ×

× × × dag ldang do /

dri zhim pa dang yid tu 'aong b'ai rlung

dag ldang ste /

rlung de dag gis mi de dag dang lha de

dag gi spos kyi bya ba kam /

kham byed do /

gal te la la zhig btag la rlung ldang

bad gyur ro /

gal te gzhan dag mi dod na /
de dag mi × × × × × p'ai rlung gyis phog
par mi gyur zhing gang dang gang gyi tse /
dod pa de dib di'ai de
dag ta la dlung ldang
bar gyur ro /
sangs rgyas kyi zhing de na da lta × × × ×
sangs rgyas kyi zhing de na /
bung med dag la yong p'ai skyon dag med na /
sangs rgyas gyi di na bud med ni mdag mi rung /
gzugs mi gas pa × × × × bris pa med × × × × ×
rjed × ×× × dod p'ai long spyod dag × × × × ×
shes pa byas pa mi bzo ba khro ba dang lce
gnyis su smra ba dang /
phrag dog dang ser n'ai chos kyis bo cengs pa dag
yin te /
sha ri'ai bu sangs rgyas kyi zhing de na /
bud med la bud med kyi skyon de dag med de /
de ni sangs rgyas kyi zhing de'ai sdon gyi smon lam
gyi khyad par gyis gyur pa yin no /
de dag gi bud med ni yon tang thams cad dang ldan
pa yin te /
bud med bud med rin mo che'ai × × × × × ×
sangs rgyas kyi zhid de na bud med kyi yon tan
yin pa de dag ni /
de dag gyi yon tan gi gal na /
bud med rin mo che'ai yon tan dag ni brg'ai char yang
nye bar mi gro /
stong gi cha dang /
brgy'ai stang gi cha dang /
bye ba brgy'ai cha dang bye ba stong gi cha dang /
bye ba brgya stong gi cha dang /

bye ba khrag khrig brgy'ai stong gi cha dang /

grangs dang × × × × × bgrangs pa dang /

dbes dang /

gyur yang mi bzod do /

sangs rgyas kye zhing na /

skyes pa dang bud med dag × × × × tu × × × pa spyad p'ai phyir /

dus sbyar med × × × × × × × × × × × × × × ×

ltas pa tsam gyis skyas pa de'ai dod chags rab tu zhi bar gyur te /

shin tu yang yid byung zhing spangs nas /

mi sdug pa la dod chags dang bral b'ai teng

de bdzin thob bo skyes pa des bud med la ltas pa tsam gyis sbrum par gyur te gnyis k'ai dod chags zhi bar gyur nas ma la na gnas p'ai khye 'au 'am bu mo lus dang sems kyis kyang de dra b'ai bde ba dper na /

gsum bcu tsa gsum p'ai lha rnams /

rin po che'ai × × × × × zhal med khang na dg'a zhing mchog tu × × × × × byed na /

× × × × × × × × × × × × × × × × ×

ba bzhin no de na ma la na gnas pa de dag nyin zhag bdun gi bar du bde ba myong nas btsa bar gyur zhing /

bud med sbrum m'ai lus dang sems kyis kyang /

bsam rtan gnyis pa la snyoms par zhung p'ai dge slong thams cad kyi thams cad du bde bar gyur pa bzhin no /

bud med bu btsa ba na yang /

mi brzang ba dang × × × × × mi × × × × × × dag med de /

sangs rgyas mi khrungs pa de'ai sangs rgyas kyi zhing na /

gang gi tshe skyes pa dang bud med × × × × × khye 'au 'am bu mo dag byan thong × × × ×

× × × × × × × × × × × × × × × ×

dogs par gyur te de zhi sngas rgyas de 'ai sden gi smon lam gyi khyad par gyis bun pa yin no de na sangs rgyas chos kyi rgyal po las rgyal po gzhan med do.

5. Tibetan Text in Classical Language

× × × × × × phel ltar ba nyam × × ×× × rang × × × × bzang por gan gyur cig /

ngangs mas mi d'a zungs × × × × × ngan /

sems can don la dgongs p'ai bla med dgon mchog gsum /

yid kyis sprul cig mtshams p'ai gnas × × × × × lus dang bcas te gshegs su × × ×× × × × /

dkon ma tshog gsum la phyag tshal lo /

dkon mtshog gsum la skyabs su mchi /

× × × × × × × skul mya dan mi da gsol

ba × × × × × × × × × × /

× × × × × dge b'ai tsa ba × × × × × /

× × × × × × sems /

dam pa bdag gis bskyed par bgyi smon p'ai sems dang rab ldan zhing /

jug pa pha rol phyin drug spyod /

× × × × × × × × × × × × × × × /

gro ba phan phyin sngas rgyas grub par shog /

phyogs bcu'ai sangs rgyas dang rgyal × × × × la sogs pa tum gsum gyi × × × × × × × × thob pa med pa × × × tha ma dal thub × × × × du /

× × × × × med pa rnam pa ldan × × × × × /

mi dge ba bnyu dang /

kh'a na ma tho ba gsum dang lci ba bzhi dang /

log pa bgyad dang /

× × × × chos la bskun ba btab pa dang /

gzhan × × × × sogs 'agas kyi dam chig dang /

× × × × byang chub sems dp'ai sdom pa dang gal bdang /

× × × tho × × × × dang gal b'ai dga chags ci mches × × × × × /

sangs rgyas × × × × × × par bgyid × × × × bdag gis dkyil khor gyi lha tshogs dang /

mi khrungs × × × bkod × × × × /

bskal pa bzang po'ai sangs rgyas stong dang byams pa dang /

rtsa brgyad la sogs p'ai rtan bzhings pa dang yum shes rab kyi pha rol du phyin ma bzhengs pa dang × × × × × sogs p'ai dus byas dang dus ma byas × × × × × dge b'ai rtsa ba ci gyis bgyis pa la bstan nas bdag × × × × × yas p'ai sems can thams cad kyi rtsa na med kyi bya × × × × thob × × gyur cig /

× × × × × × × × × × × × /

× × × × × × × × × × × × /

me tog pad ma la /

skad cig de la brdzus nas skye bar shog /

brdzus skyes skad × × × × la ni /

jam dpal lta bu stobs tang kha tog gzi brjid shes rab phran sum tshogs pa dang /

lha dang klu'ai rgyal po × × × longs spyod phun sum chogs × × × × × tshangs pa lha ng 'ai × × × × byangs /

skun pa yi × × × × × gcim ldan bde gshegs mi khrungs la /

phyag tshal mchot × × × × × × × × × ×

bsnyen bkur byed par shog kam /

6. Tibetan text in classical language on Alchi choskhor

Om kra shis par gyur cig /

× × × × rab rang bzhin jam gon la bdud de /

stan × × × × × tshod zhin pa bri bar ja na tshot dang po byis p'i dus kyi tshe /

nga rgyal rtsa dang du b'i las las med /

yon tan dag gyang bslabs pas mi lobs te /

chu la ri mo bris pa ci bzhin no bzas dang long spyod × × × × p'i tu shes med /

snyon ba dag gi shes pa dag dang tshu /

na tshod gnyis pa dar la bab p'i tshe /

so nam na bzhis bzas tang longs spyot bsag /

rgyu rtsal yig rtses phong rtsal las sogs sbyang /

thos tang bsam b'i shes rab la bad la /

rig p'i gnas lnga dag la mkhas par bslab /

yon tan med la gzhan dag bkur mi byed /

mcho ris med la gzhan dag mi bkur zhin /

yon tan can gyi thabs dun na dod /

yon tan can dang sa bdag rgyal po gnyis /

rgyal po rang gi bngas ris dag gis bkur /

yon tan can la kun kyis stod cing bkur /

de'i phyir yon tan dag la rab tu bad /

nor ni jig rten mi'i brgyan /

nor gyis blo phangs skyed p'i rgyu /

bzas tang longs phpyat la bsten nas /

dkon mchog bla ma mchot byas pa /

phyi m'i lam sna bren b'i rkyen /

nor gyis rj'i thugs kyang zin /

de bzhin phur mi'i zla yang srongs /

mnyam po 'og tu nor kyis chut /
de phyir brzas dang longs bpyot bsag /
× × × × p'i skyes bu ni /
de ni jig rten blo zat yin /
dper na shi b'i ro gzhin no /
na tshot gsum pa dar yol tshe /
snying rjes sdug cing phyongs pa bso /
byang chub sems p'i spyot pa yin /
dad pas lha dang dkon mchog mohod /
jig rten phyi m'i rgyas phye yin /
gus pas bla ma × × × × bsten /
sems nyid ston p'i me lod yin /
dang po bla ma dam pa la /
ltos pa met p'i snyen bskur gyis /
bla ma dam pa mnyes byas la /
de rjes dgong pa mnges par bya /
× × × × × byung shes rab kyis /
yang dang yang goms par bya /
sems nyid gsal b'i don rtogs na /
spyod lam rnam bzhi chos kyi sku na
tshod b'i pa rgas shing rgud p'ai tshe /
gzhon p'i lang tsho zang dang za mas zad /
mgo la skra med kha la so yang mod /
mig gis mi mthong rna ba sgra mi thos /
gro yang mi nus sgus nas gog cing gro /
dmigs pa mi gsal dran pa nyams par gyur /
nyams len mi nus tha mal dag dang tshungs /
de phyir gzhon b'i che la chos la bod /
mi lus rin can thob nas dam chos ma spyat na /

rin cān gling nas × × × × × byas pa tang /
rgya mtsho'i gling du skom trir shi ba bzhin /
te phyir gzhon b'i dus su chos la bot /
yon tan can la thams cad smon p'i gzhi
bdag med laṁ tu slongs na thar p'i lam /
dge b'i las la brtson na tho ris thob /
slong ba dag la snying rjas sbyin pa btang /
tshul bzhin tam chos spyad na byang chub thob /
khrims sdon tam la gnas pa kun kyi grogs /
'od gsal rgyut la skyes na tshe dir bras bu thob /
yon btag dge slong tshul khrims 'od /
longs spyod snyid po met pa la /
stong b'i snying po bung b'i phyir /
sku gsung thugs kyi gdung rten bzhengs /
lus kyis sgrib pa sbyang pa dang /
sprul sku thob par bya b'i phyir /
sku'i rten tu jam tpal bzhengs /
ngang gi sgrib pa sbyang ba dang /
long sku thob par bya b'i phyir /
gsung rten spyan ras gzigs dang bzhengs /
yed kyis sgrib pa sbyang ba dang /
chos sku thob par bya b'i phyir /
thugs kyi ten du byams pa bzhengs /
grags pa mtha' yas rgyal b'i dka' /
ltan pa phun tshogs × × × × bsal byas /
'od gsal zung jug rgyud la skyes /
grags ldan 'aod ches de la bgyi /
shag kya dge slong grags ldan 'od kyis
sdebs pa lags /
nongs pa mchis na bzod par gsol /

bdag cag dge b'i las rnams de dag gis /
mkhan po slob dpon dus gsum mkhyen × × × /
mtha' yas ma lus sems can thams cad × × × /
shar phyogs mngon dg'i zhing du skye bar shog /
brdzogs so /

7. Tibetan Test in classical language on Alchi Choskhor

Om kra shis par gyur cig /
rten med spyos bral nam mkh'i ngo 'ao nyid /
dmoigs med thugs rje chen po'i lho sprin phobs /
chi med bdut tsi'i char pas gro b'i /
dge b'i lo tog bskyet p'i sangs rgyas mchog /
rnam × × × × × × dbyings thar p'i jo bo las /
bsgrub p'i phags lam brgyad kyis nyi ma dkar /
ston p'i × × × × gi 'od zer phyogs bcur khyab /
gro b'i ma rig sel b'i dma chos mchot /
byang chub sems kyi sdong po snying rjes bskyet /
yon tan yal ga lo bras me tog gis /
gro b'i gdung sel lha mi'i go phang × × × × × /
chags lam bras bcas sten b'i dge dun mchot /
× × × × × × brog dgon jigs su rung bar ni /
gti mug gis stong thar × × × × × lam stor bas /
thog med dus na yun rings khyams pa la /
mig byed thar lam ston p'i bla ma mchot /
gling gi gling mchog lho'i dbram bu'i gling /
rin chen bya dung by'i × × × × × × gyis khyab /
dpag tshad drung stong lga rgya shing rt'i dbyibs /
rgyal bas byang × × × × × mchot snayes × × × × gtan /
dri met bdud rts'i byung gans rgyal po'i khab /

yon tan ltan par grags p'i gans chen mang /
a'dzam gling byang phyogs kha ba can gyi ljongs /
ri mtho sa tsang spu rgyal bot kyi yul /
byung chub sems ldan grub thob rnams kyis gang /
mkhas bstun tu m'i byung gnas mnga' ris bstod /
mar yul smad kyi la dvags A lci dir /
rtsug lag khang chen rin chen rtsegs pa di /
bzhings p'i yon bdag slob dpon tshul
Krims 'od gdung rus che × × × × ya rabs bro'i de /
dgung sngon dkyil na nyi zla gnyis po mdzes /
dog mo'i sa la gro mchog gnyis po che /
stong p'i don togs slob gnyir bya mi tshal /
rus pa bro × × × × × × × ge rtsang chat mi tshal /
s'i ber × × × × × jul ge sdu rangs kyi /
× × × × bro'i khyar bar stag bzang di /
co skyes zhang dung sa ja × × × × × nu byor /
phyi'i dgra dul nang gi bu bngas skyon /
rje'i × × × × × dogin × × × × × phyi bor bkur /
lha × × × × × skor la sogs la × × × × × × × × × /
× × × × × skabs ri tsam na /
mtso las bo zhing gangs las × × × × × × × /
× × × × × kyi nyad mar bstad /
pho byang dbang lng'i blon po byas /
× × × × rtse'i bar × × × × ×× × × × × /
kan gzhi phu mdas bar ling bcad /
gsum md'i slob dpon byang chub × × × × × /
ltsam mo khyim thab byam nas sras gsum × × /
sras kyi che shos × × × × × ldan 'od /
'od min bde ldan gnas × × × × × sum bar /
dmig med thugs rje gro b'i don la byon

mkhas btsun gnyis ldan byin rlabs nus pa che /
de lha rnam mthong sras kyis dngos brub phyul /
byor pa che zhing zas nor stong pa × × × × × /
stug phogs kun kyi gnyen mchog pha m'i go /
sku'i rgya ma dum × × × × × khang gzhings /
de'i 'ong po slob dpon chen po ni /
bstan sgron m'i × × × × × gyi dpal /
dman la snying stse bla ma mi bor bkyur /
shes rab gsum gyis × × × × nang sgro dogs bcad /
gdul bya mang po thar p'i lam la
 bkong gro b'i mgon po shag kyi seng ge'i /
bstan × × × × nub kar chos kyi rgyal mtshan btsugs /
mkhas pa chen po sle snod bsum la sbyangs /
rgyud ste bzhi'i mnga' bdag rin po × × × /
tsigs bcad /
brgyad la klag thabs drug /
dang po skyus su klang pa dang /
de na × × × × × yig klag pa dang /
dang por gnyis par tshig bar ba bdun /
phed la klag p'i thabs yin no /
de nas thur du mtshan tshan glag /
× × × × × tshil yig de bzhin × × × × × /
chigs bcad brgyad la × × × × × gyur /
brjod bya spyir bstod gsum dang ni /
× × × × × × med gyis bstod /
bcu ru shes na mkhas pa yin /
× × × × × tshigs brgyd ma mstod pa bcu /
tshig bcad nyi shur gyur × × × shag kya'i dge
 slong gar gyis bkod /

8. Tibetan Text in classical language on Alchi Choskhor, Ladakh

rtsag lag khang di zhengs p'i bsod nams kyis /

bdag dang kha' dm'i sems can rnams /

myur du bdzog p'i byang chub thob na ni /

× × × × × × × × × × × × × × × × ×

bo ban slob dpon tshul khrims × × × × ×

× × × × × rtsug lag khang bzhengs

p'i tshul mi bston chos mar me'i phreng ba zhes bya ba /

ston pa shag ky'i dge slong dngos grub

shes rab gyis bris pa las byung bsod

nams ci mchis pa /

9. Tibetan Text in classical language on Alchi Choskhor, Ladakh

spre'i gdong can gar gyis rab tu bkod /

sha ky'i dge slong gar lo tsho thul

khrims gyung drung

10. Tibetan Text in classical language on Alchi Choskhor, Ladakh

Om sva sti sid dha /

mkhyen p'i mkha' la

thugs rje'i nyi ma shar /

blo gros 'od zer phyogs bcur rab dge ras /

'agro b'i ma rig mun pa sel mdzed p'i /

drin bla ma rnams la phyag 'tshal lo /

zab bzhi spros bral 'od gsal 'du ma byas /

rtag chad mtshan mar rang grol dbu m'i lam /

phan bde byung nas ye shes byon dpe'i mzot /

yum chen pha rol phyin la gus phyag tshalo /

gzhon nu nyid las bstan las rab
tu byung bslab ma gsum la mig bras lta bur cis /
dur mig bdzin p'i mche tu bar grags p'i /
mchog las rnam rgyal zhabs gus tshal /
kye lags shes by'i mkha' la rab dkyil khor rgyas /
mdo sdags chos kyi 'od zer × × × × × × /
bska bzang du byu'i tshog rems smin mdzat
    b'i shes rab chos bzang zhabs la gus pas dut /
klong gi mtshog rgyur lho'i ddzam bu gling
kh'u khab sbyor ram sa gnyis kyi bar /
mthong ngam mdzes m'i sku mkhar mtho la btsan /
thos pas bzil non alci bri gum dir /
nam lcag thog bebas sing ge'i rtsal dang khrungs /
pha rol gra ste joms × × × × × dpun rtsal rgya /
rang ste gnyen go skyong zhing drin
can pha bas lhag mi dbang gong bkra
shis rnam rgyal la lus dga yit gsum
gus phas chag 'tshal lo /
bot yul bsot nams stos las legs /
khrungs p'i spyan ras gzigs dbang sbrul p'i myi ma shar /
bkra shis rnam rgyal rtag tu rgyal gyur cig /
Ae ma ho /
mon kha hor sogs ba dgra rnam tul /
ru dog sbi ti man cāt /
su ru hem pab kyen cat /
nang gong nub da bzang skar tshun cat
da' ris nga yog / cas /
dung pa kun brknagas rtse cas chos skot rgyud' p'i lugs la /
shes rab bsot nams btag gis bu gon cog
skyabs zhig bsot ca ba la dge b'i skul ma bye tpe grogs la /
A lci chos don dgrub blo gro lde don grub skyabs ba sbyun
    nyis /

bkra shis skyabs dongrub bkra shis don
grub pal byor tsun pa rnams kyi rtsug
la khang di la zhabstog phul /
pul kul la btag mo 'od lcam kyi drung × × ×
yu tshal bca bkut pa lags byon ris × × × ×
yu byung cig × × × × thong cig dge dge slong
bsot nam dpal byor 'i thing stang ma
khrig si drung bas rag bum cig /
drung pa lo zang bde legs kyi nat de
la nas khal rgyat chang na /
yu ru na sde pas tshal zo btun kag /
tshal li cos rdul tshal rgya rams byung /
mul be mtso – tso je mas kag /
yeng skye rag /
pho ger na tsho bcos ras lcang nang cig
    skye rgas dan na pa lcag cig byung /
dbon mo che don grub dpal /
kon cog skyabs gnga gnga rnams la zhabs tog cas /
chos ston ras bmyug ston mar bston bcas /
ton × × × × × × × × bsot nam bkra shis × × × ×
yul pa sa pi rnams sgye si ka ru tpon rnam tshim rab cas /
dge'o legs so /
bkra shis par rgyun cig /
om su bva ti ba dzu ye sva ha /
om sva ti sidham bo mo na cung nems kyi lob jang dra
    ba bzhengs /
dpon rnams shes p'i zhab tog legs phul /
bkre shis par rgyur cig /
dmon rnams sha chang kyis tshim
pad byas nas bzhing / he he he /

11. Tibetan Text in Classical Language on Alchi Choskor, Ladakh

bla ma dak rgyud sngs rgyas skal bzangs dang ma tshungs dzam gling byon /

chos rdze gro gon yab sras mnyam med rtse ba chen po yes /

rin chen nor bu dbang gi rgyal pos gro rnams tshim pa mdzat /

bla ma tsungs met gro b'i ded dpon rnams la bskyabs su mchi /

dkon mchog dri med byung ba rab kon au tu bar ba ltar /

rgyal ba mkha ltar chos dbyings dag pa lhun grub dus ma byas /

blo gros matha yas mkhyen rtse nus dang don nyis ldan pa yo /

rin po che'i byungs khungs sku gsum dbyer med sangs rgyas rnams la bstod /

dka dang bstan cos la sogs stang gi chos rnam dbang chen sa gzhi dra /

gon dzad zhi ba chags bral rgya mtsho dang mtshungs bden nyis lam /

yon tan phun tshogs stogs p'i chos ni dpag sam

shing dang tshungs /

tam p'i don ban dam chos rin chen sgron ma rnams la bstod /

drin lan gsob phyin × × × p'i dge dun rnams la rab bstod na /

ge n'i bras bus dben gyur mi log sems dap chen po rnams /

bdag gzhan thar phyin bstan p'i × × × × /

gdud khad tshogs kyi phags p'i dge dun rnam la bstod /

12. Tibetan Text in Classical Language on Alchi Choskhor

Al lci mgon gyi sku gnyer blo zang shes dab tsho zang ba × × × sung bis rten shing bras ba shag kha b'i bcis byor bas yid spro dir yang bde bar mchis tshad bul rtsa de kha gtsug lag khang gi bskor skor skyabs mgon rin po cher snyan bul zhus par rgyas pa la khri phrag cig dang brid pal stong phrag cig mtha ma lang rgya rgyas bring sdus gsum gyi bskor tshad dang kha kong gro ba rang rang gyi blo nus dang stun pa byas chog phebs byung bas dgongs jags zhu / rten phyag bdud byin rten bdu rtsi skye bdun bsang chab ril bu dang ha kha gtag dang bcas shes la sman khang nas phul /

co mo byam pa chos dzin gnyis skor tshad de zhus nas rjes su ma ri rgya rtsa gsum zheng grub pas des kyang rgyal b'i bstan pa dar rgyas par gyur cig bkris di skab su ts'u ang dul a dzo dpal ddzins ddul re byung /

Appendix 3

Tibetan Alphabet

ka	kha	ga	nga
ca	cha	ja	nya
ta	tha	da	na
pa	pha	ba	ma
tsa	tsha	dza	wa
zha	za	'a	ya
ra	la	sha	sa
ha	a		

Bibliography

Bunce, Freadric W: 'An Encyclopaedia of Buddhist Deities, Demigods, godlin,gs, Saints and Demeons; Vol I, D.K Print World Ltd., New Delhi; 1994.

Finegan Jack: 'Tibet: A Dreamt of Image, Tibet House, Delhi; 1986.

Gazetteer of Kashmir and Ladak Vivek Publishing. House, Delhi (Reprinted 1974), First Printed in 1890.

Jina, Prem Singh (1983): Boudh Bikshus of Ladakh, In All India Conference on 'Buddhist and Jaina Monasticism', Department of Buddhist Studies, Delhi University, Delhi (1984) : Buddhism in Ladakh and World Peace', In 10th International Buddhist Conference on 'Buddhism and world Peace, Japanese Temple, Both Gaya, vol. X, (1986): 'A Brief Introduuction of Ladakhi Gonpas, In All India Conference; Kashmir University, Srinagar, Department, of Centre for Contral Asian Studies.

—1986: 'A Survey of Buddhist Community in Ladakh Himalaya, In International Buddhist Conference, 'On Buddhism and Social Harmony', Japanese Temple, Bodh Gaya, Vol. XII.

— (1986): Socio-Economic and Cultural Relations between Ladakh and Lahul-Spiti, National Conference, Keylong (H.P.).

— (1987): Asangha and his constribution, In All India Conference, CIBS, Leh-Ladakh.

— (1988): 'Monasteries in the Economy of Leh-Ladakh,' in All India Conference on 'Buddhist Monasteries of Himalayan Region various Aspects, CIBS, Leh-Ladakh.

— (1998): 'Bodh Dham Leh-Ladakh (Hindi), Hindu Chetan, Vol. 7, New Delhi'.

— (1998): Ladakhi Ragao ka Both Dharam me Yogdan (Hindi, Hindu Chetana, Vol. 10.

—(1989): 'Rashtrapalparicheda Aek Drashtri', All India conference, CIBS, Leh-Ladakh.

—(1990): 'Dasvi Satabadi me Kashmir me Bodh Dharma our Uska Ladakh ki Sanskriti me Prabhav' In: All India Conference, CIBS, Leh-Ladakh.

— (1990): Buddhism and Human Values in the History of Ladakh Himalayas; In: International Buddhist Conference, Japanese Temple, Bodh Gaya, India.

— (1991): Ladakh me Bodh Kala Ka Udbhav aur Vikas' Seereja vol.6.; Feb.-March.

— (1993): Buddhism in Ladakh and its approach to material world; In: International Buddhist Conference, Japanese Temple, Bodh Gaya.

— (1994): Bhikshunis in Ladakh (Nuns in Ladakh)' In: International conference Keylong, H.P.

— (1994): Spiti ka Sanskratik Itihas, Janjati Utsav, Keylong (H.P.): 70-72.

— (1994): 'Tibet me Musalmano ka Aagama; Neeshant, March-Sept., Aligarh Muslim University, Vol. 3-12: 29-30.

— (1994): Phyang Monastery of Ladakh, Indus Publishing Company, New Delhi.

— (1996): "Ladakh: The land and the people", Indus Publishing Company, New Delhi.

— (1996): Hemis : The Biggest Buddhist Monastery of Ladakh, Yag Udbodhan, Vol. 2 No 4; New Delhi. 15.

— (1996): Lahul va Spiti me Bodha Dharma; Somsi, June-September.

(Ed) (1997): Recent Researchers on the Himalayas, Indus Publishing Company, New Delhi.

— (1997): Dasvi Sathi Avam Lahul, Somsi July-October.

— (1998): Tibetan Manuscripts and Inscriptions of Ladakh Himalaya', Sri Statguru Publishing, New Delhi.

— (1999): Some Monsteries of Drigung pa order in Central Ladakh, Sri Satguru Publication. New Delhi.

— (1999): 'Changing face of Ladakh Himalaya', Om Pub. New Delhi.

— (1999): Lamayuru monastery of Ladakh Himalaya', Om Pub, New Delhi.

— (1999): Ladakh Mera Anubhav; Anjuri, New Delhi.

— (2000): 'Ladakh: Past and Present', Gyan Publishing, New Delhi.

— (2000): 'Rinchen bzangpo's contribution in Buddhist Art: a Case Study of Sumda Chun and Suma Chenmo (Ladakh', All India Conference, C.I. B.S. LeLadalh.

— (2000): 'Alchi: A Buddhist monument in Ladakh' In: International Buddhist Confernce, Japanese Temple, Bodh Gaya.

— (ed.)(2001): Religious History of Ladakh, Sri Satguru Publishing, New Delhi.

— (2001) 'Ladakh Ki Kala Avam Sanskriti', IGNCA, New Delhi.

—(2001): 'Buddhism and Environment Pollution'; In: International Buddhist Conference, Bodh Gaya, New Delhi.

—(2002): 'Development of Ldakh Himalayas: Recent Researchers'; Kalpaz Publication, New Delhi.

—(2002): 'Second Buddhist Council', In: All India Buddhist Conference', CIBS, Leh-Ladakh.

—(2002): 'Ahinsa Avasm Jananiti'. In: International Buddhist Conference, Japanese Temple Bodh Gaya.

—(2002): First Hand Tibetan Inscriptions on Rock an Stones on Ladakh Himalaya, Sri Satguru Publication, New Delhi.

—(2003): Buddhism and Female eduaction, In: International Buddhist conference, Japanesc Temple, Bodh Gaya.

—(2004): Buddhism in the twenty First century', In; International Buddhist Conference, C.I.B. Leh-Ladakh.

—(2005): 'Chomo Lhakhang ka Adhayan (A Study of chomo Lhakhang)'; In: All india, Conference, CIBS, Leh-Ladakh

—(2005): Buddhist Paintaings in Gur Phug monastery in Ladakh; In; international Buddhist Conference; Japanese Temple Bodh Gaya.

— (2005): 'Ladakh Profile', Kalpaz Publication, New Delhi.

— (2006): Ladakh Himalaya: Past and Present, Anmol Publishing. New Delhi.

— (2006): 'Car Bhramavihara', In: All India Buddhist Confernece, CIBS Leh-Ladakh.

— (2005): Varsha vas ka Mahatava, in: All India Conference,CIBS, Leh.

— (2007): Tourist Resources of Ladakh' Anmol Publishing. New Delhi.

— (2007): Tourism and Buddhist Monasteries of Ladakh, Kalpaz Publishing. New Delhi.

— (2007): Ladakh Buddhist Culture and Tradition, Kalpaz Publishing, New Delhi.

— (2007): 'Pratityasamadpad', In: All India Confennfce, CIBS, Leh-Ladakh.

Index